# Growing Your
# *Olive Tree* Marriage

# Growing Your
# *Olive Tree* Marriage

## A Guide for Couples from Two Traditions

## David J. Rudolph

**Lederer Books**
a division of
Messianic Jewish Publishers

Unless otherwise noted, all Scripture quotations are taken from the *Complete Jewish Bible,* Copyright © 1998 by David H. Stern, published by Jewish New Testament Publications, Inc. Used by permission.

The following Bible version was also used:
*The Holy Bible, New International Version,* Copyright © 1984 by International Bible Society, published by Zondervan Publishing House. Used by permission.


Printed in the United States of America



07   06   05   04   03          6   5   4   3   2   1
ISBN   1-880226-17-0


Library of Congress Control Number:  2003104185

Lederer Books
a division of
Messianic Jewish Publishers
6204 Park Heights Ave.
Baltimore, Maryland  21215
(410)  358-6471

Distributed by
Messianic Jewish Resources International
Individual order line: (800) 410-7367
Trade order line: (800) 773-MJRI (6574)
E-mail: lederer@messianicjewish.net
Website: www.messianicjewish.net

אֵשֶׁת-חַיִל מִי יִמְצָא

"A wife of noble character who can find?" (NIV)
I did, and her name is Harumi.

This book is dedicated to my wife Harumi,
who came from the Land of the Rising Sun
to be my lifelong companion.
Thank you, my darling, for fifteen wonderful years!

# Contents

# Foreword

Intermarriage rates within the Jewish community, currently over fifty percent, may decrease or even increase in the coming years, but Jews and Gentiles will undoubtedly continue to find each other, fall in love, and join themselves in holy matrimony. This Jewish-Gentile intermarriage rate is portrayed by some as a problem, a crisis, or even a threat to the very survival of the Jewish people. But for those who share in it, intermarriage is often the source of great blessing. Whether problem or blessing, intermarriage is undeniably a challenge. Jews who intermarry, and especially their children, are often pulled away from the Jewish world. Or, if the Jewish partner remains connected to his or her community, the Gentile partner may feel like a permanent outsider.

*Growing Your Olive Tree Marriage: A Guide for Couples from Two Traditions* faces such challenges and provides a unique response. The olive tree is a metaphor in the New Testament book of Romans that describes how Jews and Gentiles come together through a common faith in Jesus, or Yeshua, as Messiah. Paul writes to the Gentile "branches" of this tree:

> *But if some of the branches were broken off, and you—a wild olive tree—were grafted in among them and have become equal sharers in the rich root of the olive tree, then don't boast as if you were better than the branches!... For if you were cut out of what is by nature a wild olive tree and grafted, contrary to nature, into a cultivated olive tree, how much more will these natural branches be grafted back into their own olive tree!* (Romans 11:17-18a, 24)

The natural Jewish branches and the wild Gentile branches share in the same rich root, and thrive in connection with the same tree. This olive tree provides a model for interfaith marriage in which both partners gain and neither remains the outsider, a model realized within the Messianic Jewish community.

As David Rudolph amply demonstrates, Messianic Judaism has much to contribute to the issue of intermarriage. It is a movement that is both deeply rooted in Scripture and its abiding truths, and innovative enough to respond to the postmodern conditions of the 21st century, including intermarriage.

Rudolph cites studies that show that Messianic Jews have the highest rate of agreement among Jewish denominations with the statement, "Being Jewish is very important in my life." This finding may be surprising, but it makes perfect sense. If being Jewish were not "very important" in their lives, Messianic Jews would have already assimilated into the Church. Instead, they have pioneered a new form of Jewish identity. Furthermore, Messianic Jews, alone of all the groups within today's pluralistic Judaism, have found the welcome mat withdrawn by the larger Jewish community. Their continuing identification as Jews, despite this rejection, gives evidence of their high level of commitment, as shown in the surveys mentioned in this book.

Messianic Judaism can claim an unusual ability to maintain Jewish identity in the friendlier, but still problematic, environment of intermarriage. Its solution is not a Jewish-Christian melting pot, but a unique Jewish community that can integrate non-Jews with integrity, without losing its essential Jewishness. Recognizing a Messiah (Yeshua, or Jesus) who is thoroughly Jewish in his identity and widely embraced by the non-Jewish world, provides the model for Jewish-Gentile marriages and a place for them within their local community. Because of the distinctive qualities of Messianic Jewish faith—its inclusiveness toward Gentiles, its adaptability to changing circumstances, its priority on loving communities—it may be able to affirm intermarriage in a deeper way than any other form of Judaism. Thanks to David Rudolph for inviting couples into this place of blessing.

Russell Resnik, 4/1/2003

# Introduction

This book is designed for intermarried couples (Jewish and Christian), those considering intermarriage, children of intermarriage, and anyone who has family or friends who are intermarried, a group that now encompasses millions of people in the United States.

Many books have been written for this group since the 1990 National Jewish Population Survey sounded the alarm over an intermarriage rate that had climbed to 52 percent (up from 6 percent prior to 1960).[1] So, you might ask, "How is this book different from all the other books on intermarriage?" Very simply, this book lays out an approach to intermarriage that has been largely overlooked in the modern literature. It is also an option that has proven to be particularly successful in meeting the needs of intermarried couples over the past two decades.[2] The approach I speak of is Messianic Judaism.

Messianic Judaism is the best kept secret in the world of intermarriage. It is an approach that honors the faith traditions of both spouses, conveys Jewish identity to the next generation and makes it possible for intermarrieds and their children to worship together comfortably as a family. What is Messianic Judaism and how is it different from the popular "Interfaith" option?

In the Interfaith approach to intermarriage, children are raised as Jews *and* Christians. The couple seeks to maintain a household that has both a Jewish and Christian expression. The child's identity is best described as "Jewish/Christian" with emphasis on the slash ("/"). This approach is generally not an attempt at reconciling the faiths but aspires to convey to the children two separate and distinct religious traditions.

By contrast, Messianic Judaism conveys a single religious identity to the children of intermarriage. Essentially, it is the removal of the slash between "Jewish" and "Christian." It is the recognition that, in the first century, at the inception of Christianity, the slash did not exist between the two faiths and that it does not need to exist today. Messianic Judaism challenges the notion that Judaism and Christianity are mutually exclusive religions and contends that it is possible to naturally reconcile these two faiths at their core. Therefore, it is perfectly acceptable to raise Jewish children who believe in Jesus and live as practicing Jews.

Often, Interfaith couples find it difficult to impart more than a minimal exposure of both faiths to their children, leaving the kids to feel neither fully Jewish nor fully Christian. Often they feel "half Jewish and half Christian."[3] It is not uncommon to hear comments like the following from adult children of intermarriage who were raised Interfaith:

> I have felt like a schizophrenic for most of my life! Or perhaps like a giant piece of taffy, constantly being stretched and pulled to capacity in both directions. . . . For as long as I can remember, I have yearned to integrate, or magically fuse, my two halves, so I wouldn't have to choose one over the other. It has always been a source of irritation, frustration, and great sadness that the two are regarded as mutually exclusive by many.[4]

By contrast, Messianic Judaism fits together pieces from both religious traditions in an attempt to restore an ancient identity. Experientially, Messianic Judaism has made two halves whole for many. It is a natural solution because children want to integrate their identities—bring them together—not separate them (a drawback of the Jewish Only and Christian Only options). Moreover, the Messianic Jewish model is rooted in the Scriptures and history, providing children with a strong sense of identity. Jesus the Jew and the first century Jews who followed him as the Messiah serve as an "identity anchor" or "identity paradigm" for twenty-first century Messianic Jews. Consequently, Messianic Jewish children can have a clear understanding of who they are.

Not only is Messianic Judaism the restoration of an ancient idea, it is thriving. Today, there are over 250 Messianic Jewish congregations in North America with thousands of intermarried couples raising their children as Messianic Jews.[5] Barney Kasdan, a former president of the Union of Messianic Jewish Congregations (UMJC), recommends Messianic Judaism for intermarried couples. Rabbi Kasdan writes:

> I believe strongly, from my personal experience, that the Messianic synagogue is the most logical common ground for any "inter-faith" family who is open to seeing a new way of looking at things.[6]

Messianic Judaism is a very good option for intermarried couples. More than other approaches, it bridges the Jewish-Christian gap for intermarried couples and their children. Reform rabbi Dan Cohn-Sherbok writes in his book, *Messianic Judaism*:

. . . this new movement has captured the hearts and minds of thousands of pious individuals from the Jewish community, as well as Gentiles who have accepted Yeshua [Jesus][7] as their Lord and Saviour. Its membership numbers over a quarter of a million individuals—no doubt the high rate of intermarriage between Jews and Christians in contemporary society has greatly contributed to such growth. Messianic Judaism provides a home for those couples who seek to integrate Jewish living with belief in Jesus.[8]

I have been a part of the Messianic Jewish community for twenty-five years and have met hundreds of intermarried families who found the solution they were looking for in Messianic Judaism. In many cases, I have heard intermarried couples express regret that they did not know of Messianic Jewish congregations years earlier, when they were just beginning to work out the religious identity of their family. What a joy it is to see an intermarried family worship together and have their needs met. What satisfaction it brings to see adult children of intermarriage find a synagogue they can call home. What a thrill it is to see second generation Messianic Jews raising their children as Jews. Yes, Messianic Judaism also contributes to Jewish continuity!

This is the first work on intermarriage that lays out the Messianic Jewish option in detail. Information about the demographic impact of intermarriage and the dilemmas that intermarried couples and their children face is provided. Intermarriage in biblical history, religious law, and genetics research, as well as how intermarried couples raise their children is also presented.

The research for this book was conducted over the course of four years and included scores of formal taped interviews with intermarrieds who attended Messianic Jewish congregations. Hundreds of other informal interviews were conducted with intermarried couples, their children, rabbis of Messianic synagogues, and leaders of Messianic Jewish organizations. The names of those interviewed and their synagogues have been changed in this book to respect privacy.

# CHAPTER 1
# Why Intermarriage is a Hot Issue

A re you intermarried or considering intermarriage? If so, you are not alone. In the United States, there are over 2 million people just like you![1] Over the last decade, one out of every two American Jews intermarried. According to the 2001 American Jewish Identity Survey:

> Of all adults since 1990, who say they are Jewish by religion or of Jewish parentage or upbringing . . . 51% are married to a spouse who is not of Jewish origins and an additional 9% are married to a spouse who is a convert to Judaism.[2]

In some parts of the country, most notably the West Coast, the intermarriage rate among Jews has topped 80 percent.[3] How are synagogues faring? Surveys indicate that it will not be long before the majority of families in Reform synagogues (the largest community of affiliated Jews in the United States) will be intermarried.[4] It has already approached 60 percent in many congregations.[5] Reform leadership families have also been profoundly affected by this trend. One study found that a third of the children of Reform leaders had intermarried and that 25 percent of the leaders themselves were intermarried![6]

Intermarriage, however, is not limited to the Reform community. Among Jews who married between 1970 and 1990, 56 percent of Reform Jews, 37 percent of Conservative Jews, and 11 percent of Orthodox Jews intermarried. Among Jews without any denominational preference, which is one quarter of all Jews,[7] the figure rose to 82 percent.[8]

According to the 1990 National Jewish Population Survey (NJPS), of the nearly one million Gentiles (non-Jews) married to Jews, approximately 95 percent chose *not* to convert to Judaism.[9]

Why is the Jewish community so alarmed about the above figures? There are many reasons. However, of utmost concern is the impact intermarriage is having on the continuity of Jewish identity. The fact is that American Jews are decreasing in numbers, primarily due to low birth rates, but also because of non-conversion intermarriage.

Consider the following population projections tabulated by Professor Sergio DellaPergola of Hebrew University:

**Jewish Population Projection—Status Quo Assumption[10]**

| Year | Size of Jewish Population [United States] |
|------|------------------------------------------|
| 1990 | 5,515,000 |
| 2000 | 5,588,000 |
| 2010 | 5,376,000 |
| 2020 | 5,204,000 |
| 2030 | 4,851,000 |
| 2040 | 4,281,000 |
| 2050 | 3,716,000 |
| 2060 | 3,228,000 |
| 2070 | 2,742,000 |
| 2080 | 2,294,000 |

How does intermarriage contribute to the disappearance of more than two million Jews in three generations? If we look at Jewish families in the United States, the number of young children with one Jewish parent already exceeds the number of young children with two Jewish parents. We now know that among "children in the age group zero-to-nine who are living with two parents, there are 410,000 living in households where both parents are Jewish, and 479,000 living in households where one parent is Jewish and the other is not."[11] Susan Schneider notes that these children of Jewish-Christian intermarriage "will comprise the majority of American Jews by the year 2050."[12] How are these children being raised?

According to the statistics, 82 percent of the children of inter-marriage are being raised Christian Only, Interfaith, or without any religion. The remaining 18 percent are being raised exclusively as Jews.[13] This notwithstanding, even the 18 percent are not committed to Jewish identity. Eight out of ten of these children say that being part of the Jewish community is unimportant.[14] Intermarriage, then, contributes to the disappearance of more than two million Jews in three generations because most of the children of such marriages are raised as non-Jews or uncommitted Jews. "There is little doubt that two generations of intermarriage will produce a third generation in which Jewishness is highly attenuated if it survives at all."[15] In light of this situation, Rabbi Jonathan Sacks writes:

Within a generation, mixed marriage has escalated with a speed that has taken observers by surprise and it now threatens the very basis of Jewish survival in one community after another throughout the world. The Jewish family—two Jews who decide to marry, have Jewish children, and thus continue the Jewish heritage—has suddenly become fragile. As a result, the great chain of Jewish tradition, stretching across three-quarters of the history of human civilization, is in danger of breaking. The future of Diaspora Jewry is at risk.[16]

The situation is indeed a grave crisis for the American Jewish community. Most intermarried couples feel that mainstream synagogues are unable to meet their unique needs. But what is the alternative if the great chain of Jewish tradition is to be preserved? This is the question we seek to answer.

# Chapter 2
# The Dilemmas of Intermarriage

When Rebekah fell in love with Mark, she adored everything about him—his love of life, his concern for others, his sense of humor, his family. The fact that Mark was a Christian didn't matter to her. Rebekah's parents liked Mark but they pleaded with Rebekah to consider the bigger picture—the breaking of tradition, the religious upbringing of their future children. Rebekah assured her parents that it would all work out in the end.

The age-old adage "love is blind" well applies to Jews and Christians when they fall in love. They rarely see the dilemmas that lie ahead. Intermarriage is often compared to a "time bomb" that quietly ticks away and goes off at transitional moments in life.[1] One may be happily intermarried, oblivious to any problems. Then suddenly, at the birth of a first child or the death of a religious parent, the issues of intermarriage explode on the scene, consuming the attention of the couple. Intermarried couples face major dilemmas, especially when it comes to parental opposition, the wedding, birth rites, the identity of Jesus, synagogue/church membership, religious life in the home, death rites, and conveying a Jewish heritage.

## Dilemma 1: Parental Opposition

Every time I see *Fiddler on the Roof*, my eyes well up at the scene when Tevye refuses to speak with his daughter because she intermarried. Parental opposition to intermarriage continues to be a problem for many couples. Frequently, concerns are voiced on the Jewish side of the family. Opposition can take the form of angry remarks or boycotting the wedding. If the family is very traditional, the couple may even be cut off. Rabbi Seigel notes:

> Some parents have become so upset with the prospect of their child marrying out of Judaism that they sit *shiva* [the seven-day period of mourning] and pronounce the child dead. Others throw the child out of the house. Others cut off financial aid. Others forbid the child from bringing the intended spouse into their home. As one parent put it to her

daughter, "Don't you dare bring that—that—that THING into my house!"[2]

The couple must then decide between appeasing the parents or forging ahead with their plans to be married. One non-Jewish woman shared with me the following tête-à-tête she had with her future husband's mother before the wedding:

> She had me sit down and talk to her one-day. It was brutal. She just did not want me to marry her son. At one point, she refused to come to the wedding. She made it very clear that she did not approve of me. . . . First she was asking a lot of background questions. Then she said, "And then there's the matter of your faith." She was very clear about it. She told me that I wasn't Jewish. She told me that Larry's uncle had married a Gentile who converted. She made sure that I understood it could be done. I said, "I'm not converting. I believe in Jesus. I'm not giving that up. That's just not an option as far as I'm concerned." My feeling was that in order to become Jewish I had to deny Christ. When we could not get the rabbi to perform the wedding jointly with the priest, she at one point said, "Well, I can't come." I said, "Mom, we're getting married. We'd really love you to be there, but if you can't I understand."

## Dilemma 2: The Wedding

Will it be a Jewish wedding performed by a rabbi in a synagogue or a Christian wedding performed by a minister in a church? The dilemma grows when it is learned that finding a rabbi to do the wedding is not an easy task unless the non-Jewish partner converts to Judaism. "The rabbinic guidelines for all four major Jewish denominations—Reform, Reconstructionist, Conservative and Orthodox—state that rabbis should not officiate at intermarriages. Reform and Reconstructionist rabbinic organizations, however, do not discipline those who digress."[3] Additionally, Jewish family members have a hard time attending a Christian wedding if the church is filled with crosses and the name "Jesus" is mentioned. Thus, the personal preferences of the intermarried couple become complicated by the sensitivities of the Jewish spouse's family and religious community.

## Dilemma 3: Birth Rites

Will the children be circumcised or baptized? This question is faced soon after birth. The intermarried couple must decide in what religious tradition their children will be raised. If the child is a boy, according to Jewish custom, he must be circumcised on the eighth day by a *mohel* (one trained to perform the surgery in compliance with Jewish law and who pronounces the appropriate blessings). If this is not done, the child will be regarded as a non-Jew according to the Torah (Gen. 17:14; Exod. 12:47–48). Some Christian traditions, such as Catholicism and Lutheranism, practice infant baptism, symbolizing the child's entrance into the Church as a Christian. If this is not done, the child is regarded as being outside the covering of the Church. Customs such as these call parents to declare the religious identity of their children early on. Young intermarried couples often put these decisions off until they are faced with parents who remind them of their religious obligations.

## Dilemma 4: The Identity of Jesus

What will the children be taught about Jesus? He said, "I AM the Way—and the Truth and the Life" (John 14:5). Was he the Messiah or not? If he wasn't the Messiah, who was he?

The average Jewish parent does not want his or her child coming home from church and speaking of "Jesus Christ" as a "personal Savior." Similarly, it can be a source of anguish for the Christian parent to hear a child explain why he or she does not believe in Jesus after coming home from Hebrew school.

Tension may also occur between husband and wife. If the Christian spouse believes that the Jewish spouse needs to believe in Jesus in order to be "saved," the couple will experience a degree of friction. Likewise, if the Jewish spouse speaks of Jesus in a pejorative way, the Christian spouse may be hurt by the lack of respect for his/her religion.

## Dilemma 5: Synagogue/Church Membership

Eventually, the intermarried couple will need to decide if they are going to join a synagogue or church in order to provide for the religious education of the children. Weddings and birth traditions may not require community affiliation. However, if a child is to have a *bar/ bat mitzvah* (a rite of passage in which a Jewish person accepts upon him/herself responsibility for the commandments of God) or a Christian confirmation, it is necessary for the family to join a local synagogue or church.

The decision will also impact the family calendar. If the couple chooses to join a synagogue, the Christian spouse will miss Christmas and Easter services. If the couple chooses to join a church, the Jewish spouse will miss the High Holy Day (*Rosh HaShanah* and *Yom Kippur*) services.

Then there is the issue of comfort level. The average Jewish spouse does not want to attend Sunday church services where he/she is surrounded by crosses and continual references to "Christ." Likewise, the average Christian spouse feels like an outsider attending synagogue services on Saturday where the liturgy is partly in Hebrew and there is a regular reference to the need for Jewish survival.

## Dilemma 6: Jewish Life in the Home

What Jewish customs will be celebrated in the home? Few intermarried couples think this through before marriage. One difference between traditional Judaism and traditional Christianity is the location of the center of ritual activity. In traditional Christianity, it is in the local church. In traditional Judaism, it is in the home. This raises a number of issues for intermarried couples to process. Will pork and shellfish be allowed in the house? Will *Shabbat* (Sabbath) candles be lit on Friday night, and will the blessings be said over the *challah* (braided egg bread) and wine? Will the family have a Passover *seder* (ritual meal recalling the Exodus from Egypt)? Will all leaven be removed from the house during the eight days of Passover and *matzah* (unleavened bread) eaten instead? Will apples and honey be eaten on *Rosh HaShanah* (the traditional New Year)? Will the family fast on *Yom Kippur* (Day of Atonement)? Will they light the Hanukkah (Dedication) candles on each of the eight days of Hanukkah? Will they have a *mezuzah* (a small box containing two handwritten biblical passages, Deut. 6:4–9 and Deut. 11:13–21, affixed to the doorposts of homes)? What about lighting a *yahrzeit* (annual memorial) candle after a parent passes away? While these customs may be important to the Jewish spouse, the Christian spouse may find some of them to be inconvenient and foreign.

## Dilemma 7: Christian Life in the Home

What Christian customs will be celebrated in the home? Will there be a Christmas tree? The Christian spouse usually has a nostalgic, "warm and fuzzy" feeling about the Christmas tree. It is a reminder of the many family Christmas gatherings that he/she experienced growing up. To abandon the Christmas tree is to abandon a piece of the Christian spouse's identity. The Jewish spouse, on the other hand, may see the tree as a religious icon. He may think it labels the family as "Christian" or "assimilated" and feel threatened by it. The tree may even be perceived as anti-Jewish due to its identification with a historic Church that persecuted the Jewish people in the name of Christ. As Judy Petsonk and Jim Remsen articulate in *The Intermarriage Handbook*:

> Most Jews are keenly aware, and most Christians are not, that for the last two thousand years Jews have suffered horribly and repeatedly at the hands of Christians. For many Jews, this history plays like a tape in the mind—a tape that is triggered by symbols such as a crucifix or a Christmas tree, and that repeats: "Crusades, Inquisition, pogroms, Holocaust."[4]

For this reason, having the tree or not having the tree is a major issue for some intermarried couples. Other Christian customs that may become an issue include prayer in the name of Jesus, hanging a cross or picture of Christ on the wall, Christmas caroling, Easter Sunday ham meals and Easter egg hunts. Like the Christmas tree, these customs can cause the Jewish spouse to feel alienated in his/her own home.

## Dilemma 8: Death Rites

What of funerals and burial customs? Young intermarried couples rarely think about death. Eventually, however, they must decide about burial arrangements. The situation is complicated by the fact that, generally, it can be difficult to find a rabbi who will officiate over the non-Jewish spouse's funeral and burial, even if he/she attended synagogue with the Jewish spouse for many years.

> A Jew who intermarried, as long as he did not convert to some other religion, would be entitled to burial in a Jewish cemetery. But traditional (Orthodox and Conservative) authorities would not knowingly permit the burial of the non-Jewish spouse or of the child of a Jewish father and non-Jewish mother in the Jewish cemetery. Reform and Reconstructionist rabbis will generally agree to bury the non-Jewish spouses and their children as long as they were active members of the synagogue and did not practice Christianity or maintain a separate church affiliation.[5]

## Dilemma 9: Taking the Jewish Initiative

Is the Jewish spouse motivated in taking the lead? The majority of intermarried couples are comprised of a Jewish husband and a non-Jewish
wife.[6] Sometimes, the Jewish husband will communicate his need to
have a Jewish home and then step back, expecting his non-Jewish wife
to carry the responsibilities, take the initiative, and learn what to do.[7]
He may even resist personal involvement in Jewish life and participate
only when pushed. This can be extremely frustrating for the non-Jewish
wife who looks at her husband and says, "If he doesn't care about these
things, and he is Jewish, why should I do all this work?" Faced with the
husband's lack of personal conviction, the wife will sometimes pull
back from taking the initiative and resume her own Christian identity in
the home, which is more natural and less time consuming for her. As a
result, the children may not be raised as Jews.

> The gender of the Jewish spouse also makes a difference
> as to whether children in an intermarriage are raised as
> Jews. When it is the wife who has a Jewish background,
> a majority (52%) report raising Jewish children; when it
> is the husband who has a Jewish background, only a mi-
> nority (25%) are raising their children as Jews.[8]

## Dilemma 10: Conveying Jewish Identity

Will the children be Jewish? Some religious leaders have referred to
the intermarriage rate in the United States as a bloodless Holocaust.
By this, they mean that annihilation of Jews occurs through assimilation rather than the ovens:

> Jews have always been a small minority, and the modern
> Jewish population suffered heavy losses from the Nazi
> Holocaust in Europe and from assimilation in America.
> Intermarriage is seen by many Jews as another equally
> serious threat to the survival of Judaism.[9]

Young intermarried couples must reckon with the fact that if they do not
consciously convey Jewish identity to their children, they are in fact
contributing to the end of the Jewish people. Study after study has
shown that intermarriage leads to assimilation by the fourth generation
if the family is not serious about maintaining Jewish identity. Rabbi
Jonathan Sacks, the Chief Rabbi of the United Hebrew Congregations of
the Commonwealth (United Kingdom), states:

In the absence of a determined effort to transmit our traditions to our children, Jewish identity persists for three generations, not longer.[10]

He continues,

There is an iron law of assimilation, first articulated in the nineteenth century: the grandfather prays in Hebrew, the father prays in English, the son no longer prays, the grandson is no longer Jewish.[11]

Historian Arthur Hertzberg concurs, "No Jewish community in Europe which lived four generations in freedom survived."[12] The majority of North American Jews are now reaching the third and fourth generation in this land of opportunity.[13] To assure that one's grandchildren will be Jewish, one must teach his/her own children that they are Jewish and so impact them with a love for Judaism that they will have the same commitment to impact their own children. If the Christian spouse has difficulty seeing the importance of this, Jewish continuity may be difficult to maintain.

Intermarriage has many challenges, but they can be overcome. Intermarried couples committed to working through the issues will discover that gold is refined in the furnace. Embracing the challenge of intermarriage can draw a couple closer together. Continual two-way communication, sacrificial love, and the prudence to consider all the options, will see a couple from two traditions through.

## CHAPTER 3

# Intermarriage in Biblical History

M any are surprised to learn that intermarriage between Jews and non-Jews is not a modern day phenomenon. During the biblical period, intermarriage was a common occurrence.[1] The big difference between then and now is that, then, conversion to Judaism was an integral part of the marriage[2] and did not involve a formal ceremony.[3] Today, it is the exception for the non-Jew to convert to Judaism, formally or informally.[4]

In the following pages, the term "intermarriage" is used to describe two kinds of marriage—conversionary and non-conversionary.[5] While some would argue that conversionary marriages are not "intermarriages" because a Jew by birth is marrying a Jew by choice, the fact remains that marriage is more than a relationship between two individuals. It is also a relationship between two families. The person who converts to Judaism brings into the marriage both their non-Jewish family and their non-Jewish cultural upbringing.[6] Thus, even after becoming the quintessential convert to Israel, Ruth was still called "the Moabitess" (Ruth 1:22; 4:10). She continued to be associated with her country of birth. Hence, even a marriage between a born Jew and a convert is a form of intermarriage.

Intermarriage receives prominent attention in the Scriptures. Example upon example is given of Israelites who married non-Jews: Judah married a Canaanite, Joseph married the daughter of an Egyptian priest, Moses married the daughter of a Midianite priest as well as an Ethiopian maiden, Samson married a Philistine woman, David married the daughter of a foreign king, Solomon intermarried regularly, and Esther married a Persian king. Half of these intermarriages are described in a positive light and half in a negative light. It all depended on whether the non-Jew embraced the God of Israel and the people of Israel as their own.

## Abraham's Sons

There is no mention that Abraham, the father of the Jewish people, ever intermarried. However, he did have a child named Ishmael with an Egyptian servant named Hagar (Gen. 16:15). Later, Abraham had another child named Isaac with his wife, Sarah (Gen. 21:5). Since Isaac was chosen by God to carry the covenant promise and to pass it on to his children, Abraham was very concerned that Isaac not marry a Canaanite woman who might lead him astray into the worship of idols. Abraham, therefore, sent his servant back to his country to get a wife for his son from among his own relatives (Gen. 24:3–4). Thus, the idea of marrying within the tribe to preserve tribal religion goes all the way back to Abraham. After Sarah died, Abraham had other children through his second wife, Keturah (Gen. 25:1–2). Was Abraham's marriage with Keturah an intermarriage? We do not know.

### Isaac's Sons

Isaac had two children with his wife Rebekah: Esau and Jacob. The Scriptures record that the Hebrew parents did not approve of Esau's choice of brides:

> When 'Esav [Esau] was forty years old, he took as wives Y'hudit the daughter of Be'eri the Hitti and Basmat the daughter of Elon the Hitti. But they became a cause for embitterment of spirit to Yitz'chak [Isaac] and Rivkah [Rebekah]. (Gen. 26:34–35)

Distraught, Rebekah cried:

> I'm sick to death of Hitti women! If Ya'akov [Jacob] marries one of the Hitti women, like those who live here, my life won't be worth living. (Gen. 27:46)

It is very likely that Esau's wives continued to worship their Hittite/Canaanite gods and sought to lure Esau into their own religion. Later, Esau married the Egyptian daughter of Ishmael (Gen. 28:8–9). Jacob, on the other hand, was sent back to his mother's country where he married one of his own relatives. Isaac charged him:

> You are not to choose a wife from the Hitti women. Go now to the home of B'tu'el your mother's father, and choose a wife there from the daughters of Lavan [Laban] your mother's brother. (Gen. 28:1–2)

Again, the marriage of the son who carried the covenant promise took place within the tribe to minimize the influence of outside religions.

## Jacob's Sons

Jacob had twelve sons and one daughter with his wives: Rachel, Leah, and their maidservants (Gen. 46:8–25). His sons became the fathers of the twelve tribes of Israel. Of these twelve sons, three married outside of the Hebrew camp. Judah married a Canaanite woman named Shua (Gen. 38:2). Later, he had relations with a non-Hebrew woman whom he had chosen as a wife for his firstborn son. Her name was Tamar (Gen. 38:6–30). Joseph married an Egyptian woman named Asenath, the daughter of Potiphera, priest of On (Gen. 41:45). Imagine, a nice Jewish boy like Joseph having an Egyptian pagan priest for a father-in-law! It is ironic that traditional Jews (who oppose intermarriage) will bless their children every *Shabbat* with the words, "May God make you like Ephraim and Manassah," even though these sons of Joseph were two children of intermarriage! Indeed, the use of the boys' names in this blessing is in keeping with the providence of God (Gen. 48:20). Simeon, also intermarried, had a child named Sha'ul by his Canaanite wife (Gen. 46:10). The leaders of a quarter of the tribes of Israel were intermarried—two couples were Hebrew-Canaanite and the other was Hebrew-Egyptian.

## Moses and His Non-Israelite Wives

Moses married a non-Israelite woman named Zipporah, the daughter of Jethro, priest of Midian (Exod. 2:16–21). She lived near the mountain where the angel of the Lord appeared to Moses. Zipporah was clearly a convert to Israel's faith, for she personally circumcised Moses' son in obedience to the covenant (Exod. 4:24–26). It is significant that God allowed his prophet Moses to marry *two* non-Israelite women, first a Midianite and then an Ethiopian (Exod. 2:16; Num. 12:1). There is no indication in the Scriptures that this was displeasing to God. The acceptability of his wives is emphasized by the special relationship that Moses had with God. He saw God "face to face" (a sign of God's favor) only after he was married to Zipporah. Moses was also Israel's first national leader and called by God to deliver the Torah's command concerning intermarriage. This command did not preclude intermarriage with all non-Jews, as traditional Judaism teaches, but only with the seven nations of Canaan. It was acceptable for Moses (or any other Jew) to marry a non-Israelite as long as the prospective spouse was not from a Canaanite nation and was willing to embrace the God of Israel and the people of Israel as their own.

A reasonable case can be made that God wanted Moses to be intermarried. It was *bashert* (Yiddish for "predestined"). Exodus 2:11–21 emphasizes the guiding hand of God in leading Moses to Zipporah, who was chosen for Moses from among Jethro's seven daughters (cf. the guiding hand of God in leading Moses down the Nile to his surrogate Gentile mother, Pharaoh's daughter, in Exod. 2:1–10). Significantly, Zipporah lived next to Horeb, the mountain of God, where Moses encountered the Lord in the burning bush (Exod. 3:1–6).

Why did God want Moses, in particular, to intermarry? One explanation is that God wanted to ensure that Israel would be forever accepting of Zipporah-like converts from among the nations. In this regard, it is ironic that traditional rabbis (who discourage intermarriage) still conclude their wedding ceremonies with the words, "In accordance with the Law of Moses and of Israel, I pronounce you man and wife." The individual whose name is spoken to declare the marriage legal was twice an intermarried Jew!

Divine approval of conversionary marriage, however, did not necessarily translate into an absence of anti-Gentile prejudice in the Israelite community. The Scriptures record that Moses was criticized by his brother, Aaron, and his sister, Miryam, "on account of the Ethiopian woman he had married, for he had in fact married an Ethiopian woman" (Num. 12:1). The Lord responded immediately to their criticism by striking Miryam with leprosy (Num. 12:4–15). Perhaps this is a lesson for God's people to not be too hasty in speaking against intermarriage, for sometimes intermarriages are made in heaven.

## Egyptian-Israelite Intermarriage

During the 430 years that the Israelites lived in Egypt, intermarriages took place between Israelites and Egyptians. The fact that Joseph had an Egyptian wife certainly set a precedent for such unions. In Leviticus 24:10–16, one such couple is mentioned. The wife was Israelite and the husband Egyptian. Both had come out of Egypt in the great deliverance. Tragically, their son had blasphemed the Lord and was put to death in accordance with the Law of Israel. The passage is very important because it gives us a glimpse into how the Torah viewed the identity of a child descended from an Israelite mother and Gentile father. Up until this point in the Scriptures, we have only seen examples of children with Israelite fathers and Gentile mothers. These children were all regarded as Israelites. From the egalitarian standpoint, one would think the Leviticus 24 child was an Israelite. And from the rabbinic standpoint, since Jewish identity is matrilineally based, one would assume that the child was an Israelite. However, during this period of Israelite history, Jewish identity was reckoned according to the identity of the father and not the mother (see Appendix

A). Thus, the child was not counted as an Israelite, as the passage makes clear. Rather, he was viewed as one of the thousands of *gerim* (resident aliens) who accompanied Israel on their way to Mount Horeb (Exod. 12:37–38). *Gerim* were tried under the same law as the native born Israelite (Lev. 24:16, 22). This is why he was put to death.

## Zimri and Cozbi

When the Israelites camped at Shittim, Moabite women came and seduced the Israelite men into worshipping Moabite gods (Num. 25). The religious ritual involved having sexual relations with these women. Because of this sin, the Lord poured out a plague on the Israelites. He also told Moses to kill the Israelite leaders who had participated in Moabite worship. One of these men was Zimri, the leader of a Simeonite family. He had taken a woman named Cozbi "into his tent." When Pinchas (Phinehas) the priest saw this happening, he impaled Zimri and Cozbi with his spear. Immediately, the plague (which had killed 24,000 Israelites) stopped. Although Zimri and Cozbi were not "married" by today's standards (i.e. they did not have a wedding), in ancient Israel, when a man brought a woman into his tent, they were considered married. The story of the Israelites at Shittim illustrates what the Lord's intermarriage prohibition was designed to prevent—the importation of foreign religious practices into the nation of Israel.

## Salmon and Rahab

When the Israelites spied out the Promised Land, they met a Canaanite prostitute named Rahab who knew the Lord was going to destroy her city. Rahab risked her life to protect the spies. Consequently, she and her whole family were spared when the Israelites took the city (Josh. 2; 6:22–25). According to Second Temple Jewish tradition, Rahab married an Israelite named Salmon (Matt. 1:5). And out of this Israelite-Canaanite intermarriage, several very famous people were born: Boaz (her son) and King David (her great, great grandson). According to later rabbinic tradition, Rahab married Joshua and became the ancestor of eight prophets, including Jeremiah.[7]

## Boaz and Ruth

Ruth the Moabitess married an Israelite man named Mahlon who had been living in Moab. When Mahlon died, Ruth chose to return with her mother-in-law to Israel and to become an Israelite herself. She declared to her Jewish mother-in-law, "Your people will be my people and your God will be my God" (Ruth 1:16). Ruth's words inspired the Sages and became the formal statement of covenant that has since been uttered by hundreds of thousands of other converts to Israel. Ruth is depicted in Jewish tradition as an ideal wife. The Proverbs 31 אשת-חיל (Hebrew, *eshet chayil*, wife of noble character) is an allusion to Ruth the Moabitess (Prov. 31:10; Ruth 3:11) and her virtues are recounted every *Erev Shabbat* (Sabbath Eve) by many Jewish men to their wives. Ruth arrived in the land of Israel and soon after married Boaz. It is significant that Boaz's mother was Rahab, a Canaanite convert to Israel (Matt. 1:5), and Boaz's wife was a Moabite convert to Israel. Imagine Rahab instructing her new daughter-in-law, Ruth, in all the laws of Israel and relating her own experiences about the difficulties of being a convert! Ruth had a lot to learn and she could not have asked for a more empathetic teacher.

As previously mentioned, Ruth continued to be called "the Moabitess," even after becoming a convert (Ruth 1:22; 2:2, 6, 21; 4:5, 10). This is clearly due to the recognition that converts did not sever themselves completely from their own family or cultural upbringing. They continued to have a tie to their nation of origin. Boaz and Ruth had a son named Obed. Obed had a son named Jesse. And Jesse had a son named David who became the king of Israel. David's great grandparents, then, were an intermarried couple, as were his great great grandparents. The book of Ruth, which is read by Jews every year during the harvest festival of *Shavu'ot* (Pentecost), memorializes the life story of Boaz and Ruth. It is an eternal reminder that even a marriage between a Jew and a Moabite can be a blessed union.

## Samson and His Philistine Women

Samson's wife was not what his Jewish parents had in mind for him. When he told them that he had picked out a Philistine bride, they replied, "Isn't there any woman from the daughters of your kinsmen or among all my people? Must you go to the uncircumcised P'lishtim [Philistines] to find a wife?" (Judg. 14:3). But Samson was not swayed. He had to have her. His wedding feast was prepared according to Philistine custom and he was given thirty Philistine companions with which to celebrate (Judg. 14:10–11). A series of events followed that led to the death of Samson's wife and his killing over a thousand Philistines. Samson eventually became a judge and led Israel for twenty years. After this time, he fell in love with another Philistine woman named Delilah. They were never married. Nonetheless, it is important to note how his love for this non-Israelite woman led to his downfall. The Philistine leaders paid Delilah to discover the secret of Samson's superhuman strength; they knew that she held the key to his heart. Through Delilah's constant nagging, Samson finally shared the secret of his strength, which led to his torture and death. The story of Samson is, in part, a reminder to Jews about the unforeseen problems that can arise from non-conversionary marriages.

### David and Maacah

King David had several wives. One of them was a non-Israelite by the name of Maacah. We do not know much about her except that she was the daughter of Talmai king of Geshur, a pagan ruler (1 Chron. 3:2). Through this intermarriage, Absalom and Tamar were born (2 Sam. 13:1). Absalom killed his stepbrother Amnon for raping Tamar and fled to his pagan grandfather's kingdom where he lived in exile for several years (2 Sam. 13:37). Absalom eventually returned to Jerusalem and led a conspiracy against his father that resulted in David fleeing the palace with Maacah. Absalom sought to kill his father but ended up being killed instead. (2 Sam. 14–18). King David also had a sister named Abigail who married an Ishmaelite named Jether (1 Chron. 2:15–17). Thus, King David's father (Jesse) had two children who intermarried.

### Uriah and Bathsheba

Uriah the Hittite was one of David's mighty men and lived in a house next to the palace (1 Chron. 11:41; 2 Sam. 11). Given his status in Israel, he was probably a convert. Uriah married a beautiful Israelite woman named Bathsheba. King David, however, was taken with Bathsheba's beauty and slept with her. Later, David killed Uriah in order to cover up the adulterous affair and took Bathsheba to be his wife. Even after becoming a convert and intermarrying, Uriah's country of origin was still tagged on to his name.

### Solomon and His Wives

Solomon's experience with women epitomizes the meaning and purpose of the command against intermarriage. Hundreds of his wives were from nations from which God forbade the Israelites to marry. His wives clung to their idols. Solomon violated God's Law repeatedly by bringing these women into his palace. Due to their seductive influence, Solomon's heart was eventually led astray after other gods and he introduced foreign religious practices into the camp of Israel. This was a very great sin and the Lord punished Solomon and the nation accordingly.

> King Shlomo [Solomon] loved many foreign women besides the daughter of Pharaoh. These were women from the Mo'avi, 'Amoni, Edomi, Tzidoni and Hitti—nations about which ADONAI had said to the people of Isra'el, "You are not to go among them or they among you, because they will turn your hearts away toward their gods." But Shlomo was deeply attached to them by his love. He had 700 wives, all princesses, and 300 concubines; and his wives turned his heart away. For when Shlomo became old, his wives turned his heart away toward other gods; so that he was not wholehearted with ADONAI his God, as David his father had been. For Shlomo followed 'Ashnoret the goddess of the Tzidoni and Milkom the abomination of the 'Amoni. Thus Shlomo did what was evil in ADONAI's view and did not fully follow ADONAI, as David his father had done. Shlomo built a high place for K'mosh the abomination of Mo'av on the hill on front of Yerushalayim, and another for Molekh the abomination of the people of 'Amon. This is what he did for all his foreign wives, who then offered and sacrificed to their gods. So ADONAI grew angry with Shlomo, because his heart had turned away from ADONAI the God of Isra'el, who had appeared to him twice and given him orders concerning this matter that he should not follow other gods. But he didn't obey ADONAI's orders. So ADONAI said to Shlomo, "Since this is what has been in your mind, and you haven't kept my covenant and my regulations which I ordered you to obey, I will tear the kingdom from you and give it to your servant." (1 Kings 11:1–11)

The difference between Solomon's non-conversionary marriages and the conversionary marriage of Boaz and Ruth is significant. In the case of Solomon's wives, there was no renunciation of foreign religious practices; there was no embrace of the God of Israel. In contrast, Ruth was a "woman of good character" (Ruth 3:11). She abandoned her Moabite religion and worshiped God. She became one of the great heroines of Israel and contributed to the Jewish religious heritage. Therefore, intermarriage can be constructive or destructive; it all depends on the character of the non-Jewish spouse and their commitment to the God of Israel and the people of Israel.

## Ahab and Jezebel

The intermarriage of Ahab and Jezebel was worse than the intermarriages between Solomon and his foreign wives. Ahab was the king of Israel and Jezebel was the daughter of Ethbaal, king of the Sidonians (1 Kings 16:31). Unlike Solomon's foreign wives who passively tempted Solomon to sin by their idolatry, Jezebel had an evil agenda to transform Israel into a Baal worshiping nation! And she was successful in her efforts. A temple for Baal worship was raised up along with 450 evil prophets (1 Kings 16:32–33; 18:22). Turning Israel away from the Lord, however, required more than the promotion of Baal worship. Hundreds of the Lord's prophets had to be killed. The royal order was given and the Lord's prophets were tracked down and murdered, with the exception of Elijah who fled for his life (1 Kings 18:4, 13; 19:2). Meanwhile, King Ahab assented to all of this. The Scriptures say of him:

> Truly, there was never anyone like Ach'av [Ahab]. Stirred up by his wife Izevel [Jezebel], he gave himself over to do what is evil from ADONAI's perspective. (1 Kings 21:25)

The intermarriage of Ahab and Jezebel represents a worst-case scenario. It is a warning not to underestimate the damage that can be done when a Jewish leader marries someone whose life is consumed by the worship of foreign gods.

## King Ahasuerus and Esther

The intermarriage between King Ahasuerus and Esther, the Jewish orphan, is probably the most famous intermarriage in the Scriptures. Haman, a trusted servant of King Ahasuerus, had devised a plan to annihilate the Jews of the Persian kingdom on a single day. With the king's permission, the plan went into effect. Only one person was in a position to save the Jews—Queen Esther. The Scriptures imply that God orchestrated the intermarriage to save his people (Esther 4:14). When Esther made known to Ahasuerus that she was a Jew, and that

Haman was planning to destroy her people, the king intervened. Instead of the Jews being killed, Haman and his anti-Semitic minions were killed instead. By God's design, this intermarried couple saved the Jewish nation from extinction. Mordecai, Esther's cousin and foster father, probably did not approve of the intermarriage between Esther and Ahasuerus in the beginning, for the king was an idolater and had no plans of becoming a convert. However, in the end, Mordecai came to see it was the hand of God. We have no record of the children of this intermarried couple. According to the patrilineal definition of Jewish identity, which was observed at that time (see Appendix A), their children would not have been regarded as Jews as long as King Ahasuerus chose not to join the nation. In all likelihood, the children assimilated into the Persian kingdom, a sad ending to a happy story.

## The Return From Exile

Israel's seventy years in Babylon was an unprecedented time of contact with other nations and naturally resulted in a higher intermarriage rate. Perhaps the royal intermarriage of King Ahasuerus and Esther also contributed to a lessening of the taboo of non-conversionary marriage. When the Jews returned to Jerusalem, they were faced with the reality of having some of these non-conversionary marriages in the camp. Nehemiah confirms that the women of these marriages were non-converts by comparing them to Solomon's wives (Neh. 13:26–27). Likewise, Ezra emphasizes their detestable practices (Ezra 9:1, 14). The number of such intermarriages was not huge. Of the 31,089 men who returned, 111 had married non-convert wives and only some had children by these marriages (Ezra 2:64–65; 10:18–44). Assuming that 80 percent of the returning men were married, the non-conversionary intermarriage rate was 0.4 percent, a tiny fraction of the population. Nevertheless, seventeen of these men were priests, ten were Levites, and several others were leaders among the people (Ezra 9:2; 10:18–24). In other words, they were a small but influential group. Ezra assessed the situation and ruled that all non-convert wives were to be sent away with their children. His motivation for taking this painful step was to prevent idolatry from entering the camp, especially through the priesthood. While traditional Judaism interprets Ezra's decision to send the children away as indicative of a change in the way Jewish identity was reckoned (i.e. from patrilineal to matrilineal), there is no Scriptural basis for this view (see Appendix A).

## Intermarriage in the New Testament

The most notable example of intermarriage in the New Testament was the one between a Jewish follower of Jesus named Eunice and a man of Greek descent in Lystra (Acts 16:1). The couple had a son named Timothy (2 Tim. 1:5; 3:15). Due to the Greek father's influence, Timothy had not been circumcised as a child and was not considered a Jew by first century patrilineal standards.[8] Ultimately, Paul circumcised Timothy (Acts 16:3; Gen. 17:9–14). A New Testament letter bears the name of this son of intermarriage.

Intermarriage is not a modern day phenomenon but has been occurring for thousands of years. Biblical precedent suggests that there is no reason for a Jew to feel he is doing anything wrong by marrying a Gentile, as long as the spouse-to-be fully embraces the God of Israel and the people of Israel as their own.[9] In this way, the Jew can keep his covenant with God and convey Jewish heritage to the next generation. Such was the way of Moses and of countless other heroes of the biblical faith.

# CHAPTER 4
# Intermarriage in Religious Law

T oday, few nations have laws regulating intermarriage between Jews and Gentiles. In ancient times, however, the situation was different. Considerable attention was devoted in early Jewish and Christian law to the subject of intermarriage.

## Biblical Law

Many people assume that biblical law prohibits Jews from marrying Gentiles. But is this actually the case? In the Torah, there are two versions of the intermarriage prohibition. I will quote them both in full:

> Adonai your God is going to bring you into the land you will enter in order take possession of it, and he will expel many nations ahead of you—the Hitti, Girgashi, Emori, Kena'ani, P'rizi, Hivi and Y'vusi, seven nations bigger and stronger than you. When he does this, when Adonai your God hands them over ahead of you, and you defeat them, you are to destroy them completely! Do not make any covenant with them. Show them no mercy. Don't intermarry with them—don't give your daughter to his son, and don't take his daughter for your son. For he will turn your children away from following me in order to serve other gods. If this happens, the anger of Adonai will flare up against you, and he will quickly destroy you (Deut. 7:1–4)

> Do not make a covenant with the people living in the land. It will cause you to go astray after their gods and sacrifice to their gods. Then they will invite you to join them in eating their sacrifices, and you will take their daughters as wives for your sons. Their daughters will prostitute themselves to their own gods and make your sons do the same! (Exod. 34:15–16)

## Intermarriage with the Seven Nations of Canaan

The intermarriage prohibition makes several points clear. First, the Israelites were to completely annihilate the inhabitants of the Promised Land—seven specific nations. No one was to survive. No mercy was to be extended. This was due to the degree of their wickedness. Lest we become compassionate toward the seven nations, the Torah reminds us, "They even burn up their sons and daughters in the fire for their gods" (Deut. 12:31). Imagine throwing your own baby into the fire as a religious sacrifice! These cultures were characterized by the sanctification of evil; they not only practiced evil, they celebrated it. Second, annihilating the seven nations meant that no one would be left with which to make a treaty or intermarry. Finally, the reason behind the commandment is that intermarriage would likely draw the Israelites away from the Lord and into idolatry.

When the Israelites entered the Land, they were not faithful to carry out the annihilation. Consequently, a chain reaction occurred: there were treaties and intermarriage, and the Israelites were drawn into idolatry. The commandment that was designed to keep the Israelites set apart to the Lord was violated and the floodgates of evil broke loose. The Scriptures cannot be more precise, "So the people of Isra'el lived among the Kena'ani, Hitti, Emori, P'rizi, Hivi and Y'vusi; taking their daughters as their wives, giving their own daughters to their sons and serving their gods" (Judg. 3:5–6). In the end, Israel adopted the wicked practices of these nations:

> They failed to destroy the peoples, as ADONAI had ordered them to do, but mingled with the nations and learned to follow their ways. They went on to serve their idols, which became a snare for them. They even sacrificed their sons and their daughters to demons. Yes, they shed innocent blood, the blood of their own sons and daughters, whom they sacrificed to Kena'an's false gods, polluting the land with blood. Thus they were defiled by their deeds; they prostituted themselves by their actions. (Ps. 106:34–39)

## Intermarriage with Non-Canaanite Nations

It is significant that only the seven nations of Canaan are mentioned in the Torah's prohibition concerning intermarriage. This is not an accident. Elsewhere in the Scriptures, this emphasis is also reiterated (1

Kings 11:1–2; Ezra 9:1–2, 10–14; 10:2, 11; Neh. 10:30; 13:1–3, 23). If God had intended to ban intermarriage with all nations, he would have certainly said so. In the ancient Near East, there were other peoples with whom the Israelites came into contact—Egyptians, Edomites, Moabites, Midianites, etc. One must assume, therefore, that intermarriage was *not* forbidden with these neighboring peoples or the more distant nations. Shaye Cohen, Professor of Hebrew Literature and Philosophy at Harvard University, concurs in his book, *The Beginnings of Jewishness*:

> Does this prohibition apply to all gentiles or only to the seven Canaanite nations? The answer is clearly the latter. Moses commands the Israelites to destroy the seven Canaanite nations because they threaten Israelite religious identity and live on the land that the Israelites will conquer. Intermarriage with them is prohibited. The Ammonites and Moabites, somewhat more distant and therefore somewhat less dangerous, were not consigned to destruction and isolation; they were merely prohibited from *entering the congregation* (Deut. 23:4). The Egyptians and Edomites were even permitted to *enter the congregation* after three generations (Deut. 23:8–9). The meaning of the prohibition of "entering the congregation" is not at all clear, as I shall discuss below, but I presume that originally, at least, it was not a prohibition of intermarriage. Other nations, even further removed from the Israelite horizon, were presumably not subject to any prohibition. Internal biblical evidence confirms this narrow interpretation of Deut. 7:3–4. The patriarchal narratives in Genesis condemn marriages between members of Abraham's clan and the indigenous Canaanite population.[1]

Deuteronomy 21 confirms the above conclusion. If the Israelites went to war against one of the non-Canaanite nations, they were allowed to take female captives.[2] Israelite men were then permitted to marry these Gentile women captives, but they had to follow a legal procedure:

> When you go out to war against your enemies, and ADONAI your God hands them over to you, and you take prisoners, and you see among the prisoners a woman who looks

good to you, and you feel attracted to her and want her as your wife; you are to bring her home to your house, where she will shave her head, cut her fingernails and remove her prison clothing. She will stay there in your house, mourning her father and mother for a full month; after which you may go in to have sexual relations with her and be her husband, and she will be your wife. In the event that you lose interest in her, you are to let her go wherever she wishes; but you may not sell her for money or treat her like a slave, because you humiliated her. (Deut. 21:10–14)

The shaving of the head, trimming of the nails, new clothes, and mourning for her parents are symbolic of the new life the woman was to begin as a member of an Israelite household. Everything was new to her, even her embrace of the one true God, for it was a capital offense in Israel to worship foreign gods. The book of Numbers records that, on one occasion, as many as 32,000 virgins from among the Midianites were added to Israel's number as war brides. Some were even given to the priests and Levites (Num. 31:25–47).

We have already demonstrated that there were many other Gentile converts to Israel who married Israelites with the Lord's blessing. The uniting of Moses and Zipporah is one such example. Zipporah was an acceptable wife for Moses because she was not from the seven forbidden nations of Canaan and she fully embraced the religion and people of Israel. Non-conversionary marriages, however, were unacceptable because they would bring a person into the camp who was unwilling to abide by the law of Israel—a law that commanded the renunciation of all foreign gods and the worship of the Lord alone. Thus, members of the seven nations of Canaan, and like-minded Gentiles,[3] were not suitable marriage partners for Jews according to the Torah. Finally, as Shaye Cohen notes:

A general prohibition of intermarriage between Jews and non-Jews does not appear anywhere in the Tanakh [the Hebrew Bible]. Leviticus lists numerous sexual taboos (Chapters 18 and 20) but fails to include intermarriage among them. Exodus 34:15 and Deuteronomy 7:3–4 prohibit intermarriage with the seven Canaanite nations, and Deuteronomy 23:2–9 prohibits four additional nations from *entering the congregation of the Lord*—perhaps (but probably not) a prohibition of marriage. But neither Exodus nor Deuteronomy prohibits intermarriage with all non-Israelites, and both of them prohibit intermarriage with Canaanites only because it might lead to something else that was prohibited (idolatry).[4]

These findings are supported by the weight of modern scholarship.[5]

## Rabbinic Law

The Sages debated whether the Torah's intermarriage prohibitions (Deut. 7:1–4; Exod. 34:15–16) referred only to the seven nations of Canaan or applied to all Gentiles:

> . . . in the Talmudic period, the Rabbis argued over the word "them" in the phrase "neither shalt thou make marriages with *them*." Some argued that it referred only to the Seven Nations spelled out in the original prohibition; but a majority view held that it represented a general prohibition against marriage with any non-Jew (*Talmud Avoda Zara 36B* and *Yebamot 77A*). From that time on, the original statement against the seven nationalities became a universal prohibition.[6]

With this reading of the text established, the next step was to decide how to deal with intermarriages once they occurred:

> One of the first acts of the Pharisees following the destruction of the Second Temple was to interpret biblical law so that intermarriage was understood as a violation of basic Jewish law. . . . The Pharisaic edict concerning intermarriage was curious. They did not *prohibit* intermarriage. A prohibition would have forbidden the act, and those involved would have been guilty of violating the law. Instead, they *invalidated* it. They simply decreed it to be a non-act. Instead of creating intermarriage as a crime punishable by law, they ruled it out of existence. A couple who intermarried did not commit a crime, did not violate a law. They simply were not married. Any child born of such a

union was illegitimate (a *mamzer*). This Pharisaic/Rab-
binic edict is still in force today in the *halacha* (Jewish law)
that is binding on all Orthodox and Conservative Jews.[7]

An intermarried couple may be legally married according to the law of
their state, but from the rabbinic perspective, they are not married in
the sight of God. They are merely two unmarried people living together and engaging in sexual relations, a great sin. For this reason,
rabbinic law eventually spelled out consequences for Jews who had
intimate relations with Gentiles. Legislation also stressed the positive
alternative—conversionary marriage:

> . . . rabbinic legislation makes a clear-cut distinction be-
> tween sexual relations with Gentiles and intermarriage
> with converts. The former is strictly forbidden in both its
> marital and extramarital varieties. If an Israelite was
> caught *in flagrante* with a Gentile woman, the "Zealous"
> were permitted to kill him on the spot, following the bib-
> lical example of Phinehas. If he committed the sin and
> was found guilty subsequently, he was flogged. In addi-
> tion to the earthly punishment, a Jew who cohabitated
> with a non-Jewish woman was believed to suffer after his
> death the fires of Gehenna. . . . As against these uncom-
> promising prohibitions, the Talmudic law developed a
> most  tolerant  attitude  toward  intermarriage  with
> converts. The Talmudic teachers went to great lengths to
> legalize marriage with Gentile converts.[8]

Rabbinic literature attests to the fact that severe punishments did take
place for Jews who cohabited with Gentiles. According to the *responsa*
(correspondence on matters of Jewish law) of Rabbi Asher ben Yehiel,
one woman even had her nose cut off.[9] One shutters to think of what
would have been done to Safiyya, the Jewish wife of Mohammed![10]

## Canon Law

Beginning in the fourth century, the Church fathers wrote down very
clear laws that prohibited marriage between Jews and Christians. The
primary motivation for these laws was anti-Semitism. Repeatedly,
these councils had to be restated as young Jews and Christians chose
to risk the consequences of falling in love. Raphael and Jennifer Patai
survey the history of these laws:

No sooner did Christianity attain a position of strength in the Roman world than it began to fight against Jewish-Christian intermarriage and extramarital sex relations. Both were sharply condemned by the Council of Elvira in Andalusia, Spain (about A.D. 300), which decreed that Christian girls must not be married to Jews or pagans and that parents who transgressed this prohibition would be excommunicated for five years. . . . In A.D. 315, Constantine renewed the old pagan Roman legislation against seduction to the monotheistic faiths, but applied it only against Judaism, threatening with the death penalty both converts and those who won them over. Even intermarriage between Jews and Christians was made a capital offense, unless of course the former abandoned their faith. The same prohibition was repeated in 339 by the Emperor Constantius, and in 388 by Theodosius the Great. . . . The Codex Theodosianus (439) treats Jewish-Christian unions on a par with adultery and imposes severe penalties on the culprits. The Council of Chalcedon (451) repeats the same injunction. . . . Alaric II's *Lex Romana Visigothorum* (506) repeats essentially the injunctions of the Theodosian Code, as do the Code of Justinian (533), and the Councils of Orleans (533), Clermont (535), Orleans (538), and Toledo (589 and 633). . . . The rulers of the Eastern Christian empire exhibited the same negative attitude toward mixed marriages between Christians and Jews. . . . As time passed, the penalties became more severe, and by the ninth and tenth centuries intermarriage was equated with adultery and was subject to capital punishment.[11]

When one stops to consider that many Jews and non-Jews were willing to risk death to marry each other, the powerful attraction of intermarriage becomes evident. Today, Christians view these ancient codes as archaic. In the Roman Catholic Church, as well as the Eastern Orthodox Church, attitudes toward intermarriage have liberalized, and the historic Protestant denominations usually offer no grounds for objection. Evangelical churches discourage believers in Jesus from marrying unbelievers (2 Cor. 6:14). The objection is not a matter of ethnic background but of marrying a person who holds to a different set of core beliefs and values than one's own.

God has an eternal covenant with Israel and it entails the obligation to pass on Jewish heritage to the next generation. Biblical law does not prohibit intermarriage outside of the seven nations of Canaan and implies that such marriages are permitted as long as the Gentile partner embraces the God and people of Israel. The rabbis of old did not recognize this and interpreted the Torah's prohibition of intermarriage in the broadest terms, perhaps as a survival measure in the Diaspora. The Christian Church was unaware of God's enduring covenant with Israel and opposed intermarriage due to its anti-Judaic theology. In each case, laws were deemed necessary to prevent intermarriage.

CHAPTER 5

# Intermarriage and Race

Some Jewish people object to intermarriage, not based on biblical or rabbinic law, but on the conviction that Jews need to preserve the purity of their race. Let us consider this view.

## Race: A Biblical Perspective

In the foundational document of Judaism and Christianity—the Torah—mankind is classified on the basis of people groups but not on the basis of race. It may even be said that dividing mankind into "races" (as the term is used today) goes against the grain of Torah since such an outlook tends to de-emphasize the common origins of all people in the first human couple.[1] The New Testament concurs that "From one man he made every nation of men" (Acts 17:26 NIV).[2] The overarching biblical emphasis is, therefore, on the human race (which bears the image of God) and not on genetic distinctions between humans.[3]

## The Myth of a Jewish Race

The concept of "race" has come under scientific scrutiny in recent years.[4] Assuming that races do exist, there has never been a "Jewish race" in the anthropological sense.[5] The biblical examples of intermarriage just described demonstrates that Israel was a nation of mixed peoples from the beginning. Even the heads of the tribes of Israel married Canaanite and Egyptian women. No one can claim to be a pure descendant of Abraham and Sarah. Harvard Anthropologist Carl C. Seltzer notes:

> . . . in the anthropological meaning of the word "race," it can be said with conviction that the Jewish people, taken as a whole, show no preponderance, nor consistency, nor exclusiveness of physical features which allow them to be classified as a unified racial group. They are a conglomerate mixture of many races in disparate proportions bound together by common religion, familial, and historical traditions, but showing in many instances varying amounts of

physical distinctiveness. We can no more classify the Jews
into a race than we can say that there is an American race.[6]

The theory that Jews are a distinct race is of nineteenth century origin.[7] Hitler popularized the notion through Nazi propaganda and
convinced even many Jews of its basis in fact. Jews who espouse this
view are ironically perpetuating a myth that Hitler introduced to the
whole world. It has not gone without notice that Jews who emphasize their blood as the basis of their being Jews are usually the least
committed to the classical teachings of Judaism. Rabbi Harold
Schulweis has observed,

> Indeed, it seems to me that the less practicing and believ-
> ing the Jew, the more insistent the contention that
> Jewishness is something born into. The weaker the Jews,
> the more powerful the attraction to make Jewishness a ge-
> netic affair[8] (see Appendix A for a detailed discussion of
> "Who is a Jew").

While it is true that the usual way a person becomes a Jew is by
birth (and entrance into the covenant of circumcision, if a boy), it is
also true that some non-Jews become Jews through a process of cov-
enant-making (e.g. Gen. 17:12–13). They are able to do this because
Jewishness, at its core, is a matter of covenant relationship with God
and circumcision is a sign of the Abrahamic covenant. Consider that
Isaac, the *full-blooded son* born to Abraham and Sarah, would not
have been reckoned a "Jew" (i.e. a member of the covenant people) if
Abraham had not circumcised him. The same was true of Jacob and
his children (Gen. 17:14). Thus, the element of volition is intrinsic to
the Abrahamic covenant and it is on this basis that converts were received into the community of Israel. The myth of a "Jewish race" can
only survive among those who know little about the history of Jewish
proselytism.

## Jewish Proselytism

*The Jewish Almanac* has a section entitled "8 Common Misconceptions Jews Have About Judaism." One of these misconceptions is that
"Judaism is a religion which never sought converts." The almanac
explains, "Although Judaism is generally thought of as a religion that
rejects the seeking of converts, proselytizing, particularly in ancient
times, was far from uncommon."[9] In fact, for thousands of years, Jews
have been a proselytizing people.[10] And from a biblical perspective,
this is good. What makes Israel a "chosen nation" is its divine calling

to bring the knowledge of God to all the peoples of the earth. Universalism—the view that all religions are equally true—is counter to the biblical Jewish mindset. The Prophet Isaiah declared that Israel would serve as a "light to the nations" (Isa. 49:6). The Prophet Zechariah spoke of a day to come when "ten men will take hold . . . of the cloak of a Jew and say, 'We want to go with you, because we have heard that God is with you'" (Zech. 8:23). Such a worldwide turning to the God of Israel was the message of the Prophet Zechariah:

> Then ADONAI will be king over the whole world. On that day ADONAI will be the only one [i.e. the only God], and his name will be the only name. (Zech. 14:9)

The Scriptures record the existence of thousands of converts in ancient Israel. On one occasion, as already mentioned, 32,000 Midianite women became Israelite wives (Num. 31:25–35). In addition to the many Ruth-like converts noted in the Scriptures, history records the existence of countless other Gentiles who joined themselves to the descendants of Abraham since the end of the biblical period. Rabbi Joseph Rosenbloom writes in his book *Conversion to Judaism: From the Biblical Period to the Present* that the population of the Roman Empire was at least ten percent Jewish as a result of proselytization:

> According to one scholar, the Jewish population of Palestine increased from 20,000 to 40,000 immediately after the Exile, to 200,000 before the expansion under the Hasmoneans, to 2,500,000 by the year 70 C.E. Adding to this the number of Jews in the diaspora, some scholars believe the Jews to have been one of the most significant groups in the region. Salo Baron estimates the Jewish population during the Roman period as 8,000,000. There were a million or more each in Syria, Egypt, Babylonia, and Asia Minor, triple the number of Jews in Palestine. While the Jews comprised 10 percent of the Roman Empire, in the most advanced Hellenestic sector of the eastern Mediterranean, they were 20 percent. *Both Baron and Joseph Klausner state that this increase is attributable primarily to proselytism.*[11] (emphasis mine)

Though Goodman and McKnight have disputed the extent of Jewish proselytizing in the Second Temple period,[12] no one denies that hundreds of thousands of converts have been added to the Jewish people over the millennia. Whole nations and entire tribes have converted to Judaism. These include the Idumeans and Itureans who were forcibly converted to Judaism in the second century B.C.E. In the Diaspora, group conversion occurred among the Adiabeneans, the kingdom of Southern Arabia, the Khazars, the Berbers of North Africa, the Abyssinians, and others.[13] Converted slaves were another demographic group that added large numbers to the Jewish people. There is evidence that "Middle Eastern and North African Jewry doubled between the seventh and eighth centuries as a result of the proselytizing of slaves."[14] From the seventeenth century to the twentieth century, there was a similar multiplication of Jewish population due to the influx of Jewish converts. Rabbi Rosenbloom notes:

> Baron estimates that the Jewish population of Europe grew from 850,000 in 1660 to 12,500,000 in 1940, a rise of 1500 percent, as contrasted with increases of 250 percent in the world population and 350 percent in the European population during the same period. Such a dramatic increase can be accounted for by better hygienic practices and large-scale conversions.[15]

Since the close of the Second Temple period, there have been many famous Jewish converts. The Torah translators, Onkelos and Aquila, were both converts. Hillel and Shammai[16] were descendants of converts, as were Avtalyon, Shemaiah, and Rabbi Meir. According to one tradition, the great Rabbi Akiba was the son of a convert[17] and married a convert.[18] In the twentieth century, Sammy Davis, Jr. and Marilyn Monroe were also converts!

How many converts are there in the Jewish community today? In her book *Embracing the Stranger,* Ellen Jaffe McClain estimates that there are "200,000 'Jews-by-choice' in the United States—about one out of every thirty American Jews. Recent estimates of how many people convert to Judaism each year in this country run between 3,000 and 5,000."[19]

This modern upsurge in conversion is a direct result of the Reform Movement's emphasis on proselytism over the last twenty years. In December 1978, Rabbi Alexander Schindler, president of the Union of American Hebrew Congregations (UAHC), called on the Reform movement (which represents one-third of organized American Jewry) to establish a Jewish "missionary" program to all religiously unaffiliated Gentiles. This call was renewed at the 1993 UAHC Biennial Convention.[20]

As a result of the UAHC embrace of missionary Judaism, the number of converts to Judaism has grown dramatically, even to the extent that half of the membership of some Reform synagogues is now made up of converts.[21] These Jews-by-choice come from a wide range of ethnic backgrounds. The conversion of adopted children from overseas has also enriched the American Jewish community with ethnic diversity. In his article "The Outreach Movement: Making Judaism an Inclusive Religion," Egon Mayer states, "With their numbers greatly increasing in the past two decades, it is entirely possible that Jews-by-choice will comprise between 7 to 10 percent of the American Jewish population by 2010."[22]

## An Intermarried People

As we have demonstrated, Jewish people have different ethnic backgrounds. All of us do not come from Russia or eat *gefilte* fish. Our people have as much "diversity of culture" as the nations in which we have lived over the last 2800 years. I have several books in my library that detail the degree to which diversity exists among Jewish communities around the globe. One of these is a work by Karen Primack called *Jews in Places You Never Thought Of*. In addition to providing profiles of these communities, it contains a fascinating photo collection of Jews from around the world.[23] There are photos of Jews with every skin color and facial feature. Ida Cowen has written a similar book—*Jews in Remote Corners of the World*. Ms. Cowen traveled the world to visit fellow Jews in such far off places as Tahiti, Fiji, New Zealand, Singapore, Burma, India, Afghanistan, Iran, Turkey, and the list goes on. She writes in her introduction:

> I attended Bar Mitzvahs in Christchurch, in Manila and in New Delhi. I participated in Rosh Hashanah services in Hong Kong, broke Yom Kippur fast with the Jews of Bangkok, crowned the Queen of Beauty chosen at the Simhat Torah Ball in Calcutta. I watched Hanukkah lights being lit in Melbourne, joined Heart's Jews at their Purim feast, observed Seder nights in Izmir and I was among those paying final respects at the funeral of Afghanistan's last rabbi.[24]

Each of these Jewish communities had, to some extent, intermarried with their host countries. Indeed, they had their own distinct cultural expressions of Judaism. And often these expressions were very different from the eastern European form of Judaism familiar to most American Jews.[25]

Every Jew is related to non-Jews. It is a fact that we are of mixed blood with the nations. Kevin Brook in his work *The Jews of Khazaria* notes that Ashkenazic Jewry is largely a mixture of Khazar converts to Judaism and others who married Jewish people:

> After considering the strong evidence for cultural, linguistic, and ethnic ties between eastern Ashkenazic Jews and the Khazar Jews, as well as the equally strong evidence for Jewish migrations into eastern Europe from the south and west, one can come to only one conclusion: that the eastern European Jews are descended from both Khazars and other converts, as well as from Judeans. The fact that most of our people descend from converts does not diminish our Jewish status, since all converts share equally in the Jewish heritage.[26]

Similarly, Paul Wexler, Professor of Linguistics at Tel Aviv University, demonstrates in his book *The Non-Jewish Origins of the Sephardic Jews*, that Sephardic Jewry is also a melting pot of national origins:

> The Sephardic Jews are largely descended from a mixed population consisting of a majority of converts of Near Eastern, Arabian, and North African origin and a small community of ethnic Palestinian Jews (and their mixed descendants). The minor Palestinian Jewish component served as the catalyst for conversion acts in Arabia, the Near East (especially Iraq) and Roman North Africa.[27]

One need only visit the State of Israel to see the extraordinary diversity of ethnic groups represented among the Jewish people.

## Genetics Research

Genetics research also confirms the claim that Jews have intermarried with the nations. In their monumental work *The Myth of the Jewish Race*, Raphael and Jennifer Patai scientifically demonstrate that Jews are a genetically mixed people:

> . . . Mourant et al. in 1978 concluded that "each major Jewish community as a whole bears some resemblance to the indigenous peoples of the regions where it first developed"; Morton, et al. in 1982 reported a high level of admixture between Jews and non-Jews; and Chakraborty

and Weiss, who calculated genetic distances for four Jewish and four non-Jewish populations, concluded that the Jewish populations were genetically closer to their neighboring non-Jewish populations. On the other hand, Kobyliansky and coworkers reported in 1982 that most Jewish populations are genetically closer to each other than to non-Jewish populations. Karlin and associates reached similar conclusions . . . the sum of the data on Jewish populations shows us both that they are genetically related to the non-Jewish peoples among whom they have lived and that they have a common Jewish gene pool. This is exactly what one would expect of a people who had a common origin and then spread out and interbred with other peoples.[28]

Some have argued on the basis of the above data that Jews are of such a mixed blood that there is no such thing as a Jewish people any longer.[29] Such a view is clearly anti-Semitic! There is a Jewish people and we are unique. The primary basis of our Jewishness, however, is not racial purity but covenant relationship with God and our fellow Jews. Just as the majority of Americans become citizens primarily through being born to American parents and secondarily through immigration/naturalization, so too, the vast majority of Jewish people enter into covenant with God by being born to Jewish parents (with covenant of circumcision, if male); the rest enter into covenant with the God and Israel through conversion. Marriage between born Jews and Jewish converts reinforces the tribal nature of Jewishness. For Americans, the terms of the covenant are found in the U. S. Constitution. For Jews, they are found in the Torah.

Today, the Jewish people are an intermarried people. The racial argument against intermarriage is based on the myth of a Jewish race and fails to deal with the long history of Jewish proselytism and its impact on ethnic diversity. Genetic research confirms this reality. Since Jewish identity is historically and intrinsically rooted in covenant, there is no reason for a Jew to feel he is doing anything wrong by marrying a Gentile, as long as the spouse-to-be covenantally embraces the God of Israel and the people of Israel as his/her own.[30] In this way, the Jew can keep his covenant with God and raise his children to follow in the way of Abraham, Isaac, and Jacob.

## CHAPTER 6

# Classic and Modern Approaches to Intermarriage

O n the practical side, how do couples with Jewish and Christian partners deal with intermarriage today? Does conversionary intermarriage work as it did in the days of Ruth? What are the alternatives? In the United States, a number of classic and modern approaches are being tried to resolve the dilemmas of intermarriage. In this chapter, we will survey the major approaches and weigh the pros and cons of each. In a later chapter, a new alternative will be presented.

## The Interfaith Option

The Interfaith approach is an American phenomenon. Here the couple seeks to maintain a household that has both a Jewish and Christian expression. The child's identity is best described as "Jewish/Christian" with emphasis on the slash ("/"). This approach is generally not an attempt at reconciling Judaism and Christianity, but aspires to convey to the children two separate and distinct religious traditions. The merit of this approach is that both parents can impart the richness of their religious backgrounds to their children, giving them the "best of both worlds."[1] Both sets of grandparents can also fully participate in the grandchildren's religious upbringing. Finally, the children become somewhat of a bridge between the two religious traditions and are more broadminded. On the flip side, the children do not have a single religious identity. Instead of feeling fully a part of both religions, they usually describe themselves as "half-Jewish and half-Christian."[2] Some experience fulfillment in this identity, but most have a sense of incompleteness and insecurity. These were the findings of Judy Petsonk and Jim Remsen:

> We have also come to the conclusion that children feel more secure if they are brought up in one religion, not two—if they have one clear religious identity. That doesn't mean the child can't be exposed to the religious background and celebrations of the other parent. But the

child raised in one religion knows who he is. He has a
definite, unambiguous label, and that label has some content. It is tied to some practices, some values, and a community of people with whom he is familiar. Children who
don't get a clear message about their religious identity
can end up struggling for much of their lives to sort it
out. . . . We found a number of adult children of two-reli-
gion or two-holiday homes who longed to commit themselves to a single religious identity, but remained
suspended, tied up in knots of religious indecision.[3]

While parents are well intentioned in seeking to raise their children in
Judaism *and* Christianity, living this out on an active level is a rare exception. It takes an extraordinary commitment to be participating
members of both a synagogue and a church community. As for the
children, there are few who desire to attend services on *both* Saturday
and Sunday, receive *both* bar/bat mitzvah and confirmation, and celebrate *both* Jewish and Christian festivals (with the exception of Hanukkah and Christmas, of course!). It is simply impossible for the
average family to manage this. Thus, the Interfaith approach usually
ends up with the children receiving only a smattering of exposure to
both traditions (what McClain calls "Dual-minimal" and Schulweis
calls "interfaithless")[4] especially as the time and energy of the parents' religious commitment dwindles. Finally, since the children are
not raised with a clear Jewish identity, the couple, without intending
it, ends up contributing to Jewish assimilation.

## The No Religion Option

The No Religion approach is a product of our secular society. Here
children are taught that they can choose a religion for themselves
when they get older. "'Let the children make up their own minds' is
the comforting slogan many parents fall back on, as they follow the
path of least resistance."[5] The merit of this approach is that the couple
does not have to choose one religious tradition over the other. At the
same time, most children who are raised in such households wish
they had received some religious upbringing to better prepare them
for life. Petsonk and Remsen concur:

People who are raised without a clear sense of religious belonging may feel a void in their lives. . . . Based on those
interviews and our talks with professionals, we have come
to feel it is not satisfactory to raise a child with no group

identification, no experience of belonging. By allying with a religious or secular community, you will be giving your child a way of understanding and explaining who she is. Because you can add to her sense of security by giving her a place to belong, and because a well-chosen community can enrich her in many ways, we recommend that you give her a clear grounding in a specific tradition.[6]

Finally, since the children will not be raised Jewish, the No Religion option contributes to Jewish assimilation.

## The Jewish Only Option

The Jewish Only approach (conversionary intermarriage) is a classic solution. Here the Gentile partner formally converts to the Jewish religion. Both spouses regard themselves as Jews and are equally committed to raising a Jewish family. The approach is relatively successful in maintaining Jewish continuity. The downside of this option (for many intermarrieds) is that it requires the Gentile partner to reject Christianity, and most Gentiles (95%) are unwilling to do this in order to convert to Judaism.[7]

In addition, conversion does not entail a total transformation of identity. It must be remembered that, among the five percent of Gentile partners who do convert to Judaism (and disavow belief in Jesus), their ethnic-religious heritage remains an important part of who they are. The Jew by choice is still connected to his/her Gentile Christian upbringing in various ways. As Egon Mayer has noted:

> . . . spouses not from a Jewish background carry within themselves all the cultural fragments and memories their own upbringing has given them. Even in conversionary families, the partner who is a convert to Judaism will very likely have ties to a Christian family network with which relationships are maintained to a greater or lesser extent. Therefore, elements of Christian religious and ethnic traditions will inevitably filter into the life-style of the intermarried family.[8]

A variant of the Jewish Only option is for the Jewish spouse to take on religious leadership in the home. The Gentile spouse agrees to have a Jewish household, is involved in Jewish life to some degree, but chooses not to convert to Judaism (he/she remains Christian). The benefit of this approach is that the children are raised in one religion,

Judaism. The drawback is that the children may perceive their identity as "half-Jewish and half-Christian" due to the Christian parent who has not converted. If the Gentile parent is the mother, the identity is even more precarious since Conservative and Orthodox Jews would not regard the child as Jewish on the basis of matrilineal definition (see Appendix A).

## The Christian Only Option

The Christian Only approach is another classic solution. Here both spouses regard themselves as Christians and are equally committed to raising a Christian family. The Jewish spouse either enters the marriage as a Christian (often raised by intermarried parents) or converts to Christianity after marriage, usually on the basis of religious convictions.[9] The benefit of this approach is that the whole family follows one religion, Christianity. While this may be wonderful for the couple and their Christian extended family, it is often difficult for the Jewish grandparents and other relatives who are not Christian. Also, since the children are not raised as Jews in a Jewish community context, the couple is contributing to Jewish assimilation. A common variant of the Christian Only option (with almost the same pros and cons) is for the Gentile Christian, married to a secular Jew, to assume religious leadership in the home. The Jewish spouse supports the goal of maintaining a Christian household but chooses not to convert to Christianity.

## The Most Popular Approaches

Of the major approaches to intermarriage we have surveyed so far, which ones are the most popular and why? The breakdown, by rank, is as follows:[10]

| | |
|---|---|
| Christian Only[11] | 33% |
| Interfaith[12] | 25% |
| No Religion[13] | 24% |
| Jewish Only[14] | 18% |

Not surprisingly, the Jewish Only approach came in last place. This is because few Gentile Christian spouses are willing to convert to Judaism and relatively few Jewish spouses stress the importance of maintaining a Jewish home.

The No Religion approach came in third place because of its seeming fairness; it is often an extreme response to the seeming inadequacy of the available options. Similarly, the Interfaith approach came in second place because it honors the faith traditions of both spouses. For both options, fairness is an overriding value.

The Christian Only approach ranked highest in popularity—a third of all intermarried couples. The primary reason for this is the large number of intermarried Jews who are also Christian.[15] Another factor that fuels the Christian Only option is the prevalence of secular Jews married to Christians.[16] If a Gentile Christian spouse wants to raise their children Christian, the average secular Jewish spouse is likely to give his/her assent.[17]

Given the large proportion of intermarried couples who are raising their children in the local church, and the potential impact this has on Jewish assimilation, we need to take a closer look at this group.

CHAPTER 7

# Intermarrieds in the Local Church

If you are an intermarried couple in a local church, you are not
alone! The number of Christians with a Jewish background is
growing rapidly in local churches, a direct result of intermarried
couples choosing to raise their children as Christians.[1] Findings from
the *2001* American Jewish Identity Survey indicate that there are more
than *one million* Christians who are Jewish on the basis of ethnic ori-
gin/ancestry, and who are either intermarried or the children/grand-
children of intermarriage.[2] How many of these one million Jewish
Christians consider their Jewish background to be important to them?
According to the *1990* National Jewish Population Survey, *21* percent
answered that being Jewish was "very important" in their life (see
Appendix D).[3] Using these statistics, we could say that this would indicate that over 200,000 Jewish Christians continue to identify in
some way with their Jewish heritage. Conversely, according to this
survey, approximately 800,000 Christians do not regard their Jewish
background as important. Jewish Christians were largely overlooked
in intermarriage studies until Bruce Phillips, Professor of Sociology at
Hebrew Union College–Jewish Institute of Religion, published his
1993 Survey on Mixed Marriage. The present chapter draws on data
from Phillips' study, as well as anecdotal research, to describe how
intermarrieds in the local church are dealing with the question of Jewish continuity. I conclude by putting forward several Scriptures that
are of particular relevance to this community.

## My Seminary Experience

When I was a graduate student at a Christian seminary, the number of
people I met who had Jewish backgrounds but did not identify as Jews
profoundly impacted me. I tried to put myself in the shoes of these
Christians of Jewish ancestry to better understand how they viewed
themselves, the Jewish community, and Messianic Jews like myself. I
came to realize that, in most cases, the disconnection from Jewish
identity was not the result of their own decision but developed from a
parent or grandparent who intermarried.

One professor learned as an adult that his father had been adopted, and that his biological grandparents on his father's side were Jewish. Some years ago, he had the opportunity to visit his Jewish grandfather, meeting him for the first time. This discovery of Jewish grandparents resulted in the professor, over the course of years, studying the Jewish roots of his Christian faith.

Another professor had a Jewish great-grandfather who was a Torah scholar. Intermarriage resulted in the family losing its Jewish identity; distant relatives are now the professor's main link to his Jewish heritage. The influence of Jewish learning, however, is not difficult to see. The professor's son is a Hebrew Bible scholar and two of his grandsons are engaged in graduate studies in the same field.

I met a number of students at the seminary who had Jewish parents and/or grandparents. One student, Josh, has memories of his grandfather speaking Yiddish and his grandmother preparing the house for *Shabbat*. Though Josh was raised Christian and attends a local church, the Jewish link has had a significant impact on his life. In college, he majored in Jewish studies and spent a semester in Israel. Last year, Josh put up a *mezuzah* for the first time.

Another student, Sam, has a Jewish mother and a non-Jewish father. Sam, who is intermarried, plans to assist in church planting after graduation. He knows that he is Jewish but he does not see the preservation of his Jewish identity as a priority. Sam's primary link to his Jewish heritage is the relationship he has with Jewish relatives.

During my three years of seminary studies, I met other students and faculty who had Jewish ancestry and attended local churches. In every case, the intermarriage of the Jewish parent or grandparent resulted in the chain of Jewish identity being broken in their lives so that none of the people I met were raised as practicing Jews.

## The Likelihood of Assimilation

It would be convenient if intermarried couples could find a home in Gentile churches and raise their children with a clear sense of Jewish identity. However, as the above statistics and anecdotal examples demonstrate, this is not what generally happens. The reason for this is simple. The Gentile Christian lifestyle is distinct from the Jewish lifestyle, and churches typically do not have the vision, leadership training, or resources to support the goal of raising Jewish children. Christian theology may even run counter to this purpose. For example, how many pastors are prepared to officiate at a *b'rit milah* (covenant of circumcision ceremony) for a Jewish child in their community? Or a *bar/bat mitzvah*? Or a Jewish wedding? These are but a few of the many aspects of Jewish communal life that the local church is not equipped to support.

Loss of Jewish identity is almost certain in the local church. I realize this is a strong statement. However, it is born out by the evidence of two thousand years. I am not aware of any historical examples—until the twentieth century—of an intermarried couple that was able to pass on Jewish identity to the next generation while raising their children in a Gentile Christian church. Millions of Jews have assimilated over the centuries. Their children lost their Jewish identity, and their grandchildren identified as Gentile Christians.

At the beginning of the twentieth century, Philip Cohen, a pioneer of modern Messianic Judaism,[4] wrote in his book *The Hebrew Christian and His National Continuity*:

> We are told that 250,000 Hebrews have been brought into the Christian Church within the last century. This sounds well, and certainly it is a cause for rejoicing that so many have acknowledged the Lord Jesus as their Messiah and Saviour, but when we ask where are they, and what has become of their children, and again when we think that these 250,000 Hebrews and their offspring are absolutely lost to the Hebrew cause, we shudder at the terrible leakage, and realize that this should be anything but a matter for rejoicing. Can this be allowed to continue?[5]

That more than 200,000 Jewish Christians in the 19th century assimilated *en masse* is confirmed by reliable sources. "Chunnelled into churches, Hebrew Christians and their progeny generally lost their Jewish affiliation through intermarriage. The ethnic bond, held to be inviolable, was thus easily broken."[6] One reads Louis Meyer's book *Eminent Hebrew Christians of the Nineteenth Century* and wonders, "What happened to their children?" The answer is that almost all of them assimilated into Protestant churches and no longer identified themselves as Jews.

In the early twentieth century, history repeated itself. Prior to World War II, tens of thousands of Jews converted to Christianity and assimilated into Gentile churches. Sir Leon Levison, president of the International Hebrew Christian Alliance in the 1930's, presented the following statistical data on Jewish Christians around the world.

"According to Levison's research, 97,000 Jews in Hungary alone accepted the Christian faith; in Vienna 17,000; in Poland 35,000; and in Bolshevik Russia 60,000 Jews became Christians. We also found Jews turning to Christ in Germany, Sweden, Denmark. Not a few have done likewise in Britain. In America, careful estimate places the number of Christians of the Jewish race at no less than 20,000." More than 230,000 Jews became Christians during the first third of the 20th century; this was far more than the 224,000 Jews during the 19th century mentioned by J. F. de le Roi (1931:905).[7]

Most of these 230,000+ Jewish Christians and their children were killed in the Holocaust. Those who survived, and those who lived in countries outside of Hitler's reach, for the most part, assimilated into denominational churches. Their children intermarried and, with rare exception, no longer identified as Jews.

What is God's perspective on this? Is it his plan for each generation of Jewish Christians to intermarry, assimilate, and disappear as Jews? Or does he want Jewish Christians to pass on the Jewish heritage to their children so that, over time, the community of Jewish believers in Jesus grows in wisdom, strength, and numbers? Cohen believed that it was God's will for Jewish Christians to maintain their Jewish identity. The prophet Jeremiah made it clear that, even in the New Covenant age, Israel was called to be a distinct and enduring people:

"The time is coming," declares the LORD, "when I will make a new covenant with the house of Israel. . . . I will forgive their wickedness and will remember their sins no more." This is what the LORD says, he who appoints the sun to shine by day, who decrees the moon and stars to shine by night, who stirs up the sea so that its waves roar—the LORD Almighty is his name: "Only if these decrees vanish from my sight," declares the LORD, "will the descendants of Israel ever cease to be a nation before me." (Jer. 31:31, 34–36, NIV)

Jewish people are irrevocably called by God to be a גוי קדוש (Hebrew, *goy kadosh*, a nation set apart; Exod. 19:6; cf. Rom. 11:29). From this perspective, Cohen viewed mass assimilation of Jewish Christians into Gentile Christianity as contrary to the Bible's teachings.

## Decisions that Affect Future Generations

Most intermarried couples join a local church because they value Christian community. They can raise their children as believers in Jesus and participate in Christian worship. They can contribute to the work of God through their church. However, the majority of these intermarried couples do not give much thought to the question of Jewish continuity or covenant faithfulness. Some are even taught in their churches that it is counter to New Testament teaching for Jewish Christians to live as Jews or raise their children as Jews.[8]

A growing number of intermarrieds in the local church see the importance of imparting Jewish identity to their children. This is what Phillips found in his study.[9] For some, it is a matter of sharing a rich ethnic heritage. For others, conveying Jewish identity is a matter of covenant responsibility. For these intermarried couples, home observance is the primary means by which they hope to maintain Jewish continuity. Among other traditions, they may light *Shabbat* candles or have an annual Passover *seder.*

While home observance is vitally important, it is not a panacea. Without Jewish communal involvement, it is extremely difficult to impart a clear and unambiguous Jewish identity to children of intermarriage. Moreover, even if the parents are successful, the ultimate question is whether their children will, in turn, raise their children as Jews. In other words, will the intermarried couple have Jewish grandchildren? Most churchgoing intermarried couples think only in terms of one generation; they do not think of their grandchildren. Jewish continuity, however, requires at least a two-generation vision.

## The Example of Abraham

When it comes to cross-generational impact, the life of Abraham is an important model for intermarried couples. Abraham (whose name means "father of many") was called by God to "give orders to his children and to his household after him to keep the way of ADONAI" (Gen. 18:19). Abraham, the quintessential father, was called to have a multi-generation vision. He was to be concerned with passing on the heritage of the Lord to Isaac as well as Jacob and his children. The sign of the covenant is but one example. The Lord said to Abraham:

> . . . As for you, you must keep my covenant, *you and your descendants after you for the generations to come.* This is

my covenant with you *and your descendants after you,* the covenant you are to keep: Every male among you shall be circumcised. You are to undergo circumcision, and it will be the sign of the covenant between me and you. *For the generations to come* every male among you who is eight days old must be circumcised . . . My covenant in your flesh is to be an *everlasting covenant.* Any uncircumcised male, who has not been circumcised in the flesh, will be cut off from his people; he has broken my covenant. (Gen. 17:9–14, NIV; emphasis mine)

Here we see that God called Abraham to instruct his future descendants in the importance of perpetuating the sign of the covenant (circumcision), a ritual that is emblematic of the totality of Jewish identity.

Abraham was to have a multi-generation outlook when it came to Jewish identity. It was not enough for Abraham to be concerned only with Isaac's upbringing; he had to also think of Isaac's children. Moreover, it is notable that the commandment to convey Jewish heritage was incumbent on the parent, and not the child, since the child was only eight days old. Genesis 17:14 teaches that Abraham held the key to Isaac being part of the covenant. If he did not convey the sign of the covenant, Isaac would be cut off from God's people along with his future descendants. In this way, the Lord made clear to Abraham the vital importance of a multi-generational vision.

Like Abraham, intermarried couples hold the key to their children being in the covenant—or not. This is a special dilemma for the 200,000 Jewish Christians who feel that being Jewish is very important in their lives. The local church is a source of spiritual life for them but it does not contribute to Jewish continuity. Ideally, these intermarrieds would like an option that provides a comfortable place for worship, honors the faith traditions of both spouses, and conveys Jewish identity to the next generation. Is there such an option? I have written this book to tell you that such an alternative not only exists, but is being explored by many intermarried couples today. It is called "Messianic Judaism."

# CHAPTER 8
# Messianic Judaism: A Natural Option

In 1990, Lee Gruzen published her celebrated book *Raising Your Jewish/Christian Child: How Interfaith Parents Can Give Children the Best of Both Their Heritages*.[1] Today, many Interfaith couples, like Gruzen, refer to their children as "Jewish/Christian." They do not use a hyphen ("-") to form the word "Jewish-Christian." Neither do they join the two words together as "Jewish Christian." Rather, they place a slash ("/") between the two religious identities to separate them. The slash is intentional and well describes the difference between the Jewish/Christian and Messianic Jewish approaches to the dilemma of intermarriage. As I stated in the Introduction, Messianic Judaism is, in short, the removal of the slash ("/") between "Jewish" and "Christian." It is the recognition that, in the first century, the "/" did not exist between the two faiths and that it does not need to exist today. As David Flusser, former professor at Hebrew University in Jerusalem emphatically stated, "Christianity and Judaism are really one faith."[2]

Can the boundary line truly be removed from the Jewish and Christian faiths? In theological circles, one of the most erroneous teachings over the last nineteen hundred years has been that Judaism and Christianity are two completely irreconcilable religions and that the core teachings of each contradict the other. Adherents of both faiths have been incorrectly taught that it is an oxymoron to join the words "Jewish" and "Christian." Nothing could be further from the truth.

## The First Christians Were Jewish

From the first to the fourth century, tens of thousands of people practiced what scholars and historians call "Jewish Christianity," "Christian Judaism" or "Messianic Judaism"?[3] Many books and articles document the history of this extraordinary movement.[4] But, you might say, "How can this be?" Let me ask you a few questions.

Q: Was Jesus a Jew or Christian?
A: He was a Jew.

Q: Did Jesus live a Jewish life?
A: Yes. *The Jewish Book of Knowledge* states:

> Jesus was a devoutly believing Jew. He himself ob-
> served, and also imposed on his disciples, the duty of
> scrupulously living according to the laws of Torah. He
> kept Sabbath, the festivals and fasts, put on *tefillin* (phy-
> lacteries) at morning prayers, fulfilled the command-
> ments to wear *tzitzit* (fringes), and observed the laws of
> *kashrut* (the dietary laws)—all of which institutions the
> Gentile-Christians later abolished.[5]

Q: Did Jesus ever renounce Judaism?
A: No. On the contrary, he upheld Judaism. To those who misunderstood his teachings, he said:

> Don't think that I have come to abolish the Torah [the
> Five Books of Moses] or the Prophets. I have come not to
> abolish but to complete. . . . So whoever disobeys the least
> of these *mitzvot* [commandments of God] and teaches
> others to do so will be called the least in the Kingdom of
> Heaven. But whoever obeys them and so teaches will be
> called great in the Kingdom of Heaven. (Matt. 5:17–19)

Q: Did Jesus disagree with some Jewish religious leaders?
A: Yes. One of the great hallmarks of Judaism is that it has a pluralistic
religious tradition. Jews can disagree, even with their leaders! Like
the prophets who came before him, many of Jesus' teachings were
of a prophetic reform nature.

Q: Did Jesus create a new religion?
A: No. On the contrary, he claimed to bring the Jewish faith to its fullness of meaning and purpose. Even Jesus' Messianic claims were
well within the boundaries of Second Temple Judaism.[6]

Q: Were the Twelve Apostles Jews?
A: Yes. They were twelve Jewish men who believed that Jesus was the
Messiah and the Holy One of Israel incarnate. Like Jesus, they
never stopped being Jewish. *The Jewish Book of Knowledge* states:

> They adhered faithfully to the Jewish religion, observed the
> Sabbath (on Saturday), kept all the festivals and fast days,

circumcised their male infants and ate kosher food. They prayed in Hebrew and devoted themselves to Torah study.[7]

Q: Did the Twelve Apostles go to church on Sunday?
A: No. They went to synagogue on *Shabbat*.

Q: Did the Twelve Apostles celebrate Christmas and Easter?
A: No. They celebrated all the Jewish festivals. They never heard of Christmas and Easter.

Q: Was the Last Supper when Jesus and the Twelve Apostles had communion together?
A: No. It was a traditional Passover *seder*.

Q: Is the New Testament a Gentile book?
A: No. On the contrary, Jews wrote it.[8]

Q: Why were followers of Jesus called "Christians"?
A: As the Twelve Apostles traveled throughout the Roman Empire and shared about the life and teachings of Jesus, many non-Jews abandoned their pagan religion to follow the God of Israel (and his Messiah). In the Greek-speaking city of Antioch, the crowds called these Gentile believers in Jesus "Christians" (i.e. followers of *Christos*, the Greek word for Messiah). The name stuck.[9]

Q: Did the Twelve Apostles believe they were part of a religion that was separate and distinct from Judaism?
A: No. They saw themselves as part of the Nazarene sect of Judaism (Acts 24:5, 14). Just as we have Orthodox, Conservative, Reform, and Reconstructionist expressions of Judaism, in the first century there existed at least five major sects of organized Jewry—Pharisees, Sadducees, Zealots, Essenes/Qumran community, and Nazarenes. Michael Cook, Professor of Rabbinic and Intertestamental Literature at the Hebrew Union College–Jewish Institute of Religion, comments:

> The earliest segment of Christianity, the Jewish Christians, were a relatively small Jewish sect in Palestine whose distinction from other Jews was their belief not that the Messiah would one day come but rather that he had already come, had died, and would soon return. Otherwise, for a number of decades, these Christians

probably continued to worship with their fellow Jews in the same synagogues, generally using similar liturgy and abiding by the Torah. What became of them we do not know—they vanished from history. But, whether or not we ever discover what became of them, it is not to these earliest Jewish Christians in Palestine that we trace the fundamental parting of the ways between Christianity and Judaism. That separation came about because Christianity took root in the Greco-Roman world of Asia Minor and flourished there in a new form—a form which had little in common with Judaism.[10]

Rabbi Cook adds, "So different was the Christianity of these Gentile believers in Asia Minor from that of the original Jewish believers in Palestine that it is almost as if Christianity had experienced a second beginning."[11]

## An Integrative Approach to the Intermarriage Dilemma

Messianic Judaism is essentially an attempt to restore the early Nazarene sect in a twenty-first century context. Gershon Nerel, Israel Secretary for the International Messianic Jewish Alliance from 1993–2001, writes:

Modern Messianic Jews find a special motivation to relate to the early Jewish followers of Jesus. This ancient heritage is grasped by them as the source of their faith. Specifically, the authentic beliefs of the first Jewish disciples of Jesus become for them the platform for constructing their own identity. In their eyes, however, a genuine Messianic Jewish identity stands in complete contrast with the "unbiblical developments" to which they point within the history of both normative Judaism and traditional Christendom. Pursuant to adopting the ancient paradigm of the primitive Jewish disciples of Jesus, Messianic Jews practically regard themselves as belonging to a restorationist movement.[12]

How is this restoration accomplished? Unlike the Jewish/Christian approach to intermarriage, which idealistically seeks to impart two distinct religious identities to a child, Messianic Judaism fits pieces together from both religious traditions in an attempt to restore an ancient identity:

## MESSIANIC JUDAISM: AN INTEGRATIVE SOLUTION

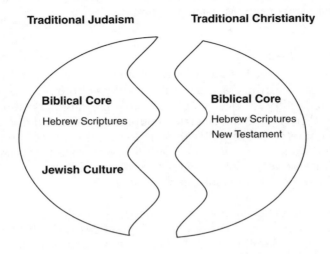

**Traditional Judaism**

**Traditional Christianity**

**Biblical Core**

Hebrew Scriptures

**Jewish Culture**

**Biblical Core**

Hebrew Scriptures
New Testament

As seen in this illustration, the overlap between traditional Judaism and traditional Christianity is in the area of the biblical core: the Hebrew Bible. Messianic Judaism views the Hebrew Bible as the Word of God. Messianic Jews also retain the traditional Jewish view that the Torah (Genesis–Deuteronomy) is the foundational revelation of God upon which all other Scripture rests.[13]

On the traditional Christian side, Messianic Judaism views the New Testament as the culmination of the Word of God and reads the New Testament through the lens of Torah.[14] In doing this, Messianic Jews see the New Testament as an essentially Jewish book, written by Jews who followed the Jewish Messiah. The traditional Christian emphasis on discontinuity between the Old and New Testament is thus replaced with a strong emphasis on continuity.

Finally, Messianic Judaism appropriates both Torah and Jewish culture in the formation of a Messianic Jewish lifestyle. This will be discussed later in greater detail. The distinction between Torah and culture is an important one for Messianic Jews and reflects the deeply held conviction in Messianic Judaism that Jewish continuity is a matter of covenant and divine mandate. Reform rabbi Dan Cohn-Sherbok writes:

> Hence, Messianic Jews see themselves as firmly rooted within the Jewish tradition. Dedicated to living in accordance with scriptural teaching, they are open to the insights of the Jewish heritage as it developed over the last

2000 years . . . they insist that they are faithful Jews, holding firm to the principles of the faith as manifest in the life and teachings of Messiah Yeshua.[15]

## A Natural Option

The Messianic Jewish approach was not created for the intermarried community. Nevertheless, a natural byproduct of the Messianic movement is its ability to serve as a home for the intermarried and their children. Why should intermarried couples be interested in Messianic Judaism? Intermarriage tends to blur the traditional boundaries between Judaism and Christianity within the average family so that a quasi- "Messianic Jewish" religious expression arises. The 1993 Survey on Mixed Marriage confirms this assertion:

> Regardless of whether mixed marriage families are more Jewish or more Christian in their practices and self-identity, such families usually evidence a mixture of influences from both traditions. Even the most Jewish of the couples maintain some Christian practices and connections, and even the most Christian mixed marrieds maintain some level of Jewish practices.[16]

Why does this happen? The initial move in this direction is often triggered by the birth of a first child who instinctively draws a sense of identity from both parents. Typically, the parents also want to convey to their child a clear and coherent identity based on their own religious backgrounds. What of non-religious parents or parents who choose to raise their children exclusively in Judaism or Christianity? Daniel Klein and Freke Vuijst, authors of *The Half-Jewish Book*, found that "Even if they tried to bring up their child as a neither-nor or as a one-thing-or-the-other, in some fundamental way, the child was going to get both cultural messages anyhow. Hardly a surprise. In all kinds of unconscious ways, a person is the embodiment of his cultural background."[17] This begs the question, "Why must a child be either Jewish or Christian?" Can't he/she be a Messianic Jew?! This is a natural solution. Children want to integrate their identities—bring them together—not separate them. They don't yearn to be half of this and half of that. They want to be whole. Messianic Judaism makes possible what many assume to be impossible. It challenges the "'law of excluded middle' by asserting that they are simultaneously Jewish and Christian."[18] Along the same lines, many intermarried couples want to be part of a community where both of their backgrounds are represented, not only one or the other. Messianic rabbi Michael Schiffman notes:

> The Messianic Jewish movement has a very high percentage of intermarriage within its constituency. This is not because Messianic Judaism advocates intermarriage, but that many intermarried couples have found a home in its midst for good reasons. Messianic Judaism provides a place where the Jewish partner feels he or she is on home turf regarding his or her background, while the non-Jew finds they can still connect to belief in Yeshua, while adjusting culturally. While neither partner may have had any Messianic Jewish involvement before their marriage, they find more comfort in a Messianic synagogue than in a traditional church or a traditional synagogue.[19]

The Messianic Jewish movement, which now includes over 250 Messianic synagogues in North America,[20] shows promise in meeting the needs of intermarried couples and giving their children a solid sense of identity. I was raised as a Messianic Jew and had a very positive experience growing up. My three daughters—Hana, Elisa, and Miryam—are also being raised as Messianic Jews. If you sense the enthusiasm in my writing concerning the Messianic Jewish option, it is only because I love being a Messianic Jew.

Messianic Judaism is a natural option for intermarried couples because it is common ground for both partners. Also, children seek to *integrate* their identities, not separate them or eliminate them altogether (a drawback of the Jewish Only, Christian Only, Interfaith, and No Religion options). In addition, the Messianic Jewish option is rooted in the Scriptures and history, providing children with a strong sense of affirmation. First century Jewish followers of Jesus serve as an "identity anchor"[21] for twenty-first century Messianic Jews. For those intermarried couples who are looking for a way to bridge both backgrounds and raise their children with a clear and complete sense of identity, Messianic Judaism is a very good option.

# CHAPTER 9

# Denise and Michael: Worshiping Together as a Family

In scores of interviews, one of the most touching statements expressed by intermarried couples who had chosen the Messianic Jewish option was that families "were now able to worship together." It was often said that worshiping together as a family had the net effect of producing a closer marriage. Issues that were off-limits to discussion or a source of contention in the marriage prior to joining a Messianic synagogue were now far less threatening because both spouses gained mutual respect for the others' beliefs. In addition, it was stated over and over that the kids were the biggest winners of all because the parents no longer fought over religious issues but found common ground in the biblical values that were taught in the Messianic Jewish community.

*As an intermarried couple, Michael and Denise have found the Messianic synagogue best suited to meet their needs. Michael is Jewish, from a Conservative background. He is not Messianic. Denise grew up Catholic. They have three children.*

MICHAEL: I was raised as a Conservative Jew. I am a computer consultant and have been self-employed for fourteen years for the most part. I had a break as an employee for a couple of years in there. I met my wife through a dating service ten years ago.

Q: Dating service? So, it works?

DENISE: No. I think we'll be the first ones. And we've told this to our children. [Laughter]

Q: How many years have you been married?

MICHAEL: Ten in October.

DENISE: Actually, we're going to renew our vows at Temple Beth Shalom this October.

Q: Congratulations. It's really good to hear. These days, so many people don't reach ten years.

DENISE: We didn't think we would for a moment, several moments there, which is why it's so special for us to renew our vows.

Q: When you first got married, were there any issues relating to the fact that you were from a Jewish background and a Catholic background?

MICHAEL: I was naïve. To me, immediately, it wasn't an issue, which was really mostly a testament to my ignorance of Christianity. To my family, it was a big issue, to the point that my parents refused to meet her until I guess a week or two before we were getting married. And they kind of said, "Well, gee, I guess they're going to do it. It might be nice to meet our daughter-in-law."

Q: They came to the wedding?

DENISE: Up to that point, they said "We are not going." I guess it was a matter of seeing whether he was going to go through with it or not. And when they figured out he was going to, they just gave in and said, "I guess we have to meet the girl."

MICHAEL: Whom they adored.

Q: How about your family Denise? Did they have any difficulties with the fact that you married a Jewish man?

DENISE: My mom became a Catholic after she married my father. To her it was not a new notion to just change your beliefs so that you can get married.

Q: How about your wedding?

DENISE: We went to the courthouse. I was willing to have a Jewish wedding. But they all refused to take part in it. We finally decided to just go to the courthouse and get married. And that's what we did. We picked a date, showed up, and the family decided to show up. That's why we're having a wedding now, because I want to have the wedding I didn't have back then.

Q: Did your different cultural and religious backgrounds become issues? What did you do about the religious holidays?

MICHAEL: I don't think the holidays themselves were an issue. The big issue was, I guess, when you started having the need to go to church.

DENISE: Up until then, we didn't go to church at all. Everything was very secular. Even Christmas was the Santa Claus thing and the gifts.

MICHAEL: We got the *menorah* and we lit it.

DENISE: Kind of the symbolic things.

Q: How long did you attend the church?

DENISE: Until 1994, about five years. I kept trying to convert him. And he kept trying not to let us talk about it. I did everything wrong in terms of sharing my faith. I was just trying to shove it down his throat.

MICHAEL: I'd go to the church.

Q: You went to the church?

DENISE: He tried it a couple of times just to be part of the family.

MICHAEL: It was like paganism. It just seemed so superstitious. I mean it wouldn't have seemed more bizarre to me if I had seen people praying to trees. The people were mumbling and talking about the blood. It was really just mumbo jumbo. If anything, it just made me more convinced. It's just "check your mind out at the door."

DENISE: To some extent, that's exactly what it was. I wasn't thinking about what I was doing. It was an automatic response, "Oh my gosh, I married an unbeliever. It's my job to save him." I was on this remote thing that I've got to get this man saved or else. They always made me feel that it was my responsibility as a wife. I was going to bring him into the kingdom and all this kind of stuff. I pretty much walked on a guilt trip all the time about it. And that created a lot of tension between us. Those first four years were very hard, to the point where I really thought, "This is not going to work and I'm going to have to divorce this man because I can't deal with this." And there were other issues . . . a lot of stress. We met in April. We got married in August. We bought our house in May. Then we had a baby. I was still working full-time nights as a nurse.

MICHAEL: Then business got slow and I decided I wanted stability. So I went back to where I used to work, which I didn't really like. Had another baby.

DENISE: We were very unhappy at the time.

MICHAEL: It was a very stressful time.

Q: How did you get out of it?

DENISE: I had a small nervous breakdown. That's pretty much what happened. I got severely depressed to the point that all I could do was cry. I just couldn't do anything to take care of the house. I didn't feel I could take care of the children. I'd call him at work and say, "You have to come home because I can't deal with it." At which point I sought out treatment. . . . They put me on Prozac. In the interim, I lost one counselor, met this other doctor who recommended this particular therapist for us, who turned out to be an incredible blessing. She was Puerto Rican. She had a Jewish father and she was a believer. She understood all our issues—from a cultural point of view and from a religious point of view. She was a godsend. And she was the one who said, "Do you know there are such things as Messianic Jewish congregations?" We both looked at each other and said, "No, what's that?" And that's when the road to recovery started. I came home, opened the phone book and it said "Messianic Jewish Congregation." Eventually, Robert [the Messianic rabbi] came here, sat down, talked, and invited us to Temple Beth Shalom. We went and we liked it. People were very warm and welcoming. We realized there were a lot of people like us, intermarriages, and people were getting along. So we decided we would try it out.

Q: Had you gone to synagogue since you were married?

MICHAEL: Basically, I had been non-practicing since high school. I remember coming home from college once and going to the High Holy Day services. I guess when I was out of college in my early twenties,

I decided to go there. I just remember leaving there and saying, "Now I remember why I haven't gone in so many years."

DENISE: I think that's one of the things that made it easier for me to be able to deny the whole issue, because he was non-practicing. I didn't have to deal with having to go to synagogue with him. And I guess that made it easier for him too because I wasn't churchgoing at the time. We weren't faced with it until later on. And it became a big issue about what we were going to do with the children.

Q: Did your parents raise these issues?

MICHAEL: No. They didn't want to talk about it.

DENISE: Total denial. Let's just pretend it's not there.

MICHAEL: And it was a very quick period of time, too.

DENISE: His father came here with a whole library of Jewish books for me to read and said, "Just so you can understand who we are." I said, "Sure, I'll read them!" And I did read most of them.

MICHAEL: He did it from the point of view, "If you just see this, you'll realize it makes sense and you'll drop this silly business of Christianity."

Q: Do you think he wanted you to convert to Judaism?

DENISE: I'm sure deep down, just like I wanted him [Michael] to convert early on.

MICHAEL: I think his point of view was, "Well, if you just get the facts, it'll be obvious."

DENISE: They were never negative about it. It was always a positive thing. "You might want to read these things and understand." He'd always present their point of view.

MICHAEL: And that was basically the same concept as the church.

Q: What was your first impression of Temple Beth Shalom?

MICHAEL: My first impression was very positive. It was very reassuring. There were people there I could talk to, that I could relate to. I'd talk to Paul a lot. I'd talk to Robert a lot and people who I understood what they believed. I wouldn't say that I agreed with them, but obviously these people had done a lot of soul-searching and had come to their own beliefs, and they didn't do it out of ignorance. Here were these people I could sit and listen to; I knew they had walked in my shoes and I wouldn't just write them off. Obviously, they could relate to what we were going through. And it was a very healing place for our family. I mean, we could go and listen without my skin crawling or without being offended.

DENISE: It was also very reassuring to see Robert and Elizabeth [the rabbi and his wife] who are intermarried and terribly in love, Paul and Suzanne [another leader and his wife], and see intermarriages that actually work. I know from my point of view, I needed to learn what makes this work, because obviously it [Messianic Judaism] does, there is something to be learned here. And for the first time, like he said, it was a healing experience for our family because we were able to go together and worship together. And the kids didn't feel like they were offending Daddy when they sang about Messiah.

MICHAEL: The kids didn't have to worry about choosing sides.

DENISE: Exactly. I think, up to then, it was very hard for them. So, we at first started getting involved with the stuff we could do. If we could bring something, we'd bring it. If they were going to build a *sukkah* [temporary shelter made of wood and foliage that is used during the Feast of Tabernacles] and Michael could bring the truck. We got involved in the service aspect of being a part of the community.

MICHAEL: It was a good support network of people who were like us. We didn't feel so isolated.

DENISE: We didn't feel out of place. Like he said, he could talk to men who understood where he was coming from. And I could talk to the women and they understood my struggles, my doubts, and could give me good advice. At first, the kids were a little leery of course, because of new people, but now you can't keep them away. They've made good friends there. I think at first, we were just relieved that there could be a place where we could be a family, and neither one of us had to feel cheated. He had his Torah reading. He'd take his Hebrew Bible and follow the Torah reading. Paul would chant in the Hebrew. To me, all that was fascinating. I had never been exposed to anything like it. And the dancing just totally won my heart. I really liked it. And I thought, "I can do this. It doesn't bother me at all.

We're all praising the same God. And if my husband is happy, that's all that matters."

Q: How about your parents?

MICHAEL: We didn't really make it high profile.

DENISE: I guess we wanted to see how it was going to work for us first before we got anybody's input about it.

MICHAEL: Basically, from their perspective, we were going to Temple on Saturday, and that was great.

DENISE: That's right.

Q: Did your parents notice your children having more of a Jewish identity?

DENISE: I think we had trained the children quite well in the sensitivity of speaking about Jesus around the grandparents. And they were very careful. So, when they did start going, it was positive in the sense that they could talk about the Jewish things and show they were gaining knowledge about it, but they were always very careful to what extent they took it and never mentioned the other part of it. But I think it was rewarding, especially for your father, to have them learn Hebrew words and what the Passover is. . . . They're not devout themselves so it's not a big issue. It's more like, "Yes, they're learning our heritage. Don't forget who we are. Learn about our history!"

MICHAEL: I think it's also closing a blind eye to the Jesus portion. Like I said, they're kind of "Great, they're going to a temple, even though it's housed in a church [building]."

DENISE: It's not a church. It doesn't have church surroundings, and that means a lot to them. They've never been there. Their first time will be at the ceremony [renewal of marriage vows].

MICHAEL: They wanted to invite all the aunts and uncles and cousins, and I said, "You know..."

DENISE: It's fascinating. We sat down and said, "You do understand that there will be some Messianic . . . it won't be blatant but something here and there." But they gave me a list of fifteen people I'm supposed to invite. So everyone's invited.

Q: And it will be a Jewish wedding? You'll have a *huppah* [wedding canopy]?

DENISE: Yes.

Q: And you'll have the breaking of the glass?

DENISE: That too.

Q: Michael, what are some of the things that make the Messianic Jewish congregation a better option for you than a church?

MICHAEL: First off, you don't see the arrogance that I know I've grown up associating with Christianity and the Church. I think they make a good case of presenting Christianity in the light of what it is, and that is, it was a schismatic splitting of Judaism in the first century. And they look at it in that light. They do emphasize the Old Testament and show the writings from Isaiah and remind me a lot of how strong "belief in a Messiah" is in how I was raised. And that is true. Those teachings were there in the synagogue. And like I say, culturally it is much more comfortable. The ceremony, even as a non-believer, I can get a lot out of it. It helps me read the Bible. It educates without beating on me with the New Testament. Whereas I'm not a believer, I'll sit and I'll listen (with, I hope, an open mind now), instead of just saying, "This is nonsense." Like I say, it's a setting where I do think I'm open-minded and I'll listen.

DENISE: And you're more open to understanding why we believe certain things, whether you agree with them or not. You can say, "Well, I see where you are coming from and why you think this because of what the Bible says," whether he chooses to believe it or not, which gives him a greater understanding.

MICHAEL: And it relieves me of trepidation that I'm going to be a failure because my kids are going to be lost to the Christians. It's put that fear to rest.

DENISE: Correct me if I'm wrong, but I think we've also found a lot of sound biblical teaching that has demonstrated that Christianity is not just an emotional thing but it can be a fact-based belief. A reason thing, not just a [staring up at heaven], which is what it was to me from the beginning, which is what he [Michael] was afraid of his children inheriting. You know, just emotionalism with no roots. Now that

I look back, he had good reason [to be concerned] because I don't want my kids to grow up like that either. The teaching we've received has been very sound and very constructive.

MICHAEL: Sound and constructive.

Q: You don't feel overwhelmed by the Jewish traditions?

DENISE: Actually, I have been totally blessed by the entire thing. I think it has enhanced who I am as a person, just understanding the roots of Christianity, understanding that Jesus was a Jew. It has put the whole concept of Judaism in a new light for me. It's taught me a lot of understanding because now I can stand on his side and say I can understand why he feels this way.

Q: You couldn't see that before?

DENISE: I couldn't see that at all. From my point of view, it was just these blind people who don't get it. But now, with having heard so much from Temple Beth Shalom about the Jewish perspective—where they are coming from, why they resist, and how they've been treated—I can understand now why he felt threatened and how my behavior before made it all worse because I was his living fear. I was acting out all his fears of what these Christians were. It's made me appreciate him a lot. This is one of the things I've learned. I've lost the arrogance also. I used to be like, "I have the truth. You just have to get it." In the process of accepting him and understanding where he is coming from, and why he feels the way he does, I have grown a lot in the understanding of why it's important to know what you believe and why you believe it. So, for me, it has cemented what I believe in because of the challenge of being married to him. I had to dig and understand, "Why do I believe these things? Do they really make sense?" because he would challenge me on the validity of these irrational things that I would say sometimes. And again, the sound teaching that we have received there [at the Messianic synagogue] has enlightened both of us. We have come to a greater understanding of each other. He can see now how it is possible that this person has a personal relationship with her God and it doesn't make me an oddball or a borderline psychotic. He might not comprehend how it all works but he sees that I am a very balanced and sane person. . . . And he can accept that. On the other hand, I can accept all the good things in him, what a good thinker he is, how he analyzes things. Even though he chooses not to accept the belief I have, I am at peace with the fact that I know he's just not blowing things off. He listens, he thinks, and ultimately the decision is his, and I have nothing to do with that.

Q: Do you feel, Michael, that you have grown closer to God through being at a Messianic Jewish congregation?

MICHAEL: Yes, absolutely. Before, I guess you would have classified me as a scientific agnostic, if there were such a thing. I certainly thought of God in a manner that was basically irrelevant in my daily life. To me, the concept of God was when Moses brought the children of Israel out into the desert. They came up with these great rules. And then, "God said so," you know, so you believe it because he said so. But I didn't really see it particularly as an issue in my daily life. And then, when I was very depressed—I mean I was very depressed—instead of my wife helping me, I felt like she was beating me on the head, telling me to quit my job and take a step out in faith. And I thought she was crazy. I was unhappy at work, I was stressed out about money, and I'll tell you, I was at the end of my rope. And I said, "OK, I'm going to try it. I don't like it." And the week I did that, things started turning up. I forget that a lot but it truly was a miracle. I was worried about money. I was constantly at work. I was squeezed between an owner and employees, trying to be fair to both sides and customers. And I turned around and I walked away from all of it. A week later I was offered a position for more money, where half of it I could do here [at home]. I didn't have to deal with any clients and it was truly a meaningful project. The offer came from someone who, at the time, I didn't think thought very highly of me. It really was amazing. That started happening. We went to Temple Beth Shalom. Life has just been getting better since.

DENISE: Maybe there is something to this God thing after all.

MICHAEL: That's right. So, I guess I do have to get hit by a ton of bricks. But it did get my attention. So, I do listen and consider. And God does have a much more important and immediate and relevant part of my life now.

DENISE: And it's a lot easier for us to communicate on each other's belief terms too. I don't have to be afraid any longer. We had a situation last night. I can just look at him and say, "God works everything for good. God is in control. God knows." And I don't have to feel that I'm offending him or beating him over the head to believe what I do. He just accepts that this is the way I see things and it helps him too. It's opened a whole new way of communication for us. We no longer are afraid of speaking. He can tell me why he doesn't believe and [and I can say] why I do. And it's not a tension. It's like, "OK, I see what you're saying." We understand where we're coming from. We do listen to each other and to the children also. We no longer have to fight over who is right or who is wrong. This is how Mommy sees things and this is how Daddy sees things. And this is why. We are teaching our children to think about why we believe these things.

Q: How do you account for the difference in communication? Has being a part of a Messianic Jewish congregation helped?

MICHAEL: I would say "yes." [Over] these past six years, Denise and I have consciously learned communications skills and we have consciously worked at improving our marriage and working it out. Is a thousand percent of it due to a Messianic congregation? Of course not, but having said that, "yes." Having the one place to go is very important because it is bringing our worship together. It is something that reinforces our family as opposed to something that would be a wedge—if she was going to church and I was going to synagogue and we believed different things, if either of us were going to either of those traditional avenues, someone would be unhappy and they would be humoring the other person. Would you agree with that?

DENISE: Yes, I do.

MICHAEL: And once again, it's a very important thing to me that there have been people who have walked in my shoes. Quite frankly, even now, someone who was born and raised a Christian, they couldn't come to me and really talk to me about what they believed. I mean, if they really wanted to do it in just the educational sense that would be one thing. But with 99% of the people, their beliefs are whatever they were raised as, and they never really examined any alternative.

DENISE: You don't consider their message meaningful at all.

MICHAEL: That's right. Because the truth is, they've never really applied any critical doubt and questioning to what they believe. At the same time, they're trying to ask for you to reject what you were raised in. But when you go to a Messianic congregation, you do see people who [did question] and obviously this was not an easy choice. They do understand the ramifications with family that they had to fight and overcome. And admittedly, they got to a point where their belief was strong enough to overcome that. Now, I'll listen to that person and I will respect their opinion, and I won't just blow that off.

Q: You could say there is some critical evaluation on the side of the non-Jew too in a Messianic synagogue because they are reexamining their childhood image of Christianity. They might have had a totally different image of Jesus, one that was entirely non-Jewish.

DENISE: I'm sure your idea of what is a believer has changed over the years just from observing these people.

MICHAEL: That's right. I've become a lot more tolerant and charitable of them espousing their beliefs to me. And I also recognize there is a wide range of people. There are certainly people who come in with the attitude, "I'm doing this service to the Lord. I'm going to save you."

DENISE: But you also see a lot of genuine people.

MICHAEL: That's right. And Robert's actually pretty good about giving a friendly restraining hand.

Q: Many books have been written on intermarriage but few mention the Messianic Jewish option. When it is discussed, it is often by a Jewish writer who states that Messianic synagogues are deceptive—they're just trying to use Jewish forms to convert Jewish people to Christianity. As an intermarried couple that attends a Messianic Jewish congregation, I would like to get your response to this.

MICHAEL: When we first started going to Temple Beth Shalom, and I would describe it to my Jewish colleagues, I would say, "Well, it's a Jewish congregation. They do believe that Jesus is the Messiah, but it's not a cult." I did come in with a high amount of suspicion. When you asked me the question, you said that the criticism is that they are deceptive and they just want to convert people. I guess I would partially agree that certainly their goal is that they would like to see the Jewish people converted but I don't think they are deceptive about it. I do think it is honest and up front. So, at that point, it is really my choice to stay and listen. And to the Jewish community, I would say that we never got a sense that there was really an option within that community. And this is a way. Whatever they classify my children, I can tell my children they are Jewish and it's OK to believe in Jesus.

DENISE: You don't feel the children are denying their Judaism just because they believe in Jesus.

MICHAEL: I don't think so.

DENISE: It used to be that you couldn't do one thing and stay the other. But within the context of Temple Beth Shalom, we have learned that you do not have to stop being a Jew just because you choose to believe in the Messiah.

Q: How did you make the jump in accepting this?

MICHAEL: That's a hard question. I'm not sure. I don't know how to answer that, how I made that jump. I guess this is really the crux of the issue why I wouldn't say I believe in Jesus. The Judaism I was taught certainly believes in Messianic prophecy. That certainly is not in question. I guess, if you come to the conclusion that you believe Jesus is the Messiah, then clearly you are fulfilling your Judaism. Now, if you do believe in Jesus, you are practicing idolatry in the eyes of a traditional Jew. You have taken another god before you. It's very clear and it's very obvious in the teachings of the Messianic temple that they are not just saying Jesus was a great guy. They are very clear in saying, "His blood cleans your sins." I mean, they're not hiding that; it's not deceptive. But from a traditional point of view, that's idolatry. I do understand why the traditional community is not very willing to accept that. But the truth is, those people raised as believers and those people raised as Jews need to understand that two thousand years ago CNN was not there, and it's very easy for someone to believe and be convinced in the rightness of what they were raised on either side. In that sense, I understand the reluctance for them [traditional Jews] to accept it, because from a traditional Jewish point of view, it is just Christianity in another guise. But the truth of the matter is, there is this large intermarried population, and if you're in that population, what are you going to do? The Messianic community certainly seems to be, by far, the best alternative for us.

DENISE: I find it interesting because, when we first started going there, that's precisely what I thought. What a clever thing, you just do this all in a Jewish context, and in the meantime, you just slip

Jesus in and it works. But this is what I learned at Temple Beth Shalom—I came to not only understand, accept and love my husband and his Judaism, but also accept the fact that whether he ever chooses to believe or not, he is still important, God still loves him, and I am to love him, regardless. The focus was no longer, "I have to save my husband." The focus turned to, "I have to be who God wants me to be so our marriage will work and be blessed." I'm no longer concerned with saving my husband. That's God's job. Do you understand what I'm saying? And that I learned from them. My mission in life was not to save him. My mission in life was to be a person of God, the wife that God had called me to be in my marriage. That has to be my concern. And as long as I'm being the wife that God has called me to be, I need to leave everything else to God. That has brought a lot of peace between us. Like I said, I no longer have to fear what I say to him because he no longer fears that I'm just trying to proselytize and convince him of something.

Q: How about your initial thought that they were just slipping Jesus in?

DENISE: That's what I'm saying. Personally, that's the idea I got at first. But they were the same ones who quickly dispelled the notion that this was why we were there, you know, in order to just coat it up so he would like it and then get it in. My purpose, and everybody's purpose there, is to come to a greater relationship with Messiah. It's individual. And within that individual growth, my marriage and everything else is going to be affected. But it's not as a guise to convince those who are not convinced.

MICHAEL: The only other thing I'd add is that we've only ever gone to this one Messianic congregation. So, it is quite possible that all the other ones deprive you of sleep and brainwash you [laughter].

DENISE: That's true. We have never visited any other Messianic congregations. Temple Beth Shalom has met our needs so well that we never felt the need to go anywhere else. So, like he says, we don't know what's out there and what the others are doing, but we do know what Temple Beth Shalom is doing [laughter].

Q: Anything you would like to add?

DENISE: Just that I am very glad we found the congregation. I don't think we'd be where we are today if it hadn't been for the support and the things we've learned, especially for me, because I've been directly discipled by people there. And that has made an incredible impact on my life.

Q: Have you met other intermarried couples in the congregation that have had similarly positive experiences?

DENISE: Yes. There are many couples there.

Denise and Michael are a good example of how the Messianic Jewish option can meet the needs of intermarried couples. Some Jewish spouses may say, "I couldn't do what Michael does. I couldn't handle going with my family to a Messianic synagogue and listening to Jesus' teachings." While this is certainly an understandable feeling, I would suggest that a broader perspective is in order. As Jews, we take pride in the value our people place on education. Judaism is a faith that encourages us to ask questions and to explore knowledge. Is there a limit to this exploration? Does the New Testament contain forbidden knowledge? Of course not!

One of the most brilliant Jews of the century, Albert Einstein, was drawn to the taboo surrounding Jesus. After studying the New Testament for himself, he concluded:

> As a child, I received instruction both in the Bible and in the Talmud. I am a Jew, but I am enthralled by the luminous figure of the Nazarene.[1]

Martin Buber, the erudite professor of philosophy at Hebrew University, wrote concerning the Jewish attitude toward Jesus' followers:

> It is a peculiar manifestation of our exile-psychology that we permitted, and even aided in, the deletion of New Testament Messianism, that meaningful offshoot of our spiritual history. It was in a Jewish land that this spiritual revolution was kindled; and Jews were those who had spread it all over the land. . . . We must overcome the superstitious fear which we harbor about the Messianic movement of Jesus, and we must place this movement where it belongs, namely, in the spiritual history of Judaism.[2]

There is nothing wrong with a Jew learning about the life and teachings of Jesus. Joan Hawxhurst, editor of a national periodical for Interfaith families, gives this counsel to intermarried Jews:

. . . learning about the life of Jesus, reading the statements attributed to him in the New Testament, or giving consideration to Jesus' philosophical teachings, in no way constitute a conversionary process. It can only add to the richness of a couple's life if the Jewish partner (and maybe the Christian partner as well) learns about Jesus' life and is familiar with the basic Christian doctrines about Jesus. I can know what is on the other side of the fence without jumping over that fence. The important point for Jews in relationships with Christians is that learning about the teachings of Jesus does not necessarily mean crossing the boundary line between Judaism and Christianity—nor does admiring the life of Jesus, nor even does being inspired by those of his statements that may resonate."[3]

I would add that learning about Jesus in a Messianic Jewish context is completely different than learning about him in a Gentile Christian context. Intermarried Jews often find the environment of a Messianic synagogue conducive for learning about Jesus because emphasis is placed on the Jewishness of his life and teachings. It is a fact of history that Jesus is the most famous Jew who ever lived. He was born in Israel, spoke Hebrew, worshipped at the Temple, taught in the synagogue, and expounded on the Torah. Any Jew who begins to study his life and teachings, in a historical Jewish context, cannot help but feel a sense of pride that he was one of us, and there is nothing wrong with that. Such is the perspective of many intermarried Jews who attend Messianic synagogues.

## CHAPTER 10

# Nate and Hannah: A Christian Wife Raising Jewish Children

---

Consider that, in 1989, two-thirds of all intermarriages were made up of a Jewish husband and a non-Jewish wife.[1] Consider further that Jewish husbands typically avoid taking on the leadership role of maintaining Jewish life in the home.[2] This creates a vacuum and places the non-Jewish wife in a difficult situation. She usually does not have the experience or knowledge to raise Jewish children and feels inadequate in taking up the slack. She is reluctant to bring the children to synagogue by herself; it is awkward since she is a non-Jew. Still, the husband may expect her to take on the leadership role. What is a non-Jewish mother of Jewish children to do in this circumstance?

In addition, there is the matter of her spiritual needs. The mainstream synagogue does not read from the New Testament, and the life and teachings of Jesus are subjects to be avoided. The non-Jewish wife with a Christian background can easily feel alienated in this environment. Is she not entitled to have her own spiritual needs met? On the practical side, it is too much to attend synagogue on *Shabbat* with the kids, and church on Sunday by herself. It is the path of least resistance to bring the kids to church on Sunday and give them a Christian religious education. But how will Jewish identity be conveyed?

As many couples are discovering, the Messianic Jewish option can be especially helpful to women in this situation. This is because the Messianic synagogue is a comfortable place for the wife to worship. She can have her own spiritual needs met, while also fulfilling her goal—to raise her children as Jews. Moreover, the Messianic synagogue will teach the wife how to keep a Jewish home and will help her to find deep spiritual meaning in a Torah-New Covenant lifestyle.

*An intermarried couple, Nate and Hannah, have found the Messianic synagogue to be an acceptable compromise solution. Nate, an Israeli professor, is Jewish but not Messianic. Hannah is originally from Germany and worked for many years as a nurse. Though non-Jewish, she is an Israeli citizen. They have six beautiful children who speak a hand-ful of languages. Both Hannah and her children attend a Messianic synagogue with Nate's full support.*

Q: How did you meet each other?

HANNAH: In Israel, in Jerusalem, in the hospital, at the night shift. Well, not just night shifts, also day shifts. [Laughter].

Q: Was the fact that you were from different backgrounds a big issue?

NATE: No, because we never thought there would be a relationship. We were just friends for many years.

HANNAH: Five years.

NATE: The religion issue was always a problem in terms of thinking about something serious.

Q: How did you deal with the wedding?

NATE: We did it very simple. Just the two of us and no family.

HANNAH: It was too far. They couldn't come anyway.

NATE: And it would be too complicated.

Q: Were you married in Israel?

NATE: In Israel.

Q: Were there any particular issues that you had to deal with when you first got married?

NATE: We could agree to get married on the basis of my philosophy that the main issue in a relationship between two persons is respect one for the other. It's not the purpose to change the other one but to help the other one to grow in their way. So, we discussed it and I be-lieved that Hannah could grow in her religion. And I would help her to grow in her ways, respecting her way of thinking and expecting the same respect. That was the basic principle that we agreed on. And we have kept to that way. We don't say, "I have the truth. You're wrong. I hope one day you will find the truth." We respect the other in his/her own way and we are helping each other to become better in her/his way. So Hannah has helped me to go to the synagogue and become more active and become more involved in Judaism. And Hannah has called on my support in her activities, which is the reason I'm here [at the Messianic congregational retreat], you see. I don't participate in her activities. I don't go to the praise because it's not my way. But if she needs help coming with the jeep and driving and the money and so on, a hundred percent. That was the main agreement.

Q: You've been married for how many years now?

NATE: Almost fourteen.

Q: Do you feel that this approach has worked out well?

NATE: Personally, I think we succeed in this approach. We have a dilemma with the children. In Israel, I believe it wouldn't be possible to do what we are doing. It would be impossible and we would have more problems. Israel is a mono-society. It is a society that has only one direction. Either you're a Jew, an Israeli, or you're out, like it or not. That was the idea of the birth of the State of Israel. It is the same in Germany. It's also a mono-society. You're either a Christian or you're out. The United States has something special—no one cares about what you do. You can be whatever you like, and that's good. In a way, you can be isolated but you can do whatever you like and nobody is killed. I mean, in Israel, the pressure of the family and the pressure of the environment is very strong. When I was young I thought we could lead and we could fight against that. I'm a little older now and I can say that it's not true. Society, the environment, the family—is a very strong factor. When you're close to the family, it's very difficult to be humanistic, as I like to say, to respect the way of the other one. Personally, if you live with me, I respect your way.

Q: How did you deal with the religious upbringing of your first child?

NATE: It was in Israel, not much discussion. The family was Jews, everybody's Jews. Hannah was a minority there. There was no problem.

Q: Were you supportive of raising the children with a Jewish identity?

HANNAH: Since we married, we have always done *Shabbat*. Of course as the children became bigger, we did more celebrations. For me, they are as important, I think, as they are for Nate.

Q: So, you have your own convictions?

HANNAH: Oh, yes. The Jewish festivals were very important for me too.

Q: Did you discuss whether your son would be exposed to teachings about Jesus?

HANNAH: In the first years when he was little, for me it was very important that he get a relationship with God by himself. At a little age, I never felt I needed to mention anything because it's something you have to understand. It took me twenty-three years until I understood about Yeshua. So, for me, it was very important first that they have a relationship with God—who God is. And that's what I do. Usually it's me, at home, who prays with the children in the evening, who sings the songs before the meal. And so I introduced them to "Someone" who is above and "Someone" who is the Creator of all of us. That was for me, in the first years, very important. During the first years in Israel I think we never really came into conflict. Our children were born in Israel. They are Israelis, so I think they have the right to be introduced to everything else that is commanded in the Torah, which I read as much as any other Jew.

Q: Are you an Israeli citizen?

HANNAH: Yes.

NATE: I'll tell you where the problem is, especially in Israel. The problem is Jesus. And this is a problem that is a theological issue and a philosophical problem. In Israel, Christianity is identified with Jesus. In the schools, they learn about "Jesus and Christianity" as the institution that has persecuted the Jews for two thousand years. The idea of "Jesus and Christianity" is one thing and is identified only with persecution and as the enemy of Judaism. So, when Asher was going to school, I started feeling that we would have troubles there because all the children in the school learn about Jesus as the enemy and nothing else. I didn't want to have my child experiencing that when he's going to the school. In the house he's learning that Jesus is God and in the school he's learning that Jesus is the enemy. That would be a conflict. And maybe that was one of the reasons I decided to take the offered position to come to the United States. It was going to be a big conflict once my child went to school.

Q: Did you agree with what the schools were teaching?

NATE: It's a sociological reality. We cannot deny something that really happened. Does it mean that the religion is wrong? That Christianity is wrong? No, of course not. The basic principles of Christianity are based on the basic principles of Judaism. And Christianity has done fantastic things in history. But it has also done terrible things. We cannot deny either one or the other. Societies have those things. They develop beautiful ideas. Then politics and power get involved . . . and we cannot deny that. Christianity did that. I know that even Israeli society is changing and it has to. Today they are presenting the other aspect of Christianity, that it is based on a Jewish monotheistic philosophy and that it changed the world. Judaism didn't spread the Jewish monotheistic philosophy. It was Christianity who did it. And they changed the philosophy of the world and based it on Christianity. No doubt! Judaism may be the father but the spread of monotheism really came from the son, which is Christianity. But the son attacked the father in order to develop its own identity. It's the same today—teenagers start attacking their fathers—they want to develop their own identity. I always see history as a human being. There is a period of childhood. You have a childhood of Christianity that was in Israel—the first Christians. You have a time of adolescence, of teenagers. That is the Middle Ages, where Christianity was looking for its own identity, and the way it did it was attacking Judaism and trying to destroy it. We cannot deny that. Now Judaism is coming back. We are trying to find our own identity again. At the beginning of the State of Israel, it denied or attacked Christianity. Now the Israeli society is becoming a more mature society. Judaism is becoming more secure. We don't need to bring up what Christianity did to us for two thousand years. But still the children are learning that Christianity was an enemy of Judaism for two thousand years.

Q: How did you arrive at the decision to raise your children in a Messianic Jewish context?

NATE: I went back to practical things. I don't intend to change Hannah's way of thinking. As for the children, in the same way that they know different languages from their father and their mother, they also need to know the way of thinking of their father and their mother. Now, the mother is the one who is in contact with the children a hundred percent of the time. Someone has to bring the money, that's natural. You see the animals in nature. The female usually is the one who is taking care and the male goes to bring the food. The human is the same. We try to change society to make it more equal. I think it's very nice but still it's not natural, in a way. I'm more feminist than anyone else. But it's the mother who has this link with the children. So we agreed. My only enemy is fanaticism. It's the only enemy. I become a fanatic when I see a fanatic. What Hannah has shown me is that she is not a fanatic. She is teaching the children values, the values that I admire. They have to learn what her background is. So she teaches them about Jesus. Yes, of course. That's what she believes. Now if she chooses the environment that she believes is easier for her to teach them, good. But again, we still have discussions to see the best way that the children also will see my side. We hope one day they will decide and maybe one would like to go to Judaism, and we will be happy.

HANNAH: They will have to make their own decision. They get exposed to both sides. They go with Nate to synagogue sometimes.

Q: A traditional synagogue?

NATE: Yes, a Conservative synagogue.

HANNAH: We go on Yom Kippur to the synagogue, all of us. They know both sides very well. They know what is Messianic Judaism and they know what is Christianity.

Q: They're probably a lot more educated in religion than most young people.

NATE: Yes, that's true.

HANNAH: They get exposed to all this religion.

NATE: That's my philosophy.

HANNAH: There comes a time and an age when they have to make their own decision. I think it is important, and I like that even, because I cannot put my religion on them and I don't want to. For me, this was very important. I found God myself, not because of my background. I was growing up in Germany and never knew who Jesus was until I came to Israel and started doing what I was doing—finding out about him through all the Jewish festivals, through Judaism, through the language, through everything. So, I think for them, they get exposed to everything, and then one day they will make their own decision. For me, it's important that they realize, first of all and most important, that there is a relationship to God. You have to know there is a Creator from whom we've received everything, who holds everything in his hands. And then we go from there. We put our steps into his hands.

Q: How is the Messianic Jewish option compared to other options?

NATE: It is very good. There is no doubt. Which is why I don't have a problem with it.

Q: You don't attend a Messianic synagogue but you are connected to the lives of people from that community through your wife and children. How do you deal with that?

NATE: I don't have any problem when people respect my way because I believe that everybody has the right to believe what they think is right. That has always been my direction. I try to stop anyone who has to convince me to become like them. And this always happens. And I understand. So immediately I'm very clear. And I say, "This is my way—respect." And you can see their faces going down and say, "Oh, he's a lost case." But I think they like it in the end because they know exactly what I am, what I think, and there is no waste of time.

Q: The two keys are clarity of communication and respect.

NATE: Yes. That's the most important thing. I make it very clear. This is what I am. I mean, I may not agree with what you do but I respect you. You have to respect me. If you respect me, we're friends. If you don't respect me, that's the end. And this has been a good thing because many of Hannah's friends are very good friends of mine. We had a guy who tried to work on me and I cut it. And the friendship with the family is finished because, you see, if I go to your house, I will respect the way that you live and I will keep my mouth shut. If you want to get close to my house, you have to accept the way we live. And the way we live, the basic principle at the entrance of the door, is respect. If you respect my way of living and you respect the way of living of my wife, we are friends.

Q: From what you're saying, it sounds like most people can handle this.

NATE: Yes.

Q: How often do you run into someone who can't meet your terms of friendship?

NATE: It has been the exception, yes. I mean one case in how many, twenty? It's very good.

Q: Do you never talk about religion?

NATE: Oh, no. I love to talk about philosophy and religion. And I say what I believe. No, I'm not afraid of that. And I'm not afraid to listen to other people. As a friend, I want to know what you think. But don't tell me that you're in the right because then we're finished. I would never tell you that I'm in the right because I may be wrong. But this is my way. And at the end of the days, if I find that I am wrong, fine, I will change; it's the only time I will change. But I give respect. Respect is a very good thing so we can have nice talks, nice exchanges of thinking. And when the friendship grows, of course I want to know what you believe.

Q: You're saying that respect nurtures trust and trust leads to greater respect for one's boundaries.

NATE: People are very nice. We just had a party. I was cooking far away, so they were discussing religion, Jesus. When Nate comes, they change the subject. [Laughter].

Q: That's very sensitive.

NATE: It's very sensitive and I respect it. Really, I think it's fantastic. And when they are discussing Jesus, OK. I don't have anything to say so I let them. It's a hundred percent OK.

Q: How do you deal with going by yourself to the Messianic synagogue?

HANNAH: From the beginning, things had been very clear to us. I knew who Nate was. It was not like I had my eyes opened after three years or something. I knew who he was and I respected and accepted him as he was and is today. So I knew that to go to congregation—I mean it's wonderful going hand-in-hand and arm-in-arm and sitting together which is great. But I think, for me, services and prayers are more than just sitting together. It's my time, what I'm offering to God. And I'm praying here to God and I do this with my heart towards Him. If Nate's not coming, it's the same for me. Of course I would prefer to have him with me. But I accepted and knew that I would go there on my own. On *Shabbat*, I'm giving my time to God.

Q: Did you ever try going only to a church or only to a traditional synagogue?

NATE: No, because that would immediately go against our basic principles. I don't want to convert her and of course I don't want her to convert me.

Q: What would you say to the one million intermarried couples about the Messianic Jewish option?

NATE: It's a good option, especially when the mother is not a Jew. It is a good option to maintain a relationship with Judaism and with the Jewish culture. And that's the reason a Jew is determined by the mother. I think that's why because the mother is really the one, in general, who is in closer contact with the children. And the way she nurses the child intellectually and emotionally—it helps for keeping both sides. The father is always an outsider in a way. It depends on the degree but sometimes we are outsiders. So, if it weren't for Messianic Judaism, maybe all the Judaism would be lost completely. In this way, the child knows some of the Jewish culture. If one day he decided to go for Judaism, it would not be something completely unknown. He's familiar with Judaism. When he goes to synagogue and they are singing all the traditional songs, he's familiar with those songs. He knows what is *Yom Kippur*. He knows what is *Rosh HaShanah*. He knows all these things. In the type of marriage where the father is a Jew and the mother is not a Jew, I think it [the Messianic Jewish option] is perfect. It is very good. It helps Judaism. For the other side, I don't know.

Q: What would you say, Hannah, to the one million intermarried couples regarding the Messianic Jewish option?

HANNAH: Messianic Judaism helps me. First of all, I am married to a Jew and I think it is important the children know about the Jewish background. In a church, you won't find that. The other thing is, yes, Messianic Judaism helps let me be who I am. It helps me also to have the Old Testament, not as an old historical book, but it keeps the Old Testament alive for me, while in Christianity it is lost. No one talks about the commandments or it is in a very different way, which I think is not right. There are many things I don't agree with in Christianity a hundred percent. And I say that because of my own experience in life—I didn't understand who God was. It took me very long and I found that through the Jewish people. So, for me, Messianic Judaism is very helpful. Also, in the education of the children, Messianic Judaism shows them that this old book, the "Old Testament" as it is called, is not an old testament; it's still alive and should be kept alive. So, for me, it's very positive. It's not always the easiest because it's a very new movement.

NATE: As the movement grows, the society also will know about it. There is the societal component. That is what we are seeing now with our children. Maybe it will be easier for the children to say, "I am a Messianic Jew" and everybody understands, and that's it. And they will really have the middle.

Q: You spoke, Hannah, about the Hebrew Scriptures, the Old Testament. Does the Messianic Jewish option provide something that a church wouldn't provide in regards to the New Testament?

HANNAH: Oh, yes, definitely. The Messianic movement also shows very clearly that Yeshua observed all the festivals from Judaism. Where I grew up, we did not know this. I had no idea that he was celebrating Hanukkah or *Pesach* [Passover]. I never understood that Yeshua did all this. I never realized it. I think in a Messianic congregation it's much clearer to me. They show me that this person I believe in did all this. I mean I'm following someone. So, if I ask myself, "Why am I doing this?" Well, if I don't have another answer, at least I can say, "Yeshua did the same thing." If he did that, and he's an example for me, I'm supposed to do that too." He never went against Judaism. He never went against the Law. Very often Christianity does go against the Law. So, I think, "Well, no, we are not against the Law. We are not against anything of Judaism." Yeshua always talked about the heart of the people. He never said what we got from Moses was wrong. So I think that is very helpful to me, and it comes from the Messianic Jewish movement.

CHAPTER 11

# Sarah and Greg: Finding a Place to Fit in

*S*arah *is a Messianic Jew from a Conservative Jewish background. Greg grew up Catholic and later converted to Judaism in a Reform synagogue. They have two daughters and have been married twenty-four years. Sarah and Greg have found the Messianic synagogue to meet their needs.*

Q: What was your religious upbringing?

GREG: I was born and raised Catholic, but not in a strict sense. My father was Protestant. Neither one of them was very religious or spiritual. My mother bought into the whole Catholic tradition. We went to the important holidays for mass—Christmas and Easter, sometimes Sunday. So when I got older, I became something of an agnostic. I believed there was a God but I didn't think he had anything personal to do with most people. When I met Sarah, I didn't know anything about Jewish people.

Q: How did you meet her?

GREG: I was at the navy hospital getting knee surgery. Sarah was there [in the administrative section of patient affairs]. I saw her in the cafeteria a few times. She was very attractive and I noticed her. Later, one of the attorneys that she had been working for got moved up to the office where I was working and he sent me down to get his stuff out of his office, and that's when I actually met Sarah. She ended up calling the attorney and saying, "I want to meet this guy." So he sent me down again.

SARAH: I picked him up.

GREG: Sarah and I hit it off and we started going out. I had a problem with my mother at home and I left home. When I left home I didn't have a place to go. [Previously] Sarah had agreed [with her parents] to move out of the house and get her own place.

SARAH: I was given an ultimatum that I either stop dating Greg or I move out.

GREG: Essentially, what happened is that I moved in with her and we lived together for about three years.

Q: When you first started dating, was the fact that you were from different backgrounds an issue?

SARAH: That was the issue. He was the first non-Jewish boy that I dated.

GREG: It wasn't an issue for me but it was for her. And I didn't realize how bad until later. What began to happen is that I was not allowed to go into the house. To me it seemed kind of archaic. I said, "What is this? This is the twentieth century already. These people aren't going to come out of the dark ages?" Of course, as I became more familiar with Jewish people, I came to understand where they were coming from, but to me it seemed very archaic.

Q: Did Sarah tell you that you were not allowed into the house?

GREG: Yes.

SARAH: When we went on a date, I met him at the bottom of the driveway. I was the oldest of three girls and my parents felt that whatever they accepted from me they would then have to accept from my sisters. They could never accept me intermarrying because that would only give my sisters permission to do the same thing.

Q: How did Sarah explain it to you?

GREG: She said, "They cannot accept the fact that you are not Jewish." And like I said, I thought it was kind of narrow-minded. But I was in love with Sarah. I said, "Well, if that's the way they want to be, that's their problem. I'm not dating them." [Laughter].

SARAH: Little did you know.

GREG: Anyway, we ended up living together. Her parents didn't know at first but eventually they figured it out. Initially, when I started living with her, I could see how this was really bothering her—what was going on between her and her parents. And I really cared for her. So I said, "Maybe what I'll do is just convert to Judaism, just on paper, so that they'll accept me and leave you alone."

Q: So your motivation was to help keep the peace.

GREG: Right. I didn't want her having strife with her mother. So I said, "I'll convert and this will alleviate this problem." It's kind of funny because after I converted I think they thought marriage was in the picture right off the bat. I hadn't intended that initially but when they talked about it and went into it, I thought, "That's not such a bad thing. Maybe I'll go with that." I wasn't intending to go that step. [Laughter]

SARAH: I didn't know that. I'm learning something new today. Stop while you're ahead! [Laughter].

GREG: I was in love with her. I hadn't given much thought about spending the rest of my life with her but I was in love with her. And then when I made the step to conversion, they invited me back into the house. It was like being with family. It seemed to fit OK. And I said, "I could do this." When I was first questioned about it, I said, "We haven't set a date."

SARAH: My mother said, "I need six months. How's June?" [Laughter]

GREG: I said, "You can take as long as you want. I'm not in a hurry." [Laughter]

Q: Did she really say that?

SARAH: Yes. My mother didn't believe in long engagements.

GREG: Anyway, I went through the conversion and then we got married. But in the process of going through the conversion, the Reform rabbi had me do some reading. I actually began to look at Scripture for the first time. I made it pretty clear to the rabbi that the purpose of my conversion was not for religious reasons, that I was doing it mainly because I wanted to make things easier for Sarah. Nonetheless, he decided to let me do it. I had to go through six months of study before the conversion. It's a good thing to have people do. So when I went through it, I actually started to read the Scripture and I began to learn things that I didn't know before. I thought I knew a lot about the Bible and then I started reading this stuff. I found things that were in conflict with what I had been taught. So that sort of opened my eyes, which actually made me a little more agnostic at first. Then I went through the conversion and we got married. Shortly after that, I worked for a while and then I went to college. I started off as an art major but later went back again to get a degree in engineering because I was trying to find a way to make a decent living. At the college, there was this fellow named Phil who was doing a lot of open air preaching in front of the student union and the library. At lunchtime I used to go down to listen to him because I thought it was interesting how he'd preach and all these people would just heckle him. I was just amazed at how he would stand there, take that, and keep doing it. And he was there every single day. I thought, "This guy must be nuts to put up with this." But he kept coming every single day. And after a while, people actually started coming to listen and started asking him legitimate questions. I started listening to the things he said, and in relation to what I was learning in my physics classes about the universe, it started to dawn on me that the universe is simple and uniform, and there had to be an outside designer. So during the summer I was doing security guard work and I said, "I'm going to read the Bible. I'm going to read the whole thing. I read some of it when I went through conversion; I'm going to read the whole thing. I'm going to start from the beginning and go all the way through."

Q: Including the New Testament?

SARAH: Correct.

GREG: I went all the way through it. It took a long time to read. And even after I read it, I didn't understand a lot of it. You need some background knowledge to completely understand the Bible. Even today, I don't completely understand a lot of it. After I got through it, I was convicted that Jesus was God and the only way for salvation was to accept him as your savior. In my heart, I accepted it then. I don't remember the exact date because it was a drawn out process over that summer. But I had come to the conviction, at that point, that this was the case . . . My coming to believe in the Lord was not a significant emotional event. It was more intellectual and came through small realizations. I came to the conclusion that this book was telling me the truth.

Q: So, then what happened?

GREG: I said to myself, "I have a problem now" [how to tell Sarah] . . . I was saying, "How am I going to do this? This is going to be like going through a brick wall," because I knew her upbringing. But it's amazing. We were lying in bed, and I decided to broach the subject with her. And I said, "I've been doing some reading and I've come to the conclusion that the Bible is right, that Jesus is God, and he is the Lord and Savior." And I said, "I've accepted him as my Lord and Savior."

SARAH: It wasn't just all of a sudden that you mentioned this to me. You had been talking to me gradually after you had finished reading the Bible.

GREG: So I explained to her how I felt. Then, I don't know what happened, but she said, "Well, ever since I was a little girl, I've thought that Jesus was the Son of God."

SARAH: I don't know why. I didn't know what that meant. I never expressed that to anybody. I don't ever remember not believing that, and I don't know why I believed it.

GREG: I wasn't expecting that. I was expecting a war. It was so easy I couldn't believe it.

SARAH: It was very easy. I don't ever remember saying, "What are you doing? Are you crazy? What am I going to tell my family?" Nothing! I'm telling you, God's hand was upon everything. It can be the only explanation.

GREG: Needless to say, I was extremely relieved. People go through their entire lives never getting their spouse to understand. I thought we were going to get divorced. That's what I thought was going to happen.

Q: Sarah, what about your background?

SARAH: Well, I was born in New York. My parents moved to this area when I was very young. The only synagogue I ever attended was Ner Tamid. I went to Hebrew school, Sunday school, I was consecrated, *bat mitzvah*ed and confirmed, and went to Hebrew high school. It was a Conservative synagogue. We fit our life around our Judaism—*Rosh HaShanah*, *Yom Kippur*, a Sabbath service. My mother was involved in the sisterhood. My father never participated in the men's part of that. He was always busy working. She sold *bat mitzvah* invitations for the synagogue and worked in the workshop. She was very involved. I loved Hebrew school. It wasn't the burden for me that it was for other people. I went three days a week and I enjoyed growing up as a Jew. I thought I was somehow better than somebody who wasn't a Jew. I always felt that it made me special. I still think it does but for a much better reason now. I was never allowed to date non-Jews. It was understood that anything but a Jewish husband would not be accepted. So that was always there. When I was about nineteen years old, I met Greg. I liked what he looked like in a uniform. He was mean, lean, and hungry. [Laughter]. My parents did not approve.

Q: Did you tell your parents that he was a non-Jew?

SARAH: Well, they saw me dating. You could look at him. And for a little while he was allowed to come to the house and pick me up. When they saw that it was getting beyond friendship, it went from— he's not allowed in the house anymore, to meeting him at the bottom of the driveway, to my father coming to me one evening and saying to me, "I love you but I love your mother and I have to live with your mother. And her happiness is more important to me. If you feel that you need to be with Greg, and that's what you need to do to be happy, then I'm happy for you. But your mother is my main concern and she doesn't have to see this. So, if you continue to date Greg, you need to find someplace else to live." Now, keep in mind, I went to a local college. I never lived anywhere but with Mommy and Daddy. I had a very special relationship growing up with my parents and I never defied them. I was a good girl. I wasn't sexually active. I didn't do drugs. So I went and found myself an apartment. Our relationship blossomed. I think for a long time I was very infatuated with Greg. In fact, we were married two years before I fell in love with him. As we were getting ready to be married—it was a wonderful beautiful wedding—and I'm walking down the aisle with my folks, and there is Greg under the *huppah*, my mother says to me, "I just want you to know, it's still not too late." She wasn't saying to me, "Don't marry this *shlump* [boring, uninspiring person]." It was more like, "Make sure of your conviction here. If you're not a hundred percent sure that this is the man you want to spend the rest of your life with, I don't care if there are 125 guests, we drop it right here." And I understood that. But here I was, looking at this man who had converted for me. We had lived together. How could I possibly not marry him? So I went through with it, scared to death. He had nothing to offer me. I came from a middle class Jewish family. I dated doctors and dentists and lawyers. And here was this backwoods, on the other side of the railroad track, poor farm boy. I never dated anybody like him, let alone I'm going to marry him. But we went through with it, under the *huppah*, the whole bit. And at that point I figured, "Oh, good, it's all over. My parents won't be pressuring me any more." But my mother was too much in the middle of our marriage. And that was predominantly my fault because I shared things with her. It was very hard in the beginning.

Q: What did you do about religious affiliation after you were married?

SARAH: I wouldn't go to a church and he wouldn't go to a synagogue.

GREG: I mentioned something about it and she said, "Well, I'm not going to go to a church." It's not that I wouldn't go to a synagogue. I just didn't find fulfillment there. There was a piece missing. So what happened is that we would go on the High Holy Days because her family would go. And because I converted, they accepted me. We didn't have any real fellowship with any believers.

SARAH: Before Rachel was born, we checked out Tikvat Israel [the Messianic synagogue] to see if it was the answer to him not going to synagogue and me not going to church. I thought the people worshipping at Tikvat Israel were crazy.

Q: Why?

SARAH: Well, first of all, at the Conservative synagogue, you didn't clap your hands. At the Messianic Jewish congregation, there were people dancing around the synagogue. There were guitars. Then we tried looking around again because Tikvat Israel was definitely not for us. So we started going on High Holy Days to different Reform congregations. Then Rachel was born. I was pregnant with Shiri. We tried Tikvat Israel again.

Q: Why did you go back?

SARAH: We were trying to find a place to fit in and we didn't know about Temple Sinai [a more conservative Messianic synagogue in the same area]. We went and tried it again. And sure enough, I still didn't like it for the same reason.

GREG: I just felt uncomfortable. Eventually, we went and saw this female Reform rabbi.

SARAH: We were looking to get Rachel into Hebrew school so she could start training for *bat mitzvah*.

GREG: We were going to explain to the rabbi straight up front, "This is what we believe. We want Rachel to have the Jewish upbringing and *bat mitzvah* training but we don't want her to deny Jesus, and we don't want her to be taught that he's not who he is. And we were just wondering if it was possible to join the congregation to get that aspect from the congregation." And she said, "No, we can't do that."

SARAH: They were sharing a building with a church and she said, "You really should be speaking to the pastor of the church because we would ask your child to deny Jesus and I would never want to put a child in that position."

GREG: If I had been smarter, I would have asked her, "Well, why don't you tell them to deny Buddha?" [Laughter]. "Why is Jesus such a particular issue?"

SARAH: Then I walked out of there and I said, "I've just been rejected by my own kind. What do I do now?" I spoke to my sister Chaiya, who is the second oldest. And she said, "Sarah, I understand that you don't want to hurt Mom and Dad, but your children need to know that they're not freaks." And it was the wisest thing that my sister Chaiya had ever said in her entire life until that point. I said to Greg, "They need to meet children who are like them. We're going to have to bite the bullet and we're going to have to check out Tikvat Israel again." So we went there.

GREG: It wasn't something we were looking forward to.

SARAH: It was *Rosh HaShanah* of 1996. We're sitting there, and who should be preaching, but Bernie [the assistant rabbi]. And what was his message on? It took the form of an introduction to him and how he came to the Lord. I kept saying to Greg, "He's telling my story." Raised in a Conservative household, grew up in Richmond, a Jewish boy. I was tickled because, all of a sudden, I wasn't alone. I could identify with this man on the *bimah* [raised platform at the front of the synagogue] like I had never been able to identify with anybody. I still was uncomfortable with the form of worship. But this time we were going to keep coming. And we have been coming ever since. We joined and became full members.

GREG: We also started getting fellowship at this point.

SARAH: We joined a home group.

GREG: We could talk to people who were like-minded. It was nice.

SARAH: I had been a Jew for over forty years, and it wasn't until coming to Tikvat Israel that I, for the first time, understood what it really meant to be a Jew, how really blessed I actually was, and how Yeshua was it.

Q: When did you tell your parents that you were attending a Messianic synagogue? What was their reaction?

SARAH: When we joined, I told them when we were attending membership classes. You know, in the traditional community, you go to a synagogue, you pay your dues, and you're a member. They don't care if you believe in God or not. But I told them that we were going to Tikvat Israel and we were attending membership classes. My father said, "What do you mean?" And I said, "Well, you know, you have to take classes to make sure we're on the same wavelength." And he said, "Well, I may not approve, but you tell them to take you."

Q: Did he understand it was a Messianic synagogue?

SARAH: Yes.

Q: Have you adjusted to the dancing and music?

SARAH: I'm more comfortable with it.

GREG: From my perspective, I actually like the worship now, the musical worship.

Q: Has the Messianic synagogue met your needs?

GREG: I would say it has.

SARAH: Yes. It is absolutely essential to my life that I am with Jewish people. That's why I'm not in a church. And even to this day, even though there are Gentile believers at Tikvat Israel that I absolutely love and adore, I do recognize in myself that I identify better with the Jewish believers.

Q: Is it important to you that your children's children are Jewish?

Both: Absolutely

SARAH: It has to be as important for us Jewish believers that the Jewish heritage continues from generation to generation. That is God's will. I think it is absolutely important that our children and our children's children have a love and an appreciation and a real respect for their Jewish heritage, because it is a rich one and it is a gift from God.

## CHAPTER 12

# Barbara and Alan: Messianic Judaism, A Marriage Saver

*B*arbara grew up Christian. Alan is Jewish but not Messianic. They
have two children. As an intermarried couple, they are raising
their daughter in a Messianic synagogue and their son in a Reform synagogue. Alan comes occasionally with his family to the Messianic service and Barbara likewise to the Reform service. The
following essay is Barbara's account of how Messianic Judaism has
helped their family.

Seventeen years ago I married Alan, who is Jewish. I am a Gentile, and
at the time of our marriage, I knew next to nothing about Judaism. I had
just accepted Jesus as my Savior the year before our wedding in 1981. I
naively did not fully understand why this caused my husband-to-be so
much anxiety. He was thirty-three and I was twenty-four when we married. We decided our love would conquer all! We even chose to recite
part of the Song of Songs to each other at our wedding. I married and
returned to my liberal Protestant Church and found that I no longer felt
comfortable there. I was now ravenous for the word of God, and no one
there seemed interested in taking the Bible so literally.

This was the beginning of several years of searching for the right
place for me to fellowship and worship. My husband, Alan, has always maintained a membership in his local Reform Jewish congregation. He would attend on High Holy Days, and a few other times
during the year. . . . Over time, I was becoming more and more depressed. I thought I had made a huge mistake marrying an unbeliever.
I thought I would continue to feel very lonely for the rest of our marriage. From my Bible studies, I understood that God hates divorce, and
being a child of divorce, I did not want to consider that as an option.

As my church activities continued, and as I served the Lord and
put him first, I was estranged more and more from Alan. I became
bitter and resentful inside while trying to have a joyful testimony on
the outside towards him. Why wouldn't he see the light?

I tried going to temple with Alan, but he wasn't interested in
going very often. I needed something more. We visited a local *havurah*

[fellowship of Jewish families who study and celebrate Jewish life to-gether]. The people were very friendly and my husband was positive about trying it. I could see after a couple of visits that they were a group of mostly intermarried Jews and nominal Christians. I couldn't commit myself to a group that completely ignored the Messiah.

I tried joining different churches and continued to be miserable in my marriage. This was a bad testimony to the rest of my family who saw my decision to be "born again" as having negative results!

To make a long story short, I truly believe that the Lord saved my marriage through introducing me to Messianic Judaism!

Nowhere else would I be able to worship my Savior in spirit and in truth, whom I now also know by his Hebrew name *Yeshua HaMashiach* [Jesus the Messiah]. Nowhere else would I be so warmly encouraged as a Gentile to learn about Judaism and the purposes of *Adonai* [the Lord] for his people, both Jew and Gentile who place their trust in him.

I have seen my husband gradually become more comfortable as a visitor of Beth Simcha [the Messianic synagogue]. He has attended a very joyful and beautiful Messianic Jewish wedding at Temple Sar Shalom [another local Messianic synagogue] and several *bar* and *bat mitzvah* services at Beth Simcha. He attends a regular *Shabbat* service with me two or three times a year. I notice he joins right in with the traditional prayers.

He occasionally sings or hums some of our worship songs as he does chores around the house! Alan genuinely likes the people at Beth Simcha. He knows they will not pressure him in any way. My friends have become his friends. Recently our daughter made plans to see a movie with my rabbi's daughter. It was my husband who suggested that we make it a double date for us parents, since we all had to do some driving anyway.

My husband is not a believer in Yeshua, but very occasionally—usually while in the car—we have some amazing conversations that reveal the depth of his inmost thoughts . . . such as, "Why did God have to require a blood atonement, anyway?"

Other blessings I have experienced through Beth Simcha:

- Friends who are truly loving and supportive in good times and in bad.
- Friends who pray!
- A whole new avenue [for me] of dance as praise and wor-ship. This led me to start taking Israeli dance at our local JCC (Jewish Community Center).
- As a calligrapher and artist, I have been greatly inspired in my work through learning Hebrew letterforms.

- Learning Hebrew is a delight. To pray in the language of the Torah feels like such a privilege. It is exciting for me to understand a few words as the Torah portion is read each week.
- Keeping *Shabbat*—Honestly, in the beginning my attitude was begrudging, "What, give up my entire Saturday?!" *Shabbat* has become the high point of my week. I look forward to the service, the time with friends, the *oneg* [refreshments after the service] (at Beth Simcha, we have lunch!), the conversation, the laughter, the rest, and the change of pace from the rest of the week.
- Another blessing is the fruit I see developing in our two children. Isaac had his *bar mitzvah* at his father's Reform temple. Since then, he has had minimal involvement in the temple. He's at the age where he is questioning everything. Recently, he had to do a collage for school (public high school), expressing his interests and identity. To my surprise, Isaac chose to include a photo from his *bar mitzvah* and a copy of the invitation. These became part of the collage, alongside photos of snowboarding, wrestling, and soccer. I feel so good about the fact that Isaac has developed a Jewish identity. I believe it has been strengthened by his Gentile mother embracing the Jewish holidays, lighting *Shabbat* candles—(even if we do it late—when Dad gets home!), and keeping *Shabbat*. I pray Isaac will come to know and love his Messiah some day. Isaac is not involved at Beth Simcha at this time. Our daughter Rachel made a profession of faith in Yeshua and has been immersed. She goes to services at Beth Simcha with me every *Shabbat*, except during the soccer season, when she has to miss quite a few! She's active in Beth Simcha's youth group. Rachel had her *bat mitzvah* in June 2000. Our whole family enjoyed this event. Oh—and I am thankful for the many positive godly role models there are at Beth Simcha and the other Messianic Jewish congregations!

*The following comments are from a follow-up interview with Alan, Barbara's husband. He did not see all the benefits of the Messianic synagogue that Barbara did. However, he was clear in saying that Messianic Jewish congregations serve a purpose and can help to meet the needs of intermarried couples.*

Q: How did you arrive at the decision to raise your children in both a Messianic synagogue and a Reform synagogue?

ALAN: We never consciously made a decision. It just evolved. My son has always gone to temple with me; our daughter has always gone with her mother; first to church, now to a Messianic synagogue. We never really planned to split the family in this fashion. For the most part, it has not evoked any problems with respect to our children being spiritually confused. I suppose we'll find out about that later on. In one sense, we were both weak in being unable to take a stand for family unity. On the other hand, we each respected the need of our spouse to maintain his/her own individual form of worship, even on opposite ends of the pole.

Q: I understand that you occasionally attend a Messianic synagogue service or event. What has your experience been?

ALAN: Let me answer this on several levels. Spiritually, I am not moved when I go to the Messianic services. The bottom line is, I don't believe in Jesus as my Lord and Savior—end of discussion on that topic. I don't, however, mind going. There are enough similarities to what I am used to that I can follow along without difficulty. It is comfortable and I do like the people. The people in the congregation, for the most part, are very aware of my views and no one tries to proselytize me; if they did, I would cut them off quickly and change the subject. I don't want to offend anyone. I have very much moderated my views, at least for this particular congregation. I regard them as Jewish people who have decided to accept Jesus. While I once considered this anathema, I now merely view it as a continuation of a broad spectrum of beliefs within the Jewish faith. I know that some of my Jewish acquaintances would be horrified to hear me say that, but the way I look at it, the ultra-orthodox Jews have held up more than one *rebbe* [teacher] as the Messiah and I didn't notice anyone throwing them out of the faith! These Messianic Jews are nice people who are maintaining their Judaism, far more so than many others I know. If they want to believe in Jesus, that is their choice. I don't necessarily agree with them, but I respect their beliefs in doing so.

Q: You are connected in some ways to the lives of people from the Messianic synagogue through your wife and daughter. How do you deal with that?

ALAN: These are among my wife's best friends. I treat them as such. I don't really care about their religious beliefs during social gatherings. With respect to their services, I am respectful. It is not something I ever have to deal with because if I am not interested in going to a function, I just don't go.

Q: What impact has involvement in the Messianic synagogue had on your children?

ALAN: On my son—none, at least not at this time. I suspect that this is the typical response of most 15 to 16 year old boys—at least the ones I know, regardless of their religious affiliations. My daughter, on the other hand, is fully involved. Her best friends are part of the synagogue, she goes to youth group; it is a big part of her life.

Q: Would you recommend the Messianic Jewish option to other intermarried couples?

ALAN: I have and I might again depending upon the circumstances. I certainly wouldn't recommend it to a religious Jew, because I don't think they would care for such an option. For intermarried couples, however, who are having great difficulty in finding a common ground, where one is not overly concerned with religion, I would suggest they check it out. I might also recommend it to a Christian spouse married to a Jew, who wants to learn more about Judaism, but cannot let go of the Jesus issues.

From the interviews presented so far, it is clear that Messianic Judaism is not simply a good idea; it is helping to meet the needs of intermarried couples and their children today. I interviewed many other intermarried couples and found that, in each case, Messianic Judaism served to strengthen the marriage relationship and embed a deep sense of Jewish identity and faith in the family. There is an element of compromise. But in almost every situation, what was gained was said to have outweighed the compromise. The children are raised with an unambiguous Jewish identity, and the husband and wife have the means to worship together if they so choose. After speaking with hundreds of intermarried couples who have never heard about Messianic Judaism, I have come to the conclusion that Messianic Judaism is one of the best kept secrets in the world of intermarriage.

## CHAPTER 13

# Joel: A Messianic Leader Reaching Out to Intermarrieds

*J*oel is the leader of Shomer Yisrael Messianic Synagogue. He is from a Conservative Jewish background. His wife Laura attended a Christian church as she was growing up. They have seven children.

Q: What do you say to intermarried couples when they come to you?

JOEL: Typically a couple will come to me as a last resort. And they will have gone to the rabbi who gave religious suggestions. Each of them is typically one who is running from institutional religious solutions. They will have gone to some counselor who will have told them, "All you do is blend. No problem. *Dreydel*s on the tree, ham on *matzah* in the spring, and you'll be amazed." It's purely a blending of symbols and traditions. And they're smart enough to know that it's superficial and vaporous. So they hear about Messianic [Judaism] and they show up, and they're desperate. What they're asking for is—beyond symbols and traditions—is there any hope? Here's what I say to them every time. I say, "I want you to dream with me. I want you to imagine sharing a mutual faith in God without either of you having to relinquish his or her own ethnic distinctiveness." They say, "It's impossible." I say, "I know this may surprise you but the source [to solve this problem] is readily available and, if you'll let me, I'd like to show you in two or three sessions how that can be possible." Then we go to Genesis and we do a little Torah study. And the exciting thing is that the Gentile, who typically has a Christian paradigm, begins to see his or her roots in Genesis. The Jew, of course, sees his or her roots in the Torah. And by the time we get to Genesis 3:15, there is at least an understanding that there is some organic link between the two cultures or identities or religions, or however they are seeing it. And it's somehow tied to this Messianic figure. So, my first goal is just to show them that it's more than ham on *matzah* or *dreydel*s on trees. It can actually be a spiritual reality, and that spiritual reality is somehow linked to the Messianic figure discovered in the Torah. That's exciting because generally they get their eyes off their own problems enough to see something that is completely new and it's linked to a source they both respect.

Q: When did you decide to reach out to intermarried couples?

JOEL: It was actually not a conscious decision. The Lord kept bringing us intermarrieds, probably because, being intermarried, I'm better able to understand and minister to them. So, after a while, you realize that the people who are calling, the people you're meeting are typically intermarried. And then you start reading books like Abrams [*Faith or Fear: How Jews Can Survive in a Christian America*] and you start reading statistics from the Jewish community and realizing fifty-two to sixty-eight percent of your community is intermarried. So, it becomes rather obvious that this is the group.

Q: What are some of the preconceptions that intermarried couples have when they come to you?

JOEL: Usually when they come to me, they honestly have no clue as to what these people are. They will understand that there is somehow a grouping of Jews and Gentiles, or as they will say "Jews and Christians." And they don't understand the link. Usually they think it's Jews who have converted but somehow maintained a friendship with their Jewishness. They can't imagine a Jew who believes in Jesus as having done anything other than convert. All kinds of misbeliefs.

Q: Do you have any intermarried couples in your congregation where the Jewish spouse is *not* a believer in Yeshua but they attend services together?

JOEL: Right now we have two intermarried couples where the Jewish partner is an unbeliever. He will regard Shomer Yisrael as his temple. He will contribute more than many of the believers. He will be involved. He will serve.

Q: Would you say that Jewish spouses who do not believe in Yeshua feel comfortable in the community?

JOEL: Generally, they choose their level of participation and they are very happy to participate in small ways. That's what they would do in *shul* [synagogue] anyway. What they really enjoy—I'm thinking of the couples themselves—is the fact that their Christian spouse, their believing spouse, is in an environment where they, the Jewish unbeliever, can also participate. When they have children, they are very excited that the spouse who is a believer can be satisfied with the children's education while the children are receiving some Jewish ethnic input. In their minds, the *Shabbat* school provides a wonderful compromise, even though Yeshua keeps popping up.

Q: So the children are a major issue?

JOEL: Huge.

Q: If you compared the Messianic Jewish option for these children to the Interfaith option, what does Messianic Judaism offer?

JOEL: Spiritual reality, relationship with God. The Interfaith option is perfect genius as long as we leave God out of the picture. It's something the children can hang around their necks like trinkets and souvenirs. They can boast to the fact that they get more gifts in the winter than anybody else. They can enjoy all the richness of tradition but they can't walk on sacred ground, because the moment they do, it forces a crisis in their lives. The genius of the Interfaith movement is it must leave God out. And that's fine for the parents, most of the time it is, until they start needing God, or one of them starts needing God. Then they begin to say, "Oh, my God, I've compromised." And they become adversary to the spouse, the children, or both.

Q: Do you think that the children who grow up in your congregation have experiences with God?

JOEL: Yes, without a doubt. Every *Shabbat*, children are sitting with Bibles open. Every *Shabbat*, they stand under a *tallit* [prayer shawl] before they are dismissed, all of them grouped together, and the fathers come up and lay hands on them. I'm crying over this because it's important to me, so I'm a little weepy. But they hear, every *Shabbat*, grownups begging God that they [the children] might follow him. And the children get it after a while—"Oh, they're not just trying to get rid of us so they can sing and dance. They're expecting something to happen in our lives." And it's happening, not with all of them, but with many. They're having experiences with God. . . . As a normative experience, they are learning Torah and *Tanakh*.

Q: What level of involvement can the non-Jewish spouse have in your congregation?

JOEL: They can have full involvement. The word is "can." That's the operative term. They can choose to be involved at almost any level.

Q: Could you have a non-Jewish elder?

JOEL: Yes, and we must. In fact, to this point, we've only had Jewish elders and it has been a source of some angst for me. Thank God we now have our first non-Jewish elder and it's very important because it represents the community.

Q: What's the percentage of intermarried couples in your congregation?

JOEL: Of our families that have a Jewish mother, father, spouse, all of them are intermarried except for I think two couples, maybe three.

Q: Do you think this is helpful to intermarried couples who come into the community?

JOEL: Do you know what it means when they come in, and at the *oneg Shabbat* I say, "Let me introduce you to the Levines, they're intermarried." Or, "let me introduce you to the Smiths, they're intermarried" and "here are the McGillacuddies, they're intermarried." They're like, "You're kidding. They're together in this and they're surviving?" It's such an impact. But not only that, they are not the exception but the rule. They're part of the majority in the community.

Q: It's really like an intermarried community.

JOEL: That's right.

Q: What impact has your community had on the success of these intermarriages?

JOEL: Of all the couples that have come to us where one, typically the Jewish partner, was a non-believer, their marriages were all strengthened, I mean logarithmically strengthened by their inclusion in the community. Because, first of all, faith elements started percolating into their marriage. They were hearing messages that, even if only in terms of coping mechanisms, helped. Plus, they found a place where they could worship together. Even among believer/nonbeliever couples, it's helping their marriages tremendously. To me, that's the most dramatic evidence of the success of the Messianic Jewish community among intermarrieds.

Q: How would you explain the higher-than-average divorce figures for intermarried couples that are sometimes quoted by Jewish leaders? Is the mainstream synagogue not working for these couples?

JOEL: Here's why I think the traditional synagogue would participate in that statistic. The traditional synagogue has not yet fashioned a niche for the non-Jewish spouse. They may be including them relationally but there still is not a place for them. So if that's part of our vision and our values, then we are going to succeed in incorporating the intermarried couple that is looking for a shared experience in God and community. We are better mobilized to do that than any other religious group.

Q: Does being intermarried yourself affect your outlook as a congregational leader?

JOEL: Completely. For instance, our focus stems from my own reality, my understanding of married people. I better understand intermarrieds than Jewish-Jewish or Gentile-Gentile. But also, it affects my leadership because I'm less inclined to say that Jewish-Gentile is an option than I am to say it is a very exciting prophetic event we're talking about. It's something that dates back to Genesis 12 with the promise to Abraham, that he would be a father of many nations . . . so, it's a celebration as opposed to a tolerance.

Q: You're saying that Israel's prophetic role among the nations is almost like a form of intermarriage.

JOEL: Definitely. Intermarriage expresses those promises and that relationship. It's beautiful. And it's exciting for the Jew and Gentile couple because he understands it from a Torah perspective in Genesis 12. She understands it from the New Testament perspective of Ephesians 2 and 3. You just can't lose. If they ascribe any authority to the Scriptures at all, they'll understand that this is something biblical they're doing.

Q: The key, then, is overcoming the danger of assimilation.

JOEL: That's correct.

Q: Let me ask you about your own family. How did you meet your wife?

JOEL: High School. She was sixteen. I was seventeen. We met at a basketball game and she was my first and last love.

Q: Was your getting intermarried an issue?

JOEL: It was bad. My parents had lined up a lot of nice Jewish girls and here I choose this blonde Gentile woman. It was pretty rough because there was only one precedent in the family. Laura grew up going to a Christian church, which was right next to her house. She began babysitting for an Orthodox Jewish family who loved her and introduced her to all the other Orthodox Jewish families. She was babysitting regularly at age sixteen for these families. Well, she's a voracious reader and she's reading everything in their homes, all the Jewish books. By the time we started dating, she knew more about Jews and Jewishness than anybody in my family. So she [impressed] them with her understanding. But it was still very intense for both sides.

Q: What did you do for the wedding?

JOEL: We couldn't have it in *shul*. We couldn't have it in the church. We had it on her front lawn. We had an arbor that looked like a *huppah*. And we had a very sweet Christian pastor who brought in Jewish symbols and terms. He was very kind and just·sensitive to the whole thing. That was it.

Q: Your children are now being raised as Jews?

JOEL: Yes. That's because my wife is so thoroughly in love with Jewish people and Jewish forms and Jewish traditions. She just doesn't see any dissonance between her faith as a believer [in Yeshua] and her heritage and these forms. The only tensions that may come up are when aunts and uncles from the Gentile side bring in Easter baskets and send me lots of Christmas cards. There is still tension over that.

Q: Where is the tension?

JOEL: Let me try to illustrate it. The kids have no problem because they love cards and candy and eggs. I would probably say something like, "Would you mind if I tell Aunt Theresa that we don't celebrate Easter? She's so sweet and we love her for thinking of us, but would you mind if we don't receive all of it?" And Laura might say, "Well, Joel, that's how she's showing love." And then she might add, "I'm not really willing." That's about the depth of our tension.

Q: Because they are members of her family and it's their culture?

JOEL: Exactly.

At this point in the interview, the phone rang in Joel's office. After speaking for a few minutes to the person on the other end, Joel said, "We just got interrupted by a phone call from Deborah who's real concerned for a couple that is Jewish-Gentile, and have been trying to blend all their traditions, but it's not working. Somebody suggested they go to a church which does both, and they said, 'There's no such thing.' And Deborah said, 'Yes, there is. I think they call it Messianic.' So Deborah is going to come here to check it out. They live in New Jersey. She's going to then go to New Jersey and take them to a Messianic congregation."

## CHAPTER 14

# The Messianic Synagogue: An Oasis for Children of Intermarriage

Intermarried couples often begin considering the Messianic Jewish option when they have small children. They see the importance of a religious upbringing and try to find a community where the needs of the whole family can be met. An integrative approach that bridges the Jewish and Christian tradition, Messianic Judaism is often very appealing to the parents. Likewise, the children want to be in a place where they can fit in.

## Fitting In

There are presently two million children of intermarriage in the United States[1] and many do not find a home in the mainstream Jewish community. Leslie Goodman-Malamuth and Robin Margolis conducted extensive research on the lives of these children. Their findings were published in the book *Between Two Worlds*:

> Scores of children and grandchildren of intermarriage, whether the offspring of Jewish mothers or Jewish fathers, have told us that they were made to feel distinctly unwelcome by the Jewish establishment. Some weathered the disapproval and became active, committed Jews, while others slunk away, wistful, disappointed, and even bitter.[2]

Many of these children also did not feel at home in the mainstream Christian community:

> Descendants of intermarriage frequently admit that they are likely to remain observers, outsiders, who feel they can never truly belong to either the Jewish or the Christian world. Regardless of how they affiliate, or would like to, 53 percent of our respondents say that it has been difficult or impossible to find a spiritual community within which they feel comfortable.[3]

In a recent study of college students, "Children of Interfaith Families: Exploring Jewish Identities," it was reported that:

> Despite a high level of personal Jewish identification, a significant minority (a little more than a third) felt some discomfort in the synagogue—and not surprisingly due to the sample, a much greater percent (about fifty-three percent) felt uncomfortable in church settings.[4]

The societal notion that Judaism and Christianity are mutually exclusive religions adds to the sense of being "out of place" in the minds of many of these children. They are thought of as "neither-nors."[5] In the Goodman-Malamuth study, one grown child of intermarriage is quoted as saying, "Society tends to dichotomize, and tries to define you. You're either one or the other, but never both. It's hard to integrate in the face of this pressure to define yourself."[6] Another said, "I think what I longed for most of all was a way to embrace both 'halves' without having to sacrifice either one."[7] For children of intermarriage, a Messianic Jewish congregation can be like an oasis in the desert, a place where they can be themselves. In the Messianic synagogue, they do not feel between two worlds. In short, Messianic Judaism bridges the gap for these children.[8] Here are a number of comments I received from children of intermarriage who grew up in a Messianic Jewish congregation:

> Being a Messianic Jew has given me tremendous identity. . . . Many people think that living a Jewish life and having belief in Jesus as the Messiah are contradictory. My personal experience is that Yeshua is the fulfillment of Jewish life and identity.

> I am thrilled with my Messianic identity, even proud of it. I would recommend it to anyone, especially children of Jewish-Christian parents.

> I think that living the Messianic Jewish life allows me to feel more complete in my walk with God and allows for a fuller view of the grand picture of what God has been and is doing.

> I like this identity very much. I feel complete, and yes, I would recommend this to other such children. I have heard that being part of families of different religious backgrounds is extremely hard, but I never felt this. Both backgrounds are my heritage and part of my identity.

The idea of half-Jewish doesn't really go through my mind. I feel that as a Messianic, being religiously different from almost everyone I know, my identity is more, and not less, complete. Difference shapes identity.

I definitely feel complete in my identity. It's a big help, though, that my non-Jewish parent took up the Messianic Jewish identity as well.

I think that living a Messianic Jewish lifestyle really affects my life in feeling more fulfilled, and understanding more of God. This means a lot to me.

Yeshua is very important in forming my identity as a Messianic Jew. It is his life that proves that being Jewish and living a Jewish lifestyle is completely in line with living a life dedicated to God.

## *Spiritual Life Emphasis*

Messianic Judaism is a faith-based Judaism. Young people in the Messianic movement are, therefore, encouraged to make God and Yeshua a part of their lives. In her research on Messianic synagogues, Rabbi Harris-Shapiro observed that children are "encouraged to talk about their personal relationship with God, to solve their problems with prayer, and to intercede for others in prayer."[9]

A twenty year-old Messianic Jewish college student and child of intermarried parents had this to say concerning the place of God in her life:

God is a very important part of my identity as a person. I try to live my life according to his plan. I pray over big and not so big decisions. I know that I am not alone in my struggles or my triumphs. I can rely on God for comfort and guidance. My relationship with God is very personal and very precious.

Other children of intermarried parents who grew up in Messianic synagogues commented:

My relationship with God is more important than anything!

God is where it all starts. Being a Messianic is meaningless without God. The whole point is to glorify Him.

My life as a Messianic Jew revolves around, and depends on, a personal, almighty, just, merciful God.

God is an extremely important part of my identity as a Messianic Jew because he is the power and source behind anything that is good in my life. He is the one that helps me get through the day and gives me understanding for things that I otherwise would not be able to comprehend.

The Messiah Yeshua is the most important part of my Messianic identity. His name is even in the title of my faith; that says enough.

The Messiah is an important part of my life because he died to give me life.

While spiritual life is ultimately a matter of choice, and not every person chooses this direction, my anecdotal research found that young people who do choose to follow the Lord in a Messianic Jewish context find abundant meaning in life.

Meeting the needs of children is the most important indicator of success in solving the intermarriage dilemma. Messianic Judaism is a very promising development because it conveys wholeness to the child's self-image and points children in the direction of God.

## CHAPTER 15

# How Messianic Judaism Promotes Jewish Continuity

Messianic Judaism is an appealing option for intermarried couples, in part, because Jewish life is fostered and Jewish identity is conveyed to the next generation. The assimilation issue is not avoided in Messianic Judaism but confronted head on. Jewish sociologist Rachael Kohn notes that Messianic Jewish leaders "frequently lament what they see as a fragile Jewish community, imperiled by assimilationist, specifically secularizing, tendencies. . . . Messianic Judaism's response to this perceived condition of a disappearing community is one of active conservation of Jewish culture."[1] A Messianic synagogue considers Jewish life and New Testament teaching to be top priorities, and the New Testament is seen as upholding Jewish identity. Though the Messianic movement is still young, there is hard evidence that Messianic synagogues are meeting success.

## *The 1990 National Jewish Population Survey*

The 1990 National Jewish Population Survey (NJPS) interviewed Messianic Jews as well as members of the rest of the Jewish community. One survey question asked: "Is being Jewish very important in your life?" According to the findings, 100% of all Messianic Jews interviewed said "Yes" to the survey question. This was higher than any other Jewish group interviewed, including Orthodox (77%), Conservative (58%), Reform (40%), and Reconstructionist (49%)[2] (see Appendix D). Professor Sergio DellaPergola, who tabulated the results, sums up the significance of this data as follows:

> Not unexpectedly, the perceived importance of being Jewish is highest among those who consistently manifest their identity via a religious definition and a clear denominational preference. The expected gradient among the major denominations (Orthodox, Conservative, Reform) emerges. Jews who are consistently secular display far lesser interest for being Jewish. The amount of interest is

quite variable, though generally low among other sub-groups with the survey population, including ex-Jews. *One small group with extremely high percentages of interest in Judaism is those preferring the Messianic denomination.*"[3] (emphasis mine)

## Additional Studies

The results of the 1990 National Jewish Population Survey have been confirmed by other studies as well. After three years of researching Messianic Judaism, Jewish sociologist Shoshanah Feher concluded that Messianic Jewish families grew in their sense of Jewish identity as a result of being part of a Messianic Jewish congregation:

> The congregants show a distinctive trend toward in-creased Jewishness: Those who grew up Jewish now value their heritage more fully; others are pleased to discover that they are Jewish; still others continue to dig through their ancestral past in hopes of finding a connection to the "Chosen People." Messianic Judaism has given Believers not only a sense of ethnicity and community, but also the feeling that they belong to an ethnic community. . . . To those who wonder whether Messianic Believers are Jews, I can only say that we must think about what we mean by being Jewish. In terms of ethnicity, they are more culturally Jewish and more proud of their Jewish heritage than many mainstream Jews."[4]

Reconstructionist rabbi, Carol Harris-Shapiro, who studied the Messianic Jewish movement for ten years and did her doctoral dissertation on Messianic Judaism, concluded her book *Messianic Judaism: A Rabbi's Journey Through Religious Change in America* with the following words:

> Until now, according to Jewish communal expectations, the amount of ritual indicates the strength of Jewish identity. Quantifiable Jewish ritual had dominated sociological research on Jewish continuity; what Jews do has classified them as "more" or "less" Jewish, more or less in touch with the "golden thread" that binds Jews to their ancestors and to each other (S. Cohen 1988; Goldscheider 1986). For example, the 1990 National Jewish Population Survey assumed individuals had a stronger Jewish iden-

tity if they had regular synagogue attendance, fasted on Yom Kippur, visited Israel, practiced Jewish holidays, did not put up a Christmas tree, and lit Shabbat candles (Kosmin, et al. 1991, 35–36). If ritual is the sole measure of Jewishness, the Messianic believers I knew in the congregation would score favorably, certainly outstripping the average "Jew by religion" in their attendance at services and possibly even doing other Jewish practices. If *doing* Jewish is *being* Jewish, ironically, Messianic Jews are more Jewish than many born Jews.[5]

## A Philosophy of Judaism

Messianic Judaism takes its name seriously. By stating that we represent a "Judaism," we acknowledge our connection to Jewish history, the Jewish community, and the Jewish religious heritage.[6] Likewise, we take the "Messianic" part of our name seriously as well. We believe that Yeshua is the long awaited Messiah, that he is worthy of worship, and that he brings Judaism to its fullness of meaning and expression. "Messianic Judaism is Judaism, in all facets of its teaching, worship, and way of life, understood and practiced in the light of Messiah Yeshua."[7] The Union of Messianic Jewish Congregations emphasizes the corporate dimension of Messianic Judaism:

> Messianic Judaism is a movement of Jewish congregations and congregation-like groupings committed to Yeshua the Messiah that embrace the covenantal responsibility of Jewish life and identity rooted in Torah, expressed in tradition, renewed and applied in the context of the New Covenant.[8]

We see ourselves as the restoration of a sect of Judaism that existed in Second Temple times and that lasted until at least the fourth century.[9] In this sense, Messianic Jews bear some resemblance to modern Zionists:

> There exists a clear resemblance between the messianic movement of Jewish believers in Jesus and the modern Zionist movement. Basically, both movements highlight the idea of bridging a historical gap between modern times and biblical times. Namely, they consciously reject allegations that they maintain anachronistic approaches. On the contrary, contemporary Jewish Jesus-believers and mainstream Zionists raise the opposite argument that they still possess a natural right to bypass the last two

millennia and directly relate to the pre-exilic period in
Israel's history.[10]

Similar to Karaite Judaism[11] and the Ethiopic variety of Judaism
(which predates Rabbinic Judaism), Nazarene Judaism did not sub-
mit to mainstream rabbinic authority but stayed connected to the Jewish community.

Contemporary Messianic Judaism continues in this same tradition. Our desire is to be honoring of the traditional Jewish heritage
and to maintain a strong connection to the Jewish community. Rather
than creating a completely new tradition, our philosophy is to enter
into conversation with the present tradition and to adapt it as needed,
especially in light of the Messianic community's conviction that the
Messiah has already come.[12]

## Torah and Culture

An important key to the maintenance of Jewish continuity in the Messianic community is the recognition that a distinction exists between
Torah and culture. When Messianic Jews say "Torah," in contrast to
"culture," they mean God's Word, God's commands, God's teachings
from the Scriptures. This is Torah. Culture, on the other hand, lacks
this authority. Torah is eating *matzah* on Passover in response to
God's command. Culture is eating *gefilte* fish. There is a difference.
And recognizing this difference—imparting this difference to our children—is an essential key to perpetuating Jewish identity.[13] Assimilation gains the upper hand when all of Jewish life becomes culture.
Messianic Jews understand this and consequently emphasize the priority distinction between Torah and culture.[14] Daniel, a twenty-some-
thing child of intermarriage who grew up in a Messianic synagogue,
put it this way:

> Jewish identity is important to my identity as a Messianic
> Jew by definition. Torah defines the contours of my rela-
> tionship with God. It is through Torah, Scripture, and to a
> lessor extent tradition, that I interact with God. I want it
> to always determine how I live.

## Jewish Grandparents

In Jewish tradition, grandparents play an important role in passing on
Jewish heritage. Jewish grandparents teach their grandchildren about

the Torah and Jewish customs. They take them to Jewish community events, tell them Jewish stories, introduce them to Jewish foods, familiarize them with Hebrew and Yiddish expressions, bring them to *Shabbat* services, and sometimes even travel with them to Israel. Messianic Judaism affirms the vital role of Jewish grandparents.

Jewish grandparents (with grandchildren who attend a Messianic synagogue) will inevitably find their involvement intersecting with the Messianic community. For example, at the grandchild's *b'rit milah*, they will meet the Messianic rabbi. At the grandchild's *bar/bat mitzvah*, they will visit a Messianic synagogue. At first this can be a very daunting experience (if they are not Messianic Jews) due to the myths that surround Messianic Judaism in some quarters of the Jewish community (see Appendix E). But, in time, as they get to know Messianic Jewish friends of the family, their concerns often subside.

Mr. Birnbaum was one of several Jewish grandparents that I interviewed. He is eighty-five years young. His son, Michael, married a Gentile woman and the couple decided on the Messianic Jewish option. When I asked Mr. Birnbaum how he felt about his son's family attending a Messianic synagogue, he replied:

> I've been to about fifty of them [services] . . . I felt comfortable. I saw some things I've never seen before but it didn't bother me.

Mr. Birnbaum remains unconvinced about Messianic beliefs, but makes it his practice to attend *Shabbat* services at the Messianic synagogue whenever he is able. He is very clear that whatever makes his grandchildren happy is fine with him.

In the end, most Jewish grandparents are like Mr. Birnbaum. Their primary concern is the happiness of their children and grandchildren. "If you're happy, I'm happy," sums up the average Jewish grandparent's philosophy. Some, however, don't fully appreciate the Messianic Jewish option, tending only to compare it to the Jewish Only option in raising the children. They forget that if the parents had chosen the Christian Only option or the Interfaith option, they would be visiting a Christian church and meeting a minister. Likewise, if the family had chosen the No Religion option, the grandchildren would be missing out on their Jewish heritage. As time goes by, and the grandparents see that their grandchildren are being raised with good values and a solid Jewish identity in the Messianic synagogue, most cannot help but admit that Messianic Judaism has had a positive influence.

## *Jewish Education*

Religious education is emphasized in the Messianic Jewish community. National organizations make available *Shabbat* School curriculums that are designed to lay the foundations of Jewish learning for Messianic Jewish young people. Messianic synagogues also offer *bar/bat mitzvah* classes that lay the foundation of Torah and New Testament study by age twelve or thirteen.

A growing trend in the Messianic Jewish community has been the establishment of Hebrew schools. My oldest daughter, Hana, attended a Messianic Jewish Hebrew school in the Boston area and loved it. I am proud to see her growing up with a solid understanding of the Hebrew language and her Jewish heritage.

Messianic day schools are also being established. One of the oldest is Ets Chaiyim School in Gaitherburg, Maryland, which opened its doors in 1980. Ets Chaiyim serves as a good example of how the Messianic Jewish community is committed to raising children with a strong sense of Jewish identity. One of its graduates, Jeremy, a child of intermarriage, had this to say:

> I have had a wonderful experience growing up in the Messianic Jewish community. I attended a Messianic Jewish day school and learned Hebrew. I minored in Hebrew in college as well. The emphasis on family life and developing long-lasting relationships is also a part of Jewish life that has made a deep impact on me. I would definitely recommend this life to other children. Messianic Jewish life offers a culture rich in tradition, and an eternity rich in heavenly treasure.

Ets Chaiyim's enrollment was 166 students as of the 2002–2003 school year; spanning kindergarten to twelfth grade. The school has programs in Hebrew language, Biblical/Messianic Jewish Studies, and Jewish History, covering ancient Judaism and modern Israel. Jewish calendars hang on the walls of the classrooms and the students follow the weekly *parashot* (portions of the Bible that are part of the synagogue Scripture reading cycle). In addition to *Kabbalat Shabbat* (Welcoming the Sabbath) services that are celebrated every Friday afternoon, the school observes all of the Jewish festivals throughout the year. The students put together an indoor *sukkah*, and hold Hanukkah parties, Purim plays, and Passover *seder*s. The older students are taught Jewish folk dances as part of the winter physical education program, and Jewish art can be seen lining the walls of the classrooms. Even the athletics program incorporates Jewish identity, as spectators cheer at basketball, volleyball and soccer games: "Go, Lions of Judah!!"

The administration of Ets Chaiyim embraces a student body that is both Jewish and non-Jewish. Such an outlook is a strong testimony of the egalitarian and inclusive nature of Messianic Judaism. Some students come from Messianic Jewish families and others from Christian families. Christian parents send their children to Ets Chaiyim School because they want their children to participate in the richness of Jewish life, a heritage to which they feel connected through their own Messiah. These non-Jewish children will grow up to be advocates of the Jewish people, opponents of anti-Semitism and bridges of peace between Jews and Christians. The success of Messianic day schools like Ets Chaiyim is a promising development in the Messianic Jewish movement.

Messianic Jewish summer camps are another source of Jewish education. There are several in the United States such as Simchat Yeladim and Camp Shoshanah. Messianic camps are staffed by rabbis, teachers, parents, and college students who love the summer camp experience and know how to make Jewish life fun and interesting for young people. Camp is also a time when many youth grow in their experience with the Living God.

Regional and national youth conferences are additional opportunities to grow in Jewish areas of study. Both the Union of Messianic Jewish Congregations and the Messianic Jewish Alliance of America have established youth organizations that seek to involve young people in Jewish life. The Young Messianic Jewish Alliance (YMJA) began in 1967 and has helped to bring together young Messianic Jews from around the world at their annual conferences.

## Jewish Community Involvement

Intermarried couples who join Messianic synagogues are encouraged to be involved in the local Jewish community. The Jewish Community Center (JCC) is an especially important area of communal activity. Rabbi Harris-Shapiro notes, "Members of the Messianic community have long been members of local Jewish community centers."[15] One Messianic Jewish leader is the basketball coach of a JCC team in a major city. When someone questioned the appropriateness of his level of involvement in the JCC, the whole team rallied around him. In another city, a Messianic Jewish parent coaches the JCC soccer team. The parents could care less that he's a Messianic

Jew because he's not teaching about the Messiah; he's there to coach the kids. Several members of the college-career group of my former Messianic synagogue took a course on *Pirke Avot* (Sayings of the Fathers) at the local JCC. The Orthodox rabbi teaching the class was impressed to discover that the majority of his students were from a Messianic synagogue.

Support for Israel is another way that intermarried couples who attend Messianic synagogues connect to the larger Jewish community.[16] Feher observed that "in their support for the State of Israel, Messianic Believers are generally politically aligned with the Jewish community at large."[17] Rabbis encourage congregants to visit the Land and to consider making *aliyah* (immigration to Israel). As a result, there is a vibrant and growing Messianic Jewish community in Israel.

Giving *tzedakah* (charity) is another way that intermarried couples connect to the worldwide Jewish community. This was Rabbi Carol Harris-Shapiro's observation as she traveled throughout the Messianic Jewish movement:

> In the Florida Messianic congregation that I visited, children contributed faithfully to the Jewish National Fund, well-known for its program of planting trees in Israel. In 1995, Congregation Rosh Pina in Baltimore gave five thousand dollars for a new reservoir (Hardie 1995, 2). Another purchase of trees, this time by the MJAA for fifty thousand dollars (Henry 1996, 8), was eventually scuttled by the Jewish community when the gift became widely known.[18]

American Messianic synagogues help Russian Jews immigrate to Israel and hold special fundraising drives to aid Jewish communities around the world, even in such remote places as Ethiopia and India. Privately, Messianic Jewish families give to a range of Jewish organizations and actively support Jewish and non-Jewish causes.

## Synagogue Service and Liturgy

Intermarried couples discover that the Messianic *Shabbat* service is much more upbeat than the traditional synagogue service. Modeled after worship described in the Psalms, Messianic Jewish services commonly incorporate song, dance, and instrumental music (usually guitar and piano). Many traditional Hebrew liturgies are also included in the service (usually with English translation). Readings from the Torah and the New Testament are also typical in most Messianic synagogues. While it is not an Orthodox synagogue service, the celebratory Messianic Jewish service is rooted in the Temple tradition and young people find it easy and enjoyable to worship. Feher found that "Messianic services are joyful; singing and dancing are part of the experience, and there is an effusive vitality that is rarely felt in mainline synagogues or churches."[19] As a cultural expression, she described the Messianic *Shabbat* service she attended in the following way:

> To an individual walking in from the street, the services are seemingly Jewish. Worship takes place on Saturday morning, congregants are dressed "Jewishly" in skullcaps and prayer shawls, many of the prayers and songs are in Hebrew, songs are often set to music faintly reminiscent of *klezmer*, and the congregants dance in Israeli style.[20]

One woman I interviewed said, "A lot of my Jewish friends that have come to various occasions, whatever their belief system is, their comment is always, 'Boy, you guys really have fun. You really enjoy your services.'" Rabbi Harris-Shapiro compares the Messianic *Shabbat* service to a Jewish wedding:

> The dancing and music together resemble nothing so much as a Jewish wedding, a similarity that congregants themselves recognize, thus joining Jewish ethnic celebration with the spiritual "joy in the Lord."[21]

While the average Messianic synagogue service fits Harris-Shapiro's description, there are some congregations that follow a classic synagogue model, based on the *Siddur* (prayer book). High Holy Day services in Messianic synagogues also tend to be more traditional and replete with Hebrew liturgy. In studying the messages of one Messianic rabbi, Rabbi Harris-Shapiro found that "the phrase 'our people' is never far from the speaker's lips."[22] This natural sense of connectedness to the broader Jewish community is reflective of our philosophy of Judaism described above.

Finally, whereas only 13 percent of Reform, Conservative and Orthodox synagogue members attend services regularly (i.e. several times a month),[23] the figure rises to over 90 percent in Messianic Jewish congregations. This is clearly related to the sense of fulfillment that members have in being part of a Messianic Jewish community.

## Festivals

Intermarried couples participate in all festival events in a Messianic synagogue. On *Rosh HaShanah*, families gather for a High Holy Day service[24] and enjoy festive meals together. Among the traditional foods eaten are apples and honey. As in all synagogues, the New Year greeting "*l'shana tova*" (to a good year) is heard throughout the day.

On *Yom Kippur*, another service is held. Typically, liturgy from the *Machzor* (prayer book for the High Holy Days) is included as well as other prayers that thank God for sending Yeshua, the ultimate atonement.[25] Adults in the community fast on *Yom Kippur* and, in some synagogues, gather after the service to study the book of Jonah. In the evening, everyone breaks the fast together.[26]

*Sukkot* (the Feasts of Booths or Tabernacles) is a fun festival for intermarried couples and their children. It is a week of celebration. The *Sukkot* service typically includes the special *parashot* for the festival in addition to readings from the New Testament. The blessings over the *lulav* (made of palm leaves as well as other species) and the *etrog* (a citrus fruit) are recited, and Yeshua's own celebration of *Sukkot* is usually recalled (John 7).[27] Many families build their own *sukkah*; the rest visit friends who have a *sukkah*.[28] After *Sukkot*, Messianic synagogues observe *Simchat Torah* (a festival in which the Torah is celebrated and the synagogue Scripture reading cycle is begun anew). Often, children parade around the synagogue with singing and dancing,[29] the Torah scroll is rolled back to Genesis 1 and the congregation celebrates the goodness of God's Word.[30]

Hanukkah is a joyful celebration. Families gather for a festival service,[31] light the candles of the *hanukkiyah* (Hanukkah menorah), recite Hebrew blessings, and give presents. Sometimes, the congregation has a Hanukkah party where all of these activities are done. As Feher observed, "Messianic Believers celebrate Hanukkah as a time of praise and thanksgiving to God."[32] Children spin *dreydels*, eat Hanukkah *gelt* (chocolate money), and feast on *latkes* (potato pancakes). From the *bimah*, Messianic rabbis encourage children to recall the story of the Maccabees and the lesson it holds for resisting assimilation in our own time. Visiting intermarried couples are always surprised to learn that Yeshua himself recognized Hanukkah (John 10:22).

As for Christmas, Messianic synagogues typically do not celebrate the birth of the Messiah at this time.[33] More commonly, his birth is remembered as a community event during *Sukkot*, when the symbol of the booth reminds us of how Yeshua, the *Shekhinah* (the manifest presence of God) took on flesh and dwelled among us. According to many scholars, fall is also the more likely time that he was born. However, many intermarried Messianic Jewish couples do have Christmas trees in their homes.[34] It is a personal decision. Feher remarks, "Christmas, then, is a holiday that is sometimes celebrated at the individual level but is not part of the congregation's communal festivities."[35]

Purim is a joyful occasion for Messianic intermarrieds, a time when parties, carnivals, and plays are held in the Messianic Jewish community. People dress up as characters from the book of Esther and *nosh* (snack) on *hamantashen* (triangle-shaped cookies with fillings inside). It is a time to have fun and be silly. At Purim plays, the mention of the name "Haman" is echoed by the sound of noise-makers and "boos." The name "Mordecai" prompts a chorus of "Hoorays" with the crowd shouting, "May the name of the righteous be blessed." Messianic rabbis highlight the role that Esther and King Ahasuerus, an intermarried couple, played in saving the Jewish people.[36] Likewise, it is often emphasized that the unity of Jew and Gentile in the plan of God will result in great blessing for the world.

In the Messianic synagogue, Passover is a very special experience for intermarried couples and their children. This is because the Passover *seder* bridges the gap between Judaism and Christianity. Messianic *haggadot* (handbooks used at Passover *seder*s to guide families through the order of the ritual meal) focus on the Exodus of our people from Egypt by great signs and wonders as well as the Exodus of mankind from sin and judgment through the Messiah Yeshua. Messianic *haggadot* compare the sacrificial role of the Passover lamb to the sacrificial role of the Messiah. A Messianic *haggadah* also draws from New Testament references to Yeshua's celebration of Passover. During Passover, we remove all leavened products from our homes and eat *matzah* instead. Easter Sunday is not celebrated in Messianic synagogues. The Messianic Jewish celebration of Passover emphasizes the death and resurrection of the Messiah.[37]

Other festivals are also celebrated in a Messianic synagogue (e.g. *Shavu'ot*, the Feast of Weeks or Pentecost, when the book of Ruth and Acts 2 is read).[38] These descriptions of festivals should give you a good sense of what to expect if your family joined a Messianic synagogue or visited during festival times. The celebrations are full of joy and thanksgiving to the Lord. I grew up celebrating all the Jewish festivals in a Messianic synagogue. Looking back, it was a wonderful experience, one that I recommend to any intermarried couple.

## Lifecycle Ceremonies

From birth to death, Judaism has a ceremony to mark every passage of life. This reflects the Jewish view that God is intimately involved in his creation. No area of life is so mundane as to be overlooked by the King of the Universe. Every event must be set apart to him as holy. Intermarried couples and their children can participate in the full range of ceremonies and rites of passage in a Messianic synagogue.

The *b'rit milah* ceremony is viewed as a divine commandment that is binding on Jewish parents (intermarried or not) when they have a son.[39] There is little difference between a traditional Jewish *b'rit milah* and a Messianic Jewish *b'rit milah*; the Hebrew blessings are usually the same.[40] Portions from the Torah and the New Testament are read which affirm the importance of circumcision on the eighth day in accordance with God's command; often reference is also made to Yeshua's own *b'rit milah* (Luke 2:21). The Messianic rabbi will usually conclude a *b'rit milah* with prayers and blessings over the child. At present, there are only a few Messianic Jewish *mohelim* who serve in the United States.[41] Consequently, intermarried families typically use a *mohel* from the Jewish community who is not Messianic. Most of the *mohelim* I've spoken with are very impressed by the *kavanah* (heart-felt devotion and connection to God) they sense at the *b'rit milah*. Intermarried couples especially appreciate the Messianic Jewish *b'rit milah* because both sets of families can find common ground in the event. Jewish family members feel they are in Jewish space; Christian family members connect to the Jewish roots of their New Covenant faith.

As an intermarried couple, you will find that the Messianic Jewish *bar/bat mitzvah* is much the same as the traditional ceremony. The young adult prepares, through considerable Hebrew training, to chant or read a portion of the Torah and *Haftarah* (Prophets). There is usually a procession with the *bar/bat mitzvah* child carrying the Torah scroll. Hebrew blessings are recited[42] and a speech is given before the congregation. The parents also say a special blessing over their child. One distinctive part of the Messianic ceremony is the reading of a portion from the New Testament that is thematically linked to the *parashah*. The rabbi may also remind the congregation that when Yeshua was *bar mitzvah* age, he was brought to the Temple in Jerusalem where he asked insightful questions and amazed the elders of our people by his understanding (Luke 2:41–47). At a Messianic Jewish *bar/bat mitzvah*, Jewish grandparents will feel that they are in a *shul*; non-Jewish grandparents will feel fully welcomed by the community. Messianic synagogues also invite the full participation of the Gentile parent in the *bar/bat mitzvah* ceremony.

Intermarried couples married in a Messianic synagogue experience the joy of a traditional Jewish wedding ceremony. The couple is married under a *huppah* and a *ketubah* (marriage contract) is signed. The seven Hebrew blessings[43] are chanted and a glass is broken to shouts of "*Mazel Tov!*" ("Congratulations!"). Usually, the rabbi will read from the Hebrew Bible and New Testament to exhort the couple in their covenantal obligations to one another. Most Messianic Jewish wedding receptions have a lot of dancing with, as in Jewish tradition, the couple being carried around by family and friends on raised chairs. The Jewish family members of the couple will feel perfectly at home at a Messianic Jewish wedding. Christian family members will likewise enjoy the event, as they will find familiarity in the New Testament readings and depth of meaning in the Messianic Jewish marriage ceremony.

A Messianic Jewish funeral is based on the traditional model with most Messianic rabbis drawing from the *madrikh* (a handbook for rabbis). The body is buried within twenty-four hours if possible. *Kaddish* (a prayer of praise to God during mourning) is recited along with other traditional Hebrew prayers. *Keriah* (tearing of the garments) is performed. One addition to the traditional service is the reading of verses from the New Testament as well as the Hebrew Bible. Typically, the rabbi also takes time to speak of the resurrection life and hope that is found in the Messiah. In my experience, Jewish and non-Jewish family members of intermarried couples always feel comforted and touched at a Messianic Jewish funeral. Messianic Jews are often buried in Jewish cemeteries[44] and in traditional pine boxes. It is typical for a Messianic Jewish family to sit *shiva*, light *yahrzeit* candles and consult their rabbi about the traditional mourning process.[45]

Messianic synagogues are serious about Jewish continuity and are finding success in this endeavor. We have a clear philosophy of Judaism whereby all of Jewish life takes on new meaning as a result of the coming of the Messiah. Joy and devotion to the Lord characterize the Messianic Jewish lifestyle. The children of intermarriage find a clear paradigm for Messianic Jewish living in the first century Messianic Jewish community, where Torah and tradition were observed. We enter into conversation with Jewish tradition as it has come down to us today, and adapt it as needed to meet the needs of our community. The important role of Jewish grandparents, Jewish education, Jewish community involvement, synagogue service and liturgy, festivals and lifecycle ceremonies are all upheld in a Messianic Jewish congregation. It is a huge task for a young movement and we are not always successful. But we are finding encouragement in the many intermarried couples and their children in our midst who, out of their devotion to God, are maintaining the great chain of Jewish identity in their families that stretches all the way back to our father Abraham.

# Final Thoughts

I hope this book has been helpful to you. If you would like to learn more about the Messianic Jewish option, I suggest that you visit a Messianic synagogue. You can find one by looking under "Synagogues" or "Churches" in the Yellow Pages. Appendix C contains a list of organizations that can help you find a Messianic congregation.

If you decide that Messianic Judaism is not the best option for your family, I hope that the information in this book has enriched your understanding. No option is perfect, and Messianic Judaism is no exception. Please remember, however, the door of the Messianic synagogue is always open to you. I know I speak for all Messianic rabbis in saying that intermarried couples and their children are always welcome at Messianic Jewish congregations.

In assembling the chapters of this book, I decided that some relevant material was too detailed or too lengthy to include in the main section. Therefore, I included this information in Appendices A–E. These contain much valuable information, as well as lists of helpful resources, so please take some time to peruse them.

I love being a Messianic Jew and I love being married to my wife Harumi. Both experiences are sources of joy and inspiration in my life. Working together to form a Messianic Jewish identity for our family has succeeded, and we highly recommend it. Although no option is perfect in resolving all of intermarriage's challenges, Messianic Judaism comes close. As someone said, "Try it! You'll be glad you did."

# Who is a Jew?

When a Jewish couple has children, the children are clearly Jewish. However, when an intermarried couple has children, the identity of the children is less clear. Are they Jews? Half-Jews? Is Jewish identity passed through the mother or father? Intermarriage begs the question: Who is a Jew?

## The Messianic Consensus

While there is no center of *halakhic* (legal) authority in the Messianic Jewish movement to rule on the issue of "who is a Jew,"[1] the movement as a whole is generally supportive of *both* the patrilineal and matrilineal definitions of Jewish identity.

> Messianic Judaism has concurred on this issue with the Reform movement, and considers the children of intermarriage Jewish regardless of whether their Jewish status is through the father or mother."[2]

This is the official position of the International Messianic Jewish Alliance (IMJA)[3] and the International Alliance of Messianic Congregations and Synagogues (IAMCS), and is affirmed by the majority of leaders within the Union of Messianic Jewish Congregations (UMJC).[4] In addition, there is the recognition of converted Jews, i.e. Jews by choice, who have gone through a formal conversion ceremony under a recognized authority.[5]

## Patrilineal Definition

Messianic rabbis generally uphold the patrilineal definition of Jewish identity because it is the standard established by God in the Torah. Ancient Israel was a patriarchal society and family genealogies were reckoned according to the father's identity (Gen. 5:1; 10:1; 11:1; 1 Chron. 23:6).[6] The male head of household spoke on behalf of the entire family unit and the wife would follow in the way of her husband. Shaye Cohen explains this ancient Near Eastern social dynamic:

> If a gentile man married a Jewish woman, in all likelihood he would not thereby enter the Jewish community, since a wife would normally join her husband's house and family. In contrast, if a gentile woman was married to a Jewish man, she too was supposed to join her husband's house and family, thereby becoming part of the community to which her husband belonged. There was no ritual of conversion; the act of marriage to a Jewish husband was de facto an act of conversion—that is, an act of integration into the Jewish community.[7]

On a spiritual level, Jewish identity is a matter of covenant. According to the Torah, a Jew is an individual who abides in the Abrahamic covenant of circumcision. It is the object of this covenant to walk before God and be blameless (Gen. 17:1). While females do not bear the sign of the covenant, they appropriate it through either their father or husband.

The patrilineal definition of Jewish identity is implied in virtually every case of intermarriage in the Scriptures.[8] For example, Moses and Zipporah's children were Jews because Moses was a Jew. Boaz and Ruth's children were Jews because Boaz was a Jew. 1 Kings emphasizes the fact that King Rehoboam's parents had intermarried. His mother was an Ammonite (1 Kings 14:21, 31) and his father, Solomon, was a Jew. Rehoboam was, consequently, a Jew. King Ahaz married Jezebel, a Sidonian. The royal children of this intermarriage were Jews because King Ahaz was a Jew. Jezebel was certainly not a convert to Judaism (1 Kings 16:31–33; 18:4).

In the Scriptures, the only seeming exception to patrilinealism is the intermarriage between an Egyptian slave named Jarha and his Israelite owner's daughter (1 Chron. 2:34–35). According to Professor Cohen, the biblical passage suggests "the offspring of Israelite women and foreign men were judged matrilineally only if the marriage was matrilocal—that is, only if the foreign husband joined the wife's domicile or clan. . . . The marriage was probably a form of adoption."[9] It is significant that this passage occurs in the middle of a genealogy. The verses before 2:34 read, "The son of . . . the son of . . . the son of . . . " The verses following 2:34 read, "The father of . . . the father of . . . the father of . . . " There is clearly no break in emphasis on patrilinealism. One might conclude from this context that an adoption, or even a recognized conversion, took place whereby the children of Jarha would be reckoned as continuing the genealogy of his father-in-law, thus upholding the patrilineal principle.

The patrilineal principle continues to be upheld today according to traditional *halakhah* (the application of Jewish law). For example, a person is reckoned a *cohen* (a descendant of a priestly family) according to the identity of his father, not his mother.[10] The Talmud states, "The family of the father is considered family, the family of the mother is not considered family."[11] This is derived from a Torah passage that identifies families with fathers (Num. 1:2).[12] Many synagogue traditions are, despite assertions to the contrary, based on patrilinealism:

> The same holds true for naming children with the formula *son or daughter of the name of the father*. The mother's name is not included. And if the father is a *kohen* or a *Levi* or the mother is the daughter of a *kohen* or a *Levi*, no *pidyon haben* [redemption of the firstborn son ceremony] takes place, a further nod to patrilineal descent. Patrilineality is also reaffirmed when a man is called to the Torah for an *aliyah* by his name and his father's name. The traditional marriage contract, the *ketubah*, records the names of the groom and the bride and their father's names respectively. The witnesses to the *ketubah* sign their own names along with the names of their fathers. At no time is the mother's name mentioned in any of the examples cited above.[13]

In Jewish history, Karaite Jews (who recognized the authority of the Hebrew Bible but not the Oral Torah) upheld the patrilineal standard of Jewish identity.[14]

The worldwide Jewish community recognizes that six million Jews were killed in the Holocaust. Many of these martyrs, however, were Jews according to the patrilineal definition of Jewish identity, including the daughter of Theodore Herzl, the founder of modern Zionism. She died at Theresienstadt concentration camp because she was a Jew, even though her mother was a Gentile.[15]

In 1968, Reconstructionist Judaism accepted the patrilineal principle as a standard of Jewish identity:

> In the first centuries of our era—*only* eighteen or nineteen centuries ago—the Tannaitic rabbis decided that Jewish identity would be transmitted only through the mother

(matrilineal descent). Current research indicates that before that time, identity had been transmitted through the father. When the rabbis made that reversal, they lived in a Roman empire in which the matrilineal principle was the norm for all matters of personal status. . . . The Reconstructionist movement, since 1968, has recognized the Jewishness of the child of a Jewish father and a non-Jewish mother when that child is raised and educated as a Jew (patrilineal descent).[16]

At the 1983 Central Conference of American Rabbis (CCAR), Reform Judaism included patrilinealism as a standard for Jewish identity under certain conditions:

> The conference voted to override the *halachah*, which recognizes matrilineal descent; that is, the child is automatically Jewish if born to a Jewish mother. Instead, the CCAR declared that in an intermarriage where either the father or the mother is Jewish, the child is "under presumption of Jewish descent." In other words, descent alone is not sufficient. Such a child will be considered Jewish only after identifying with the Jewish community by fulfilling the *mitzvot* and participating in Jewish life. Indeed, the CCAR's position is even more stringent than that of the *halachah*, which confers automatic Jewishness if the mother is Jewish, regardless of how the child is reared.[17]

Patrilinealism is a view widely held by lay members of the modern Jewish community. As many as "70 percent of Conservative Jews say they would consider their grandchildren Jewish even if their mother was not."[18] Approximately ten percent of Orthodox Jews are also accepting of patrilinealism.[19] In a 1990 survey of B'nai Brith women, eighty percent said they would regard their grandchildren as Jews even if the mother was not Jewish.[20] A similar study found that seven percent of Orthodox rabbis and forty-one percent of Conservative rabbis would consider their grandchildren Jewish by patrilineal definition. Similarly, among board members of local Jewish community organizations, seventeen percent of those Orthodox and seventy-nine percent of those Conservative would embrace patrilinealism.[21] According to Egon Mayer, such surveys reveal that patrilinealism is receiving a "growing acceptance" in the Conservative and Orthodox Jewish world.[22]

## Matrilineal Definition

Given the ancient roots of patrilinealism, how does one explain the origin of the matrilineal definition of Jewish identity? It is often claimed by traditional Jews that the matrilineal definition is rooted in the return of the Babylonian exiles to Jerusalem, among whom were Jews who had married foreign women and who had children by these unions. The Scriptures relate that Ezra sent away the children of inter-marriage from the camp of Israel (Ezra 10), along with their Gentile mothers, an act taken by traditional Jews to mean that the children were not accepted as Jews. It is suggested by some that the paternity of these children was in question, compelling Ezra to switch the basis of Jewish identity from patrilineal to matrilineal since the mother's identity is almost always known.[23]

There are a number of issues related to these assumptions. First, the text does not explicitly state a change in the definition of who is a Jew. Second, Ezra is described as a devout observer of the Torah (Ezra 7:6, 10), a legal tradition that upholds patrilinealism. Third, of the 31,089 men who returned from exile, 111 had married non-convert wives and only some of these wives were mothers (Ezra 2:64–65; 10:18–44). Assuming that 80 percent of the returning men were married (a conservative estimate), the non-conversionary intermarriage rate would be 0.4 percent. It is a stretch to believe that Ezra, the Torah-faithful scribe, would have changed the basis of Jewish identity for all future generations, affecting millions of Jews, in order to deal with 111 couples and their children. Finally, in Israel's history, there were numerous times when Jewish men married foreign women. However, the inability to establish paternity never undermined the patrilineal standard of Jewish identity.

In my view, there is a better explanation for why Ezra sent away the children—their Gentile mothers had clung to their foreign gods.[24] They were not righteous converts like Ruth but idolaters like Solomon's foreign wives (Neh. 13:26). Support for this view is found in the fact that Ezra emphasized their detestable practices (Ezra 9:1, 14). Ezra knew that keeping these women in the camp of Israel would have introduced a corrupting element into the community.[25] Since Ezra was intent on rededicating the community to the service of God, the women were a clear impediment; even some of the priests of Israel had intermarried with them (Ezra 9:1–2), compromising the integrity of the priesthood. The pagan wives, therefore, had to be sent away.

This interpretation is confirmed by Ezra's and Nehemiah's reiteration of the commandment that prohibited Jews from marrying peoples (male or female) of the land (Ezra 9:10–14; 10:2; Neh. 10:30; 13:1–3, 23–27; see also Deut. 7:1–4; Exod. 34:16; Josh. 23:12; 1 Kings 11:1). The basis for this law was that such marriages would introduce idolatrous practices into Israel. If the foreign women had been righteous converts like Ruth (who abandoned the Moabite religion and clung to the God of Israel), Ezra would not have had a problem with the intermarriages. Ezra's concern was rather with the Torah commandment, which, in principle, prohibited marriages with Canaanite-like women.[26] This was the post-exilic situation. If Jewish women had returned from captivity with pagan husbands, he would have sent the pagan husbands away as well, for they would have also tainted the camp!

Sending the children of intermarriage away did not imply that they were non-Jews or that their identity was suspect. On the basis of Torah, the fathers were Jews and so the children were Jews. The issue was more likely a matter of custody. Ezra's decision was consistent with Near Eastern divorce laws that gave custody of the children to the mother. Such was the Babylonian tradition, even as it is the American tradition today. Moreover, Ezra would have been lacking in compassion had he kept these Jewish children from their non-Jewish mothers, especially the babies.

Where, then, did the matrilineal principle come from? In addition to the traditional explanation, Professor Cohen presents six other possible explanations for the origin of matrilinealism. The two most compelling theories, he states, are that it derived from Roman law or from the rabbinic view of forbidden mixtures.[27] Whichever is the case, it is likely that the matrilineal principle did not exist before 70 c.e.

> I conclude that the matrilineal principle was not yet known in second-temple times. This conclusion is supported by an argument from silence and an argument from positive testimony. The argument from silence is that none of the works of "the Apocrypha," "the Pseudepigrapha," or the Qumran scrolls knows, assumes, mentions, or applies the rabbinic matrilineal principle. The argument from positive testimony is that in various scattered passages Philo, Paul, Josephus, and Acts make statements or assumptions that cannot be squared with the rabbinic matrilineal principle. . . . The matrilineal principle is first attested in the Mishnah.[28]

At some point after the Second Temple period, we may assume that nascent Rabbinic Judaism switched the standard of Jewish identity from patrilineal to matrilineal. This means that matrilinealism has no basis in the Hebrew Bible or New Testament.

Messianic Judaism seeks to honor the tradition of the fathers, but it seeks to honor God and his Word above all. In this regard, most Messianic Jews cannot support the rabbinic view that it was permissible to deviate from the Torah's standard of Jewish identity. From the Messianic perspective, then, the switch from patrilinealism to matrilinealism was unauthorized. How can modern Jews continue to call themselves Jews if their identity is based on an errant definition of Jewishness? In my opinion, there is only one answer—matrilineal Jews are Jews on the basis of covenantal declaration and not ancestry alone. Behind the Messianic Jewish recognition of matrilineal Jews as Jews, therefore, is the implicit recognition that a person can become a Jew, even without undergoing a formal conversion ceremony.[29] It is enough that a person is raised as a Jew (and is circumcised if a male), thinks he is a Jew, declares he is a Jew, and is received by the community as a Jew.[30] One might call such a person a "common law Jew."[31]

## Conversion

All the evidence suggests that, in ancient Israel, Ruth-like converts did not undergo a formal conversion ceremony to become Jews. Professor Cohen explains: "The woman was joined to the house of Israel by being joined to her Israelite husband; the act of marriage was functionally equivalent to the later idea of 'conversion.'"[32] The Torah's silence on the issue of formal conversion implies that the need for it did not exist in ancient times. Instead, the Torah emphasizes the importance of a wife submitting to her husband. In this context, a Gentile woman married to an Israelite man was called to embrace the God of Israel and the people of Israel as her own. In the rare instance of a Gentile man marrying an Israelite woman, it is possible that a form of adoption took place whereby he would enter the wife's family and carry on the name of her family (e.g. 1 Chron. 2:34–35). In such a case, he would also be expected to embrace the God of Israel and the people of Israel as his own. Why didn't the Jewish woman take on her Gentile husband's religious identity? It is because Israel is a nation in covenant with God. Jews are obligated to circumcise their sons and pass on Jewish heritage to the next generation (Gen. 17). If a Jewish woman marries a Gentile man and she converts to her husband's religion, she cannot fulfill her covenantal obligations pertaining to Jewish continuity. The covenant with God is violated. However, if the Gentile husband converts to Judaism, from the biblical perspective, no covenant violation occurs. Such is the biblical rationale for conversion from Gentile to Jew and not the other way around.[33]

The world has changed much since ancient times, especially in regard to gender roles. In the United States, in particular, women do not automatically follow their husband's religion. The idea of a husband marrying into his wife's family is an alien concept. Conversion is no longer assumed or normative in cases of intermarriage. Consequently, it is expedient for the Gentile spouse to formally convert to Judaism, if only so that the children can have a clear and unambiguous identity.[34]

The debate over "who is a Jew" is still in session in the Messianic Jewish community. While a consensus exists in some areas, in others (such as standards for formal conversion) there is much diversity of opinion. What else would you expect from a truly Jewish movement? In seeking to be Scripture-based and tradition-honoring, Messianic Judaism must question the traditional boundaries that have been passed down from ancient times. The result is a fresh look at this millennia-old issue.

# Why Messianic Jews Believe Yeshua is the Messiah

Many intermarried Jews wonder why Messianic Jews believe Yeshua is the Messiah since he died two thousand years ago. Isn't the Messiah supposed to bring peace to the world? The key biblical text that Messianic Jews point to in support of their belief is Isaiah 53, which speaks of a suffering servant, sent by God to lay down his life as a ransom for sin. The writers of the New Testament, all Jews,[1] believed that Yeshua was this suffering servant that Isaiah foretold (Matt. 8:17; 27:27–66; Acts 8:32–33; 1 Pet. 2:22–25). Significantly, many Chabad *Hasidim* (members of the largest sect of ultra-Orthodox Jews) concur with Messianic Jews that a suffering Messiah is depicted in Isaiah 53 (they point to the Talmud [*b. Sanh.* 98b]); but instead of believing that Yeshua is the suffering servant, they believe that Menachem Schneerson, the Lubavitcher *rebbe*, fulfilled this prophecy when he died in 1994 (see Appendix D).[2] What does the prophecy actually say? Read it and judge for yourself. Does any Jewish person in history fit this portrait?

> In fact, it was our diseases he bore,
> our pains from which he suffered;
> yet we regarded him as punished,
> stricken and afflicted by God.
> But he was wounded because of our crimes,
> crushed because of our sins;
> the disciplining that makes us whole fell on him,
> and by his bruises we are healed.
>
> We all, like sheep, went astray;
> we turned, each one, to his own way;
> yet ADONAI laid on him
> the guilt of all of us.
>
> Though mistreated, he was submissive—
> he did not open his mouth.

Like a lamb led to be slaughtered,
like a sheep silent before its shearers,
he did not open his mouth.
After forcible arrest and sentencing, he was taken away;
and none of his generation protested
his being cut off from the land of the living
for the crimes of my people,
who deserved the punishment themselves.
He was given a grave among the wicked;
in his death he was with a rich man. (Isa. 53:4–9)

Today, most of our rabbis interpret Isaiah 53 exclusively as a reference
to the nation of Israel. This view finds its origin in the writings of
Rashi (1040–1105 C.E.).[3] Nevertheless, the more classic interpretation,
and the one that countless of our rabbis agreed upon until the time of
Rashi, is that it is a depiction of the sacrificial death of the Messiah,
the one-man Israel. The Chabad Hasidic view, then, is essentially the
restoration of a teaching that has been encapsulated in biblical and
rabbinic literature for centuries.[4]

What Chabad rabbis recently discovered, Messianic Jews have
been teaching since the first century. The key difference between the
two positions is the matter of who has the credentials to be the Messiah. From the Messianic Jewish perspective, Yeshua's credentials are
exceptional. One only needs to read the New Testament to see that
Yeshua's life was one of humbly ministering to the people of Israel. He
healed the sick and raised the dead. Like the prophets of old, his
words cut to the heart and revealed the thoughts of men. Like Jeremiah and Ezekiel, he too was rejected by the religious establishment
but received by the common people. The Messiah is referred to in the
Hebrew Bible as being "a light to the Gentiles" (Isa. 49:6–7). Through
Yeshua's life, hundreds of millions of Gentiles have turned from idol
worship to the God of Israel. What other Jew has caused this to happen? The timing of Yeshua's death was in accord with the prophecy of
Daniel (Dan. 9:24–26). And the manner of his death was in accord
with the Prophet Isaiah (Isa. 52:13–53:12). Yeshua said that he would
come again to fulfill the rest of his mission. Until then, Messianic Jews
wait and seek to observe his teachings faithfully.

The following interpretations of Isaiah 53 are from the book
*The "Suffering Servant" of Isaiah According to the Jewish Interpreters*
by S. R. Driver and Abraham Neubauer. It is the most complete collection of Jewish commentary on Isaiah 53 ever compiled and trans-
lated. Additional texts from the Cairo Geniza, the Dead Sea Scrolls,
and other manuscripts that have come to light in recent years can be

found in the doctoral dissertation of Rabbi Asher Soloff, "The Fifty Third Chapter of Isaiah According to the Jewish Commentators, to the Sixteenth Century."

Rabbi Mosheh El-Sheikh taught:

> I may remark, then, that our Rabbis with one voice accept and affirm the opinion that the prophet is speaking of the King Messiah, and we shall ourselves also adhere to the same view . . .[5]

Rabbi Naphthali Ben Asher Altschuler taught:

> I will now proceed to explain these verses of our own Messiah, who, God willing, will come speedily in our days! I am surprised that Rashi and R. David Qamhi have not, with the Targum, applied them to the Messiah likewise . . . the Parashah refers to our Messiah . . . he suffered in order that by his sufferings atonement might be made for the whole of Israel, as it is said of the prophet Micah, that the blood issuing from him made atonement for all Israel. The sickness which ought to have fallen upon us was borne by him: the prophet means to say, When Messiah son of Joseph shall die between the gates, and be a marvel in the eyes of creation, why must the penalty he bears be so severe? . . . *for the transgression of my people* had this *stroke* come upon the Messiah.[6]

Rabbi Don Yitz'chak Abarbanel taught:

> The *first* question is to ascertain to whom it refers: for the learned among the Nazarenes expound it of the man who was crucified in Jerusalem at the end of the second Temple. . . . Yonathan ben Uzziel interprets it in the Targum of the future Messiah; and this is also the opinion of our learned men in the majority of their Midrashim.[7]

The Babylonian Talmud (*b. Sanh.* 98b) states:

> The Messiah—what is his name? . . . The Rabbis say, The leprous one [those] of the house of Rabbi [say, the sick one], as it is said, 'Surely he hath borne our sicknesses,' [Isa. 53:4] etc.[8]

*Midrash Rabbah* (a homiletical commentary on Scripture) states:

> Another explanation (of Ruth 2:14)—He is speaking of
> the king Messiah: 'Come hither,' draw near to the throne;
> 'and eat of the bread,' that is, the bread of the kingdom;
> 'and dip thy morsel in the vinegar,' this refers to the chas-
> tisements, as it is said, 'But he was wounded for our
> transgressions, bruised for our iniquities.' [Isa. 53:5].[9]

The *Zohar* (a commentary on Torah from the perspective of Jewish
mysticism) states:

> There is in the garden of Eden a palace called the Palace
> of the sons of sickness: this palace the Messiah then en-
> ters, and summons every sickness, every pain, and every
> chastisement of Israel; they all come and rest upon him.
> And were it not that he had thus lightened them off Israel
> and taken them upon himself, there had been no man
> able to bear Israel's chastisements for transgression of the
> law: and this is that which is written, 'Surely our sick-
> nesses he hath carried.' [Isa. 53:4].[10]

A *Musaf* (additional morning) service prayer written by Rabbi Eleazar
Kalir in the 7th century, and included in the *Machzor*, states:

> We are shrunk up in our misery even until now! Our rock
> hath not come nigh to us: Messiah, our righteousness,
> hath turned from us: we are in terror, and there is none to
> justify us! Our iniquities and the yoke of our transgres-
> sions he will bear, for *he was wounded for our transgres-
> sions*: he will carry our sins upon his shoulder, that we
> may find forgiveness for our iniquities, and *by his stripes
> we are healed* [Isa. 53:5]. O eternal One, the time is come
> to make a new creation: from the vault of heaven bring
> him up, out of Seir draw him forth, that he may make his
> voice heard to us in Lebanon, a second time by the hand
> of Yinnon [Messiah]![11]

The Targum (an Aramaic paraphrase) of Isaiah 52:13 reads:

> Behold, my servant Messiah shall prosper.[12]

In *P'siqtha* (a homiletical commentary on Scripture), it is written:

The Holy One brought forth the soul of the Messiah, and said to him, Art thou willing to be created and to redeem my sons after 6000 years? He replied, I am. God replied, If so, thou must take upon thyself chastisements in order to wipe away their iniquity, as it is written, "Surely our sicknesses he hath carried." The Messiah answered, I will take them upon me gladly.[13]

In *Sifrei* (an exegetical/homiletical commentary on Scripture), it is written:

R. Yose the Galilean said, Come forth and learn the righteousness of the King Messiah and the reward of the just from the first man who received but one commandment, a prohibition and transgressed it: consider how many deaths were inflicted upon himself, upon his own generations, and upon those that followed them, till the end of all generations. Which attribute is the greater, the attribute of goodness, or the attribute of vengeance? He answered, The attribute of goodness is the greater, and the attribute of vengeance is the less; how much more, then will the King Messiah, who endures affliction and pains for the transgressors (as it is written, "He was wounded," etc.) justify all generations! And this is what is meant when it is said, "And the Lord made the iniquity of us all meet upon him."[14]

Rabbi Mosheh Ben Maimon (Maimonides) taught:

What is to be the manner of Messiah's advent, and where will be the place of his appearance? He will make his first appearance in the land of Israel. . . . And Isaiah speaks similarly of the time when he will appear, without his father or mother or family being known, *He came up as a sucker before him, and as a root out of the dry earth* [Isa. 53:2], etc.[15]

Rabbi Shimon Ben Yohai taught:

. . . and Messiah, the son of Ephraim, will die there, and Israel will mourn for him. And afterwards the Holy One will reveal to them Messiah, the son of David, whom Israel will desire to stone, saying, Thou speakest falsely; already is the Messiah slain, and there is none other Messiah to stand up (after him): and so they will despise him, as it is written, "Despised and forlorn of men;" but he will turn and hide himself from them, according to the words, "Like one hiding his face from us."[16]

Rabbi Elijah de Vidas taught:

> *But he was wounded for our transgressions, bruised for our iniquities* [Isa. 53:5], the meaning of which is that since the Messiah bears our iniquities, which produce the effect of his being bruised, it follows that whoso will not admit that the Messiah thus suffers for our iniquities, must endure and suffer for them himself.[17]

Rabbi Yepheth Ben 'Ali taught:

> By the words "surely he hath carried our sicknesses," they mean that the pains and sickness which he fell into were merited by them, but that he bore them instead: the next words "yet we did esteem him," etc., intimate that they thought him afflicted by God for his own sins, as they distinctly say, "smitten of God and afflicted." And here I think it necessary to pause for a few moments, in order to explain why God caused these sicknesses to attach themselves to the Messiah for the sake of Israel . . . by the Messiah bearing them they would be delivered from the wrath which rested upon them.[18]

Rabbi Mosheh Kohen Ibn Crispin taught:

> The expression *my servant* they [certain contemporary commentators] compare rashly with [Isa.] 41:8 'thou Israel art my servant,' where the prophet is speaking of the people of Israel (which would be singular); here, however, he does not mention Israel, but says simply *my servant*; we cannot therefore understand the word in the same sense. . . . I am pleased to interpret it, in accordance with the teaching of our Rabbis, of the King Messiah, and will be careful, so far as I am able, to adhere to the literal sense: thus, possibly, I shall be free from the forced and far-fetched interpretations of which others have been guilty.[19]

## Appendix C
# A Guide to Messianic Jewish Organizations

To learn more about Messianic Judaism or to find a local synagogue in your area, please contact the following organizations:

Messianic Jewish Communications
6204 Park Heights Avenue
Baltimore, Maryland 21215
Telephone: (410) 358-6471
Website: http://www.MessianicJewish.net

Union of Messianic Jewish Congregations (UMJC)
529 Jefferson Street N.E.
Albuquerque, New Mexico  87108
Telephone: (800) 692-UMJC/8652
Website: http://www.umjc.org

Messianic Jewish Alliance of America (MJAA)
P.O. Box 274
Springfield, Pennsylvania  19064
Telephone: (800) 225-MJAA/6522
Website: http://www.mjaa.org

International Messianic Jewish Alliance (IMJA)
P.O. Box 6307
Virginia Beach, Virginia  23456
Telephone: (757) 495-8246
Website: http://www.imja.com

# The Growing Acceptance of Messianic Judaism

All religious movements within Judaism go through a process of proving themselves before receiving acceptance in the American Jewish community. In recent times, this was the case with Reform Judaism, Conservative Judaism, Reconstructionist Judaism, and Humanistic Judaism.[1] In each case, these groups were initially misunderstood, maligned and even attacked as threatening the very existence of the Jewish people. Over time, they won general acceptance in the American Jewish community. Messianic Judaism is following the same course and will inevitably find a place at the table with other segments of the non-Orthodox Jewish community.[2]

Acceptance in the Christian community is a somewhat different situation. Messianic Judaism is already well received by many Protestant/Charismatic denominations. Where this is not the case, such as among some liberal Protestant and Catholic leaders who are part of the ecumenical movement,[3] the key to Messianic Jewish acceptance is for mainstream Jewish leaders to give their nod of approval. Therefore, in this section, I will focus on the growing acceptance of Messianic Judaism in the American Jewish community. This trend has direct relevance to intermarried couples considering the Messianic Jewish option.

## Sources to Learn About Messianic Judaism

Over the past two decades, the Jewish community has been aided by the academic study of Messianic Judaism on the postgraduate level. Nine Ph.D. dissertations on the subject of Messianic Judaism have been made available as a result of this research, making accurate information about the Messianic Jewish movement more readily accessible to the public and Jewish leaders in particular. Most of these doctoral dissertations on contemporary Messianic Judaism can be ordered through Inter-Library Loan (ILL) at college/public libraries:

Leigh Paula Berger. "Messianic Judaism: Searching the Spirit." Ph.D. diss., University of South Florida, 2000.

Shoshanah Feher. "Passing Over Easter: Constructing the Boundaries of Messianic Judaism." Ph.D. diss., University of California, Santa Barbara, 1995.

Ruth I. Fleischer. "The Emergence of Distinctively Jewish Faith in Jesus, 1925–1994." Ph.D. diss., King's College, University of London, 1995.

Carol Harris-Shapiro. "Syncretism or Struggle: The Case of Messianic Judaism." Ph.D. diss., Temple University, Department of Religion, 1992. An updated version of this dissertation for popular reading is available at major bookstores. It is entitled *Messianic Judaism: A Rabbi's Journey Through Religious Change in America* (Boston: Beacon Press, 1999).

Rachel Kohn. "Hebrew Christianity and Messianic Judaism on the Church-Sect Continuum." Ph.D. diss., McMaster University, Department of Religious Studies, 1985.

Gershon Nerel. "Messianic Jews in Eretz Israel, 1917–1967: Trends and Changes in Shaping Self Identity." (Hebrew). Ph.D. diss., Hebrew University, 1995.

Bruce Stokes. "Messianic Judaism: Ethnicity in Revitalization." Ph.D. diss., University of California, Riverside, Department of Anthropology, 1994.

Walter Riggans. "Messianic Judaism and Jewish-Christian Relations: A Case Study in the Field of Religious Identity." Ph.D. diss., University of Birmingham, 1991.

Jeffrey Wasserman. "Messianic Jewish Congregations: A Comparison and Critique of Contemporary North American and Israeli Expressions." Ph.D. diss., The Southern Baptist Theological Seminary, 1997.

Notably, four of the dissertations were written by mainstream Jews (Berger, Feher, Harris-Shapiro, Kohn). Of particular interest to Jewish leaders is that these empirical studies confirm that Messianic Judaism contributes to Jewish continuity. Messianic Jewish success in steering exogamous Jews in the direction of halakhic Jewish lifestyle has consequently taken many Jewish leaders by surprise and contributed to a new openness to learning about the American Messianic Jewish community.

Concurrent with the publication of postgraduate research on Messianic Judaism has also been the collection of statistical information on Messianic Jews by Jewish demographers working for national Jewish organizations. For example, in the 2001 American Jewish Identity Survey (AJIS Report), sponsored by The Graduate Center of the City University of New York, the questionnaire asked, "What is your religion, if any?"[4] Number three on the list of forty six possible answers was "Messianic Jew," just under "Jewish/Judaism" and "Jewish and another religion."[5]

Few people realize that the 1990 National Jewish Population Survey interviewed Messianic Jews as well as members of the rest of the Jewish community. One survey question asked: "Is being Jewish very important in your life?" The results were compiled by the North American Jewish Data Bank and sponsored by the Council of Jewish Federations (CJF). Professor Sergio DellaPergola of Hebrew University tabulated the results and presented these findings: [6]

*Percent of Respondents Agreeing That*
*"Being Jewish is Very Important in Your Life"*
By Denomination, USA, 1990 (weighted sample)

| Respondent's Denomination | % Agree |
| --- | --- |
| Messianic | 100 |
| Orthodox | 77 |
| Multiple denomination | 61 |
| Conservative | 58 |
| Reconstructionist | 49 |
| Reform | 40 |
| Just Jewish | 29 |
| Jewish + other religion | 27 |
| Christian | 21 |
| Don't know | 21 |
| Secular | 16 |
| Non-participating | 13 |
| Other religion | 5 |
| No answer, refuse | 4 |
| Agnostic/atheist | 0 |

According to the above data, one hundred percent of all Messianic Jews surveyed said "yes" to the survey question, thereby indicating that being Jewish was "very important" in their lives. This was higher than any other Jewish group interviewed.

Numerous doctoral dissertations and demographic studies that cast a favorable light on Messianic Judaism do not, in and of themselves, represent a growing acceptance of Messianic Judaism. However, they do provide a basis for acceptance if Jewish leaders hold up Jewish self-identification and contribution to Jewish continuity as the minimal standards for acceptance in the Jewish community. As I will seek to demonstrate, such leaders do exist and are increasingly going on record in support of Messianic Judaism. Moreover, some Jewish leaders see the acceptance of Messianic Judaism in the American Jewish community as inevitable by virtue of the lack of any single standard that would exclude Messianic Judaism while accepting other modern forms of Judaism, such as Humanistic Judaism, Reconstructionist Judaism, Reform Judaism, and Chabad Hasidism. In other words, many Jewish leaders are beginning to acknowledge that the days of the double standard are drawing to an end.

## The Growing Acceptance

The strongest statement, by far, from the mainstream Jewish community in support of Messianic Judaism has come from Dan Cohn-Sherbok, a Reform rabbi and professor of Judaism at the University of Wales. Rabbi Cohn-Sherbok received a Ph.D. from Cambridge University as well as an honorary Doctorate in Divinity in 1996 from Hebrew Union College–Jewish Institute of Religion. Among the fifty books he has written on Jewish history and theology are *The Jewish Faith*, *Atlas of Jewish History*, *Modern Judaism*, *The Future of Judaism* and *Understanding the Holocaust*. I say this to underscore the point that Rabbi Cohn-Sherbok is one of the top thinkers in the Reform movement. Far from being uninformed about the boundaries of Judaism, he is a specialist on the topic.

In July 2000, Rabbi Cohn-Sherbok published a book entitled *Messianic Judaism*, the result of six years of research. That same year he addressed a large gathering of Messianic rabbis at the summer conference of the Union of Messianic Jewish Congregations. While making clear that he was not an adherent of Messianic Judaism, he related that Messianic Judaism, in his view, is a vibrant form of Judaism and one that is capable of making an important contribution to the Jewish world. On the subject of Messianic Judaism's acceptance in the American Jewish community, he stated, "I see Judaism as widening, and yes, I do think you will get into the country club. It is going to happen in the 21st century."[7] He added, "I do regard Messianic Judaism as rooted within the evolution of Judaism. . . . To me, it is totally inconsistent and illogical to exclude you."[8]

In *Messianic Judaism*, Rabbi Cohn-Sherbok suggests that he is not alone in adopting a sympathetic approach to Messianic Judaism. There are many "pluralists" in the Jewish community who accept Messianic Judaism as a legitimate expression of Judaism and reject the double standard:

> A very different approach to the issue of Jewish authenticity is espoused by thinkers who advocate a more tolerant view of the Messianic movement. Given the multi-dimensional character of modern Jewish life, they contend that Messianic Judaism should be regarded as one among many interpretations of the Jewish faith. The central difficulty with the non-Orthodox exclusion of Messianic Jews, they point out, is that the various non-Orthodox movements are themselves deeply divided over the central principles of Judaism. As we have seen, many Humanistic, Reconstructionist, Reform and Conservative Jews seek to redefine the concept of God; these movements even include adherents who have totally abandoned a belief in a supernatural Deity. In the view of Jewish pluralists, this state of affairs makes it absurd to exclude the Messianic movement from the Jewish community. The same applies across the range of religious beliefs. Doctrines concerning creation, revelation, divine action, omniscience, omnipotence, providence and salvation have been either redefined or abandoned by many members of all these movements. In addition, the multifarious laws in the *Code of Jewish Law* have been largely neglected by the various non-Orthodox movements. No longer is Jewry united by belief and practice; instead the various branches of the modern Judaic establishment have radically separated themselves from their past. In the light of such an abandonment of the tradition, pluralists maintain that the exclusion of Messianic Judaism from the circle of legitimate expressions of the Jewish heritage is totally inconsistent.[9]

Pluralist Jewish leaders like Rabbi Cohn-Sherbok are not afraid to admit that Messianic Judaism rivals other branches of Judaism in important areas of Jewish life and thought. Observing the Messianic Jewish commitment to the God of Israel, the Torah and Jewish continuity, as well as noting the absence of any uniform standard of who is a Jew in the American Jewish community, these leaders suggest that it is more than appropriate to regard Messianic Judaism as a legitimate expression of the Jewish faith alongside other modern forms of Judaism. To illustrate this point, Rabbi Cohn-Sherbok includes in his book a picture of a seven-branched *menorah* that represents the seven branches of the twenty-first century Jewish community.[10] Each branch is labeled according to its kind of Judaism. Messianic Judaism is the seventh branch:

> This shattering of the monolithic system of Judaism has become the hallmark of contemporary Jewish life. In this light, Jewish pluralists argue, Messianic Judaism should be seen merely as one among many expressions of the Jewish faith. Alongside Hasidism, Orthodox Judaism, Conservative Judaism, Reform Judaism, Reconstructionist Judaism, and Humanistic Judaism, Messianic Judaism offers a pathway through the Jewish heritage. Admittedly, unlike the other branches of Judaism, this movement is firmly rooted in the belief that Yeshua is the long-awaited redeemer of Israel. Yet such a belief is in principle no more radical than the Reconstructionist and Humanistic rejection of a supernatural deity. Indeed, as we have seen, in many respects Messianic Jews are more theistically oriented and more *Torah*-observant even than their counterparts within the Conservative and Reform movements. . . . In accordance with this, the seven-branched *menorah* in which all denominations, including Messianic Judaism, are represented, is the only reasonable starting point for inter-community relations in the twenty-first century.[11]

The publication of *Messianic Judaism* has caused many in the Jewish community to rethink their stance toward Messianic Judaism. It has also emboldened some pluralist Jewish leaders to speak out in support of the Messianic Jewish movement. One such voice of affirmation has come from Rabbi Sherwin Wine, who, in the 1960's as a Reform rabbi, pioneered the first secular humanistic Jewish congregation.[12] According to the 2001 AJIS Report, Rabbi Wine's movement of Humanistic Judaism presently has 40,000 adherents, thus surpassing Reconstructionist Judaism, which has approximately 35,000 adherents.[13] Rabbi Wine endorsed the back cover of *Messianic Judaism* in saying, "Finally, someone in the Jewish world has the courage to say what needs to be said. Dan Cohn-Sherbok, with his usual lucidity and analytic skills, has demonstrated that Messianic Jews have the right to be included in the Jewish people."

Another voice suggesting that the winds of change are among us has come out of the Reconstructionist branch of Judaism. Rabbi Carol Harris-Shapiro, who wrote her doctoral dissertation on Messianic Judaism in 1992, and published an updated version of it in 1999 entitled *Messianic Judaism: A Rabbi's Journey Through Religious Change in America*, has suggested that the double standard by which Messianic Judaism is judged cannot stand up under scrutiny. Acceptance of Messianic Judaism, in her view, is already a *fait accompli* in segments of the Jewish world. Rabbi Harris-Shapiro writes:

> Given the large variation within what is generally accepted in the community as "Jewish" and "Judaism," is it possible to find a single definition of either that includes all groups considered normative in American Jewish life but excludes Messianic Jews and Messianic Judaism? Messianic Judaism challenges the normative Jewish community to articulate its own boundaries. A seemingly simple task on the surface, it proves surprisingly difficult. A partial acceptance of Messianic Jews has proven inescapable, even by those organizations most set against the Messianic Jewish movement.[14]

The growing acceptance of Messianic Judaism has also been evident among Conservative Jewish centrists. Dennis Prager, the nationally syndicated Jewish talk show host, wrote in the June 2000 issue of *Moment* magazine that the time has come for the Jewish world to partially accept Messianic Judaism. Arguing that "we Jews accept among us a variety of messianic beliefs—but what we do not accept is a variety of divinities,"[15] Prager proposed that Messianic Jews should be accepted as full members of the Jewish community, even while believing that Jesus is the Messiah, as long as they deny Jesus' divinity. Prager was clearly responding to his concern that a new double standard existed in the Jewish community, no longer just on the left, but now on the right. By 2000, tens of thousands of ultra-Orthodox Jews had become more vocal in their belief that the Lubavitcher *rebbe*, Menachem Schneerson, who died in 1994, was the Messiah; moreover, that he died for the sins of Israel, and would come again after being resurrected to establish the kingdom of God on earth.[16] Prager makes clear that this similarity to Messianic Jewish belief is his underlying concern:

> In Judaism there is an enormous difference between erroneously believing that a certain man is the messiah and

believing that this man is God. There is, after all, a belief in Judaism that someone will be a messiah, and, at different times, many Jews have believed that someone was the messiah without being read out of the Jewish people. At this very moment, there are some wonderful Chabad Jews who believe the last Lubavitcher rebbe was the messiah and no one is calling, nor should anyone call, for their removal from the Jewish people.[17]

By drawing the line at belief in a divine Messiah, Prager hoped to include these ultra-Orthodox Jews in the Jewish community along with some heterodox Messianic Jews while excluding traditional Messianic Jews. Prager was clearly concerned that, without doing something to remove this double standard, Messianic Judaism might be considered doctrinally equivalent to Chabad Hasidism in the Jewish community.

Prager, in his foresight, was correct. The double standard has been taken by many in the Jewish community to support the acceptability of Messianic Judaism. Messianic Judaism is effectually riding on the coattails of Chabad Hasidism. As but one instance that occurred on an Interfaith newsgroup, a rabbi argued by e-mail that Messianic Jews were not Jews. I responded that his view was not consistent with Talmudic law, which does regard Messianic Jews as Jews (*b. San.* 44a).[18] Then, a Jewish (non-Messianic) fellow named Eric, sent his reply:

> I've read some of the emails on the Messianic Jews. . . . It sounds alright with me. This is how I look at it. The first ones to believe in Jesus were Jews. So, does that mean 2000 years ago the second a Jew said he believed in Jesus he wasn't Jewish anymore? To say a person is no longer Jewish just because they believe in Jesus doesn't make any sense to me. That would mean one would be defining a Jew by a negative, i.e. a Jew is someone who believes that the Messiah has not yet come. Isn't a Jew a lot more than that? This seems like a very narrow definition of a Jew. Another way to view it is—what happens the next time a being arrives on this planet and several thousand Jews believe he is the Messiah and several thousand don't? So, then does that mean those that do believe he is the Messiah are no longer Jews also? I heard that many Jews believe that Rabbi Schneerson was the Messiah. I don't think they'd be very happy if someone came up to them and said "Sorry, you're no longer a Jew, you're now

a Schnersonite, because a Jew is defined as someone who believes the Messiah has not yet come." These are my thoughts. Any feedback is welcome. [19]

Eric picked up on the double standard that Prager was concerned about and interpreted it to mean that Messianic Judaism was an acceptable expression of the Jewish faith.

As well meaning as Prager was in writing his proposal, it was flawed on two accounts. First, it was unrealistic. Conservative Jews lack the credibility in Orthodox circles to take positions on matters such as Messianic doctrine. Rabbi David Berger, a modern Orthodox rabbi and Professor of History at Brooklyn College, concurs, "Once you deny the essentials of a particular doctrine, you lose your standing in a debate about its details. Most Conservative and all Reform Jews have long ago relinquished the belief in a personal Messiah. . . . Moreover, non-Orthodox Jewry lacks institutional leverage in dealing with Hasidim of any variety." [20] For these reasons, Conservative Jews have stayed out of the debate over Menachem Schneerson's Messiahship and the double standard between Lubavitch Jews and Messianic Jews remains.

Second, it is now clear that Lubavitch Jews also believe in the divinity of their Messiah, just like Messianic Jews! In other words, the gap has closed between the two groups concerning their Messianic beliefs. Either both are in or both are out. Rabbi Berger sums up the present ultra-Orthodox view:

A significant segment of this movement now declares openly that the Rebbe is not only the Messiah but God. In the last year and a half various Lubavitch writings have called the Rebbe 'our Creator', 'the Holy One Blessed be He', the 'ba'al habayit [master] of all that occurs in the world', 'omnipotent', 'omniscient', 'our God', 'indistinguishable' from God, one who underwent an 'apotheosis' on 3 Tammuz 5754, whose 'entire essence is divinity' and to whom one may consequently bow in prayer. These formulations, complete with prooftexts, appear in publications in which Lubavitch educators participate and reflect views that can be found not only on the movement's periphery but also at its core. [21]

Rabbi Berger, who has mounted a seven-year campaign to exclude ultra-Orthodox Jews from the Jewish community on account of their doctrines of a Second Coming and a divine Messiah, admits that he receives little support in his endeavor from the Orthodox community.

Hence, the provocative title of his book: *The Rebbe, the Messiah and the Scandal of Orthodox Indifference.* An important reason for this indifference is that Lubavitch leaders hold key positions of rabbinic authority and control nodal points of social services in the Jewish world.

> Hasidim who proclaim this belief, including some who have ruled that it is a belief required by Jewish Law, routinely hold significant religious posts with the sanction of major Orthodox authorities unconnected with their movement. These range from the offices of the Israeli rabbinate to the ranks of mainstream rabbinical organizations to the chairmanship of rabbinical courts in Israel and elsewhere, not to speak of service as scribes, ritual slaughterers, teachers, and administrators of schools and religious organizations receiving support from mainstream Orthodoxy. For much of Orthodox Jewry, then, the classic boundaries of the messianic faith of Israel are no more.[22]

Moreover, the Chabad-Lubavitch movement has an international presence, with emissaries in 107 countries.[23] This flows out of its outreach vision to bring non-religious Jews back to Orthodoxy:

> Chabad boasts more than 2,600 institutions throughout the world, with 3,700 married couples serving as emissaries. . . . Chabad rabbis constitute 50 percent of the rabbinate in England. . . . Any Jewish traveler to France, where the Lubavitch directory lists 35 major emissaries, will testify to the visibility and significance of Chabad institutions and services there. . . . The head of the rabbinic court for the entire city of Montreal is a Chabad rabbi. In a significant number of American communities, anyone seeking an Orthodox presence—sometimes any religious Jewish presence—will find it only in Chabad. As for Israel, the movement is disproportionately represented there among the country's rabbis and religious functionaries. . . . Finally, the role of Chabad in the former Soviet Union, a vast territory with a population of a half-million Jews, deserves special mention. The recently formed Federation of Jewish Communities has installed a Chabad emissary named Berel Lazar as the country's chief rabbi . . . the activities of Chabad dwarf those of all other Jewish religious movements.[24]

The point of this documentation is that Chabad Hasidic Jews are here to stay. Much of the worldwide Jewish community is dependant on them for their study of rabbinic law and their commitment to Jewish social services. Non-Orthodox Jews simply lack the credibility to exclude them from the Jewish community. It is a "catch twenty-two" for Orthodox Judaism and non-Orthodox Judaisms alike. Consequently, to the extent that ultra-Orthodox Jews continue to embrace a Second Coming Judaism and a divine Messiah, to that same extent the door is left open for Messianic Jewish acceptance in the American Jewish community.[25] Rabbi Berger admits that the boundaries of Judaism vis-à-vis Jewish Messianic belief have been changed dramatically, and perhaps irreversibly, as a result of Chabad Hasidic Judaism. In September 2001, he wrote in *Commentary* magazine:

> In the course of the last seven years, a revolutionary development has quietly overtaken the Jewish religion. Unless it is somehow rolled back, Jews will soon have to confront the fact that one of the key pillars of their faith has been thoroughly undermined, and even the most elementary primer on the differences between Judaism and Christianity will have to be rewritten. The matter at issue is what Jews believe about the messiah. . . . For Christians, of course, the messiah decidedly *could* die in the midst his redemptive mission. Indeed, Jewish denial of this proposition became one of the central points of contention in the millennial debate between the two religions. . . . Incredibly, however, over the course of the last seven years, Orthodox Judaism has effectively declared that, with respect to this fundamental issue of principle, Christians were correct all along and Jews profoundly mistaken.[26]

Michael Wyschogrod is another voice within the modern Orthodox community whose writings suggest a growing acceptance of Messianic Judaism. An esteemed professor of Jewish philosophy and a key participant in the Jewish-Christian dialogue movement, Wyschogrod has argued that Jews who believe in Jesus are Jews and have the continuing obligation to live according to the Torah:

> In the past, when a Jew accepted baptism, he severed his bonds with the Jewish people and with Judaism. Being a Jew and a Christian were thought to be incompatible by

the adherents of both religions. While everyone knew that
Judaism and Christianity had some beliefs in common,
most Jews and Christians focused on the differences and
these were important enough to convince everybody that
a choice had to be made: one was either a Jew or a Christian but one could not be both. From the Jewish point of
view—and probably also from the Christian—this state of
affairs had its advantages. Both faiths required clear identities. Because there was a time long ago when the two
communities were one, both have been anxious over the
centuries to define their identities in contrast to the other.
This effort would be ill served by any degree of toleration
of dual citizenship. One had to make a choice. It was an
either/or situation. But, as we have seen, that situation is
now changed. There are Jewish Christians. . . . So I return
to your claim that you remain a Jew in spite of having
become a Christian. Is this a claim I can accept? Of
course, I can. . . . Now the point is that once someone is a
Jew, he always remains a Jew. Once someone has come
under the yoke of the commandments, there is no escap-
ing this yoke. So baptism, from the Jewish point of view,
does not make eating pork into a neutral act. In fact, nothing that a Jew can do enables him to escape from the yoke
of the commandments. This proves like nothing else that
a Jew who has converted to Christianity remains a Jew,
albeit one who has done something he should not have
done. . . . Having established that we agree that you are a
Jew, we must now ask what significance this fact has for
the situation in which you find yourself. Let us start by at-
tempting to answer this question from a Jewish point of
view. Because you are a Jew, you are obligated, like all
Jews, to obey the *mitzvoth* (e.g. tefilin [phylacteries] in
the morning, kashrut, sabbath, etc.). Like all other Jews,
you are not perfect. You have violated some of the commandments of the Torah and you (and I) should repent of
these violations. If, in your conscience, your conversion
to Christianity is in accord with God's wishes and therefore not a sin, then you have no reason to repent of that
particular act. But in any case, from the Jewish point of
view you are obligated to live in accordance with the
mitzvoth just like any other Jew. . . . Are you not obligated
to obey the dietary laws, the sabbath, the Jewish festivals,

etc.? It is clear that such a decision could cause problems both for the Church and for Jews. But that cannot be the decisive issue. If you, in your conscience, become convinced that because you are a Jew you are obligated to lead a life in accordance with the Torah, then you must do so, no matter what the consequences.[27]

In a rejoinder article entitled "Response to the Respondents," Wyschogrod addresses the communal aspect of Messianic Judaism. He notes that rabbinic law cannot sanction a Messianic Jew's participation in acts that require a *minyan* (a quorum of ten Jews). This would include, for example, being counted in a *minyan* for prayer or serving as a valid witness in a rabbinic court.[28] There is no basis, however, to exclude Messianic Jews from other aspects of Jewish communal life that do not require a *minyan*.[29] Moreover, Wyschogrod regards Torah-observant Messianic Jewish congregations that promote "sustained Jewish Torah observance"[30] as completely acceptable, "No Torah-observing Jesus-believing communities have survived past the first few centuries. But if my advice is accepted, such communities will arise. It is better for Jews to obey some of the commandments of the Torah even if they disobey others."[31]

For a growing number of Orthodox Jews like Wyschogrod, Messianic Judaism is not that different from Conservative Judaism or Reform Judaism; some even view Messianic Judaism as closer to Orthodoxy. Jonathan Rosenblum, director of Jewish Media Resources, a leading Orthodox Jewish media organization, wrote in his weekly column in the *Jerusalem Post*:

Though American Jews may be certain that they are far better Jews than those who identify themselves as Messianic Jews, it would be a valuable thought experiment to ask themselves why. That question would force them to consider—perhaps for the first time—the crucial issue of what determines legitimacy of a particular belief or practice in Jewish terms. . . . Why is the acceptance of Jesus as the messiah more un-Jewish than rejection of God as lawgiver? Why is Jewish atheism less oxymoronic than Jewish Christianity? . . . How can 4,000 delegates to the recent Reform convention in Dallas gulp down non-kosher food without qualms? Messianic Jews accept most of Maimonides' 13 principles of faith; most American Jews would be hard-pressed to affirm more than a few, if they

knew what they were. Many groups of Messianic Jews are
halachically observant to a far greater degree than most
Reform and Conservative Jews. So why is one group
Jewishly illegitimate and the other legitimate? . . . The issue of legitimacy is not merely theoretical. It lies at the
heart of the pluralism debate in Israel today. If the state
puts its imprimatur on Reform conversions, why not on
those of Messianic Jews, who outnumber Reform Jews in
Israel today? . . . If neither history nor Halacha are any
longer a guide to legitimacy—as must be the case to classify the Reform and Conservative movements as merely
different 'streams' of Judaism—then history and Halacha
cannot be used to deny equal rights to Jews for J.[32]

Another prominent voice in the Jewish community is that of Marty
Lockshin, Professor of Rabbinics at York University. In Lockshin's article "Judaism, Christianity and Jewish-Christianity: What the Future
May Hold," he acknowledges that the Messianic Jewish community is
multiplying, "While precise statistics are difficult to find on this subject,
there is evidence that the phenomenon of Jewish Christianity is currently growing in numbers. There are ample reasons why a development like this might be occurring now, at the end of the twentieth
century, and why this tendency might grow even more in the twenty-
first century."[33] For Lockshin, the Jewish community's acceptance of
Messianic Judaism is almost inevitable due to several factors. First, the
Jewish community is exceedingly diverse. There is no standard of
Jewishness that can maintain present levels of inclusiveness and, with
consistency, exclude Messianic Judaism. Second, the Jewish Federations' standard of inclusiveness is Jewish self-identification and support
for Jewish continuity, a standard that Messianic Judaism meets. Finally,
Messianic Judaism has mass. There are presently over 250 Messianic
Jewish congregations in the United States and scores of others around
the world,[34] compared with only ninety-eight congregations in the
Reconstructionist movement.[35] For Lockshin, it is just a matter of time
before the Jewish community opens its doors to Messianic Judaism:

How long will the organized Jewish community succeed
in maintaining that the community is open to any and
all theologies and to atheists, to the widest varieties of
Jewish world outlooks, but it is not open to Jews who
believe that Jesus was the Messiah? How long will the
community say that one God is fine, no gods is fine, but
three-gods-who-are-one is unacceptable? How can an

atheist agree to cooperate with monotheists, but not with Trinitarians? How can the serious religious Jew find halakhic grounds for cooperating with atheists but find no grounds cooperating with Jewish-Christians? In what sense is Jewish Christianity halakhically worse than Jewish atheism? . . . Why should the value of pluralism extend to some groups but not to all? . . . Academic voices are beginning to argue that current Jewish opposition to messianic Judaism is illogical or worse. In a paper presented at the Association for Jewish Studies, Howard Bernstein argued, "If only messianic Judaism is condemned, on what rational basis does this condemnation lie? In view of the fragmentation of today's Jewish community and the wide variation of belief and practice ranging from Orthodoxy to humanistic and other Judaisms, not to mention the value placed on pluralism by so many Jews today, on what basis do they declare that messianic Jews are not Jews and that messianic Judaism is not Judaism?" As Federations grow in strength, as Federation identity begins to replace older forms of Jewish identity, what will be the fate of Jewish-Christians? Federations generally promote the one unassailable Jewish value—continuity. But they refuse to associate continuity with a specific set of Jewish values and they refuse to define who is a Jew. "What we need," they often say, "is to ensure that there will be more Jews (i.e. more people who call themselves Jews and are proud of that identity). If there really are 50,000 or more Jewish-Christians in the USA, and these people, presumably, take their Jewish identity seriously, how long will it be before these Jewish-Christians become part of the organized Jewish community? What factors other than inertia will isolate these people from Judaism? If all else remains the same (and it never does), I do not think that North American Judaism will continue to be an inclusive community that simply defines Judaism as un-Christianity. It seems inevitable that . . . [they] will take their place alongside of other Jewish denominations.[36]

The fact remains that no segment of the Jewish community is without its critics. Reform Judaism regards Reconstructionist Judaism as an aberration. Conservative Judaism regards Reform Judaism as illegitimate. Orthodox Judaism regards Conservative Judaism as outside the boundaries of Judaism. In his book *Must a Jew Believe Anything?*, Menachem Kellner, Professor of Jewish Religious Thought at Haifa University, writes:

> Orthodoxy is unwilling to do anything which might be construed as conferring legitimacy upon Conservative, Reform, and Reconstructionist Judaism. The reason for this is quite simple: non-Orthodox Judaism is heresy. This comes out very clearly in the many responsa of the late Rabbi Moses Feinstein (1892–1986), in which the subject comes up directly or indirectly. He forbids, for example, an Orthodox service in a Conservative synagogue building (not just in the main sanctuary, but in any room in the building), since 'it is well-known that they [Conservative Jews] are deniers [*koferim*] of many Torah laws'. Most Conservative and Reform rabbis can be assumed to be 'deniers of God and His Torah'. All the people buried in Reform cemeteries are 'evil-doers who have denied our holy Torah'.[37]

Ultra-Orthodox Judaism, likewise, views modern Orthodox Judaism as deviant. Reb Elya Meir Bloch, the Telshe *Rosh Yeshiva* (head of the Telshe seminary), summed up this attitude: "We no longer have to fear Conservatism—that is no longer the danger. Everyone knows that it is *avoda zara* [foreign worship; idolatry]. What we have to fear is modern Orthodoxy."[38] Within this no-denomination-is-fully-accepted framework, Messianic Judaism is receiving growing acceptance.

Voices of change can be heard across the Jewish spectrum, from Humanistic Judaism to Orthodox Judaism. Prominent Jewish leaders, like Rabbi Dan Cohn-Sherbok and Rabbi Sherwin Wine have stepped forward as advocates of the Messianic Jewish movement. Other leaders, like Dennis Prager, have called for partial acceptance of Messianic Jews in the Jewish community. Still others, like Michael Wyschogrod, have gone on record as supporting the existence of Torah-observant Messianic synagogues and Messianic Jewish involvement in all aspects of Jewish life where a *minyan* is not required. Finally, others like Rabbi Carol Harris-Shapiro, Rabbi David Berger, Jonathan Rosenblum and Marty Lockshin, are critics of a double standard that they acknowledge to be unacceptable. They are proponents of evenhandedness. The Jewish community cannot exclude Messianic Jews and simultaneously accept atheistic Jews and Chabad Hasidic Jews who regard their *rebbe* to be a divine Messiah. All of these Jewish leaders are profoundly aware that the classic boundaries of the Jewish faith vis-à-vis Christianity are changing before their very eyes, thus opening the door wide to Messianic Judaism.

Intermarried couples can be encouraged by this development. It means that an intermarried family no longer has to choose between being either Jewish or Christian. It is increasingly acceptable to be both and to raise one's children as Messianic Jews. Advocates (full and partial) for this option can be found in every branch of modern Judaism. There is really no cogent argument against Messianic Judaism for those who hold to the legitimacy of non-Orthodox expressions of Judaism. Even the ultra-Orthodox must admit that Messianic Jews should not be excluded on account of their theology, for the *Hasidim* too believe in a divine Messiah who died as a ransom for sin according to Isaiah 53 and is coming again to establish the kingdom of God on earth (see Appendix B).

# Prejudice, Insecurity, and Myths About Messianic Judaism

How is it that one can be a Jewish Buddhist, a Jewish New Ager, or even a Jewish atheist, but one cannot be a Jewish believer in Jesus the Messiah? Rabbi Harris-Shapiro notes:

> Under Messianic Jewish scrutiny, the American Jewish reasoning that accepts secular Jews but not Christian Jews as Jews, practicing Christian spouses of Jews as members of liberal synagogues but not Messianic Jews as members of liberal synagogues can appear fragile, fuzzy even self-contradictory.[1]

In my opinion, there is only one explanation for this double standard—prejudice. Prejudice is rooted in the emotions and is essentially irrational and self-contradictory.

## Disagreement and Prejudice are not the Same

It is one thing for a segment of the Jewish community to disagree with Messianic Jews over the Messiahship/divinity of Jesus; it is quite another for that group to harbor prejudice. The distinction between disagreement and prejudice is an important one. Prejudice goes beyond disagreement. According to Webster's dictionary, "prejudice" is:

1. A bias for or against something formed without sufficient basis.
2. Irrational intolerance of or hostility toward members of a certain race, religion, or group.[2]

Those who are intolerant of Messianic Judaism,. or simply oppose it without understanding it, reveal their prejudice. People can learn to disagree without crossing the line of prejudice. Opinions should be based on knowledge.

## Knowledge About Messianic Judaism

As previously mentioned, a number of academic studies on the Messianic Jewish community are available (see Appendix D). Additionally, *Messianic Judaism* by Dan Cohn-Sherbok is also a valuable scholarly work, the result of extensive research. However, the best way to learn about Messianic Judaism is to visit several congregations in your area.

## Human Relationships are the Key

Even after recognizing that a stereotype has no basis in fact, the lens of prejudice may still exist. Human relationships are key in breaking the bonds of prejudice. Even after many white southerners realized that their prejudice against blacks was unjust, their feelings remained unchanged. Often, their feelings prevailed until the white person developed a relationship with a black person and realized that both whites and blacks are part of the same human race. By developing relationships with Messianic Jews, Jews who don't believe that Yeshua is the Messiah may overcome their prejudice.

## The Insecurity of Anti-Jesus Judaism

Behind prejudice, concerns about Messianic Judaism are often rooted in the insecurity of anti-Jesus Judaism. American Jews have largely adopted a negative definition of what it means to be Jewish. When it comes right down to it, what makes many Jewish is that they are not Christian:[3]

> A group easily assimilable into the Christianized culture of the United States, as well as a group internally pluralistic in religious and ethnic practice, the Jewish community needs a sense of "who we are not" to maintain its group cohesion and integrity. The one surety for even the most inactive Jew is that "Jews are not Christians.[4]

Dennis Prager concurs that Jewishness for many Jews means being different from Christianity:

> A lifetime of work in Jewish life has convinced me that many Jew's beliefs are shaped more by reactions to Christianity rather than anything related to Judaism. Many Jews have adopted important beliefs and attitudes solely

because these beliefs are the opposite of what they believe Christianity and Christians believe.[5]

Hence, rejection of Messianic Judaism is often motivated by insecurity
about one's own Jewishness and the corresponding need for Jewish
validation. For such people, the removal of the "Jesus boundary line,"
through the growing acceptance of Messianic Judaism, means the di-
minishment of a clear sense of Jewishness in their lives. Consequently, they are defensive about the subject of Messianic Judaism.

## Myths About Messianic Judaism

One of the results of this prejudice-insecurity is the spread of myths
about Messianic Judaism. Intermarried couples who begin to explore
Messianic Judaism are likely, at some point, to encounter this unfortu-
nate reality.[6] Therefore, to help alleviate any concerns, I would like to
address each one of these myths and offer a thoughtful response. The
chief myths about Messianic Judaism are as follows:

Messianic Judaism is a missionary scheme.
Messianic Judaism is philo-Judaic Christianity.
Messianic Jews are not Jews.
Messianic Judaism is not Judaism.

### Myth #1: Messianic Judaism is a missionary scheme

Some say that Messianic Jewish congregations put on a veneer of religious Jewish practice in order to lure Jewish people into a belief in
Jesus.[7] It is suggested that Messianic Jews substitute Christian terms
with Hebrew equivalents in order to mask true Christian identity.[8] A
related argument is that Messianic synagogues misuse Jewish rituals
when they attach New Covenant meanings to them.[9]

Often, those who have never visited a Messianic synagogue or
taken the time to discuss their concerns about Messianic Judaism with
a Messianic rabbi protest the most. Those who do take the time to do
their homework discover that the allegations of deception are false.
Indeed, the culture of a Messianic congregation is based on a sincere
love for Torah and traditional Jewish heritage. Messianic rabbis, like
their traditional counterparts, recognize the dangers of assimilation
and work hard to convey Jewish identity to the next generation of
Messianic Jewish families. One Messianic Jewish leader has written:

There is absolutely no truth that Messianic congregations are merely for marketing. The men who lead these congregations have sacrificed quite a bit to do so. They endure ongoing criticism for the stand they have taken—from both the Jewish *and* Christian communities. . . . Messianic rabbis have deep convictions concerning their heritage. When we celebrate the Sabbath and other holidays, we do so with great joy, excitement and devotion to God. Our goal is not to see our Jewish members funneled into churches, but to see more and more Jewish believers who have assimilated into Gentile culture return to their Jewish roots—just the opposite of what we are accused of doing.[10]

Messianic Jewish use of Hebrew expressions (even for New Testament terms) is in keeping with this spirit of resisting assimilation pressures in order to preserve Jewish identity. In addition, it must be remembered that Jesus and the Apostles were Jews and taught in Hebrew. New Testament teaching was originally Hebraic. Messianic Judaism, therefore, sees the use of Hebraic New Covenant terminology, such as the name "Yeshua" instead of "Jesus," as a restoration of something that is historically accurate.[11] It links Messianic Jewish families to their first century roots. Shoshanah Feher observed in her doctoral research that "restoring the original" is a central focus of Messianic Judaism:

> Believers use the early church as a governing metaphor to reconcile Jewish with Christian symbols and to create a sense of historical community. Messianic Judaism has combed the past in order to create a new form of tradition (see also Morgan 1983). They make use of early texts, reading the Gospels and other first-century works, as well as tracing Jewish Christians through the centuries, in order to establish a symbolic social cohesion with roots in antiquity (see also Gusfield 1975; Hobsbawm 1983). . . . Messianic Jews use ritual to create a sense of continuity."[12]

Additionally, some Christian terms and symbols may be offensive to Messianic Jews and therefore are avoided in a Messianic synagogue. For example, almost all Jews are raised with a natural aversion to the term "Christ" as well as to the emblem of the cross[13] (since they are reminders of religious persecution). This feeling doesn't automatically change when one becomes a Messianic Jew. Substituting the Hebraic term "Messiah" for Christ and taking down crosses or covering them up (if a church building is used for *Shabbat* services), then, is not primarily for visitors but for the Messianic Jewish families themselves. The fact that Jewish visitors may have the same sensitivities only adds to the importance of the matter.

Finally, the fact that Messianic Jews inculcate some Jewish traditions with New Covenant meaning only supports the argument that Messianic Jews are up-front about their beliefs. It is natural that Jews would use Jewish ritual to express their devotion to God. Even Orthodox Jews believe that some Jewish ritual will be modified when the Messiah comes.[14] Messianic Jews agree and have made the necessary changes since, in their view, the Messiah has already come. The Messianic Jewish community is no different from the Reform and Reconstructionist communities that also engage in ritual formation to express the distinct values of their own branches of Judaism. Rabbi Harris-Shapiro concurs:

> Messianics are not the only ones to legitimate their Jewishness with religious ritual. Because ethnicity has been wrapped in a religious container, one of the only ways to express Jewish ethnicity is through religious language. . . . This would explain the use of Jewish ritual by groups who transform the meaning of the very rituals they use. The presence of the ritual confirms the Jewish ethnic orientation of the group, but the original meaning of the ritual has been altered to express the core values, not of traditional Judaism, but of the group utilizing the ritual. Even small portions of the ritual or liturgy are sufficient to give the value expressed a "Jewish flavor." . . . Liberal Jewish seders regularly transform the meaning of the traditional service from emphasizing the saving acts of God to the courage of humanity, as in the Reconstructionist Haggadah, which sharply elevates the role of humanity in the Passover story (Kaplan et al. 1941). Other holidays, such as Hanukkah, also reflect prevailing American values or secular Zionist achievements rather than a rabbinic religious message. . . . Just as Jewish religious forms express Jewish ethnicity or secular values in a number of transformed rituals, so too when Messianic believers sought to express ethnic continuity, they chose to infuse forms of Jewish life with new, Christological meaning.[15]

## Myth #2: Messianic Judaism is philo-Judaic Christianity

Sometimes Messianic Judaism is compared to philo-Judaic Christian groups (churches that observe Jewish customs such as the Sabbath).[16] The argument is that Messianic Judaism is just another Christian group that does Jewish things but is not Jewish.[17] Such a statement represents an ignorance of Messianic Judaism. To begin with, the Messianic Jewish movement is largely comprised of Jewish people and led by Jewish people.

> . . . the name Messianic Judaism implies that our movement is fundamentally among Jews and for Jews. It may include non-Jews, but it is oriented toward the Jewish people, and those non-Jews within it have a supportive role.[18]

This is a key distinction. Philo-Judaic groups are almost entirely non-Jewish in leadership and membership. Second, Messianic Jewish families are integrally connected to Jewish community life, even more so than most Jews. They often attend traditional Jewish synagogues, join Jewish Community Centers, take classes at Jewish colleges, work for Jewish organizations, support Jewish causes, shop at Jewish bookstores, and *shmooze* (pass the time talking) at Jewish delicatessens. Philo-Judaic Christian groups, on the other hand, generally do not involve themselves deeply in the Jewish community. Third, Messianic Judaism, by definition, claims to be a Judaism. It is a restoration of Nazarene Judaism in a twenty-first century context that seeks to enter into conversation with the traditions of our people. Philo-Judaic Christian groups do not make such a claim. They typically regard themselves as part of a religion that is separate and distinct from Judaism, albeit, one with Jewish roots. Finally, Messianic Judaism stands in agreement with Rabbinic Judaism that God's covenant faithfulness to Israel endures to this day. Messianic Jews see themselves as being under this covenant. In contrast, most philo-Judaic Christian groups are adherents of replacement theology and believe that God abandoned the Jewish people and made Christians the new people of God.

## Myth #3: Messianic Jews are not Jews

Sometimes it is said that Messianic Jews are no longer Jews because they believe in Jesus. There are several problems with this statement. First, it is historically inaccurate. Tens of thousands of first century Jews believed that Jesus was the Messiah and were accepted as Jews by the Jewish world.[19] Second, the view that Messianic Jews are no longer Jews may be based on insecurity. Jews who are insecure about their own identity may feel the need to exclude others from the Jewish community in order to enhance their own sense of Jewishness. This explains why it is often non-traditional Jews who make this statement.[20] Third, Orthodox Jews commonly acknowledge that Messianic Jews are Jews. Professor Michael Wyschograd is one such Orthodox rabbi who has written in support of this view. In his letter to a Jewish Christian friend, he writes:

> So I return to your claim that you remain a Jew in spite of having become a Christian. Is this a claim I can accept? Of course, I can. . . . Now the point is that once someone is a Jew, he always remains a Jew. . . . According to authentic Jewish teaching as I understand it, a Jew remains a Jew no matter what religion he adopts and this basic truth cannot be changed for political or prudential reasons.[21]

Rabbi Dan Cohn-Sherbok concurs:

> . . . Jewish law provides a clear basis for determining the status of a convert to another faith. According to the *halakhah*, it is technically impossible for a person born to a Jewish mother or converted to Judaism through the traditional procedure to change his status. . . . In the view of the medieval scholar Nahmanides, this attitude is based on the fact that the covenant between God and Israel was made 'with him that standeth here with us today before the Lord our God and also with him that is not with us here today' (Deuteronomy 29:14). For an individual who is born a Jew, Jewish identity is thus not a matter of choice: that person remains a Jew regardless of his religious beliefs.[22]

David Novak, Professor of Jewish Studies at the University of Toronto, sums up the Orthodox position in his essay "When Jews are Christians":

> The important thing to remember when dealing with the issue of the Jewish Christians is that according to normative Judaism, they are still Jews. . . . No one who accepts the authority of normative Judaism can rule that Jewish Christians are not Jews.[23]

The Orthodox view makes sense. In the Hebrew Bible, the Prophets re-buke Israel again and again for worshipping foreign gods but there is never an indication that the people are no longer Jews. The conclusion that Messianic Jews are Jews is also supported by the rulings of Rabbi Zadok ha-Kohen of Lublin and Rav Yosef Caro.[24]

As noted in Appendix D, many *Hasidim* believe that the Lubavitcher *rebbe* is the Messiah and the Creator of the Universe. Are they no longer Jews? Many second century Jews, including Rabbi Akiba, believed that Bar Kochba was the Messiah. Were they no longer Jews? And what of those Jews in the seventeenth century who believed that Sabbatai Sevi was the Messiah? Did they abandon their identity as Jews? Likewise, it is irrational to argue that Jews who believe Jesus is the Messiah are no longer Jews. The fact is that Jesus is the most famous Jew who ever lived. It is because of Yeshua ben Yosef (Jesus son of Joseph) that hundreds of millions of people on the earth worship the God of Israel and embrace the Scriptures of Israel as their own.[25] If one of the key roles of Messiah is to be a light to the nations, I can think of no other Jew as well qualified as Yeshua to be the Messiah. If you can be a Jewish Buddhist, or a Jewish atheist, you can certainly be a Jew who believes that Jesus is the Messiah.

### Myth #4: Messianic Judaism is not Judaism

Sometimes it is stated that Messianic Judaism is not a legitimate form of Judaism. The assumption here is that Rabbinic Judaism is the only form of normative Judaism. However, this was not the case two thou-sand years ago and it is not the case today. Philip Alexander, Professor of Jewish Studies at the University of Manchester, explains:

> Rabbinic Judaism cannot easily be equated with norma-tive Judaism before the third century C.E., and even then only in Palestine. The reason for this is that it was not until the third century that a majority of the Jews of Pales-tine accepted the authority of the Rabbinate.[26]

Today, authentic Rabbinic Judaism is anything but normative. Only six percent of American Jews are Orthodox.[27] The other ninety-four percent have rejected even the most basic tenets of Rabbinic Judaism. Based on the 1989 National Survey of American Jews, Steven Cohen has noted:

> If at one time Orthodoxy could successfully lay claim to near-exclusive authenticity among the laity, recent years

have seen an evaporation of the potency of that claim. Respondents today resoundingly reject Orthodoxy's assertion of primary authenticity. Just 18 percent agree with the statement "Part of me feels that Orthodox Jews are the most authentic Jews around," and even fewer (13 percent) agree with a parallel statement about Hasidic Jews (Note that the statements include the qualifier "part of me feels . . ." so as to elicit the broadest possible concurrence. Without the qualifier, it is likely that even fewer would have agreed.)[28]

If nonconformity to Rabbinic Judaism is the basis for Messianic Judaism's illegitimacy, then the same must hold true for every non-Orthodox form of Judaism, including Conservative and Reform. This is, in fact, the official position of Orthodox Judaism. All modern, non-Orthodox expressions of Judaism are considered illegitimate. Professor Cohn-Sherbok explains:

> According to traditionalists, there is only one legitimate form of the faith: Orthodox Judaism. Any deviation from *Torah*-observant Judaism as practiced by Jews through the centuries is heresy, no matter what its practitioners believe. In this connection it should be noted that this is true, not only of Messianic Judaism, but of all the non-Orthodox Jewish movements which currently exist in the modern world. Hence, not only is Messianic Judaism an illegitimate interpretation of Judaism, so too is Conservative Judaism, Reform Judaism, Reconstructionist Judaism, and Humanistic Judaism. The Orthodox model thus not only excludes Messianic Judaism from the circle of authentic Judaism, but also excludes all other branches of Judaism in contemporary society.[29]

The irrationality of the Orthodox view is evident when one considers that Messianic Judaism has its origins in Second Temple Judaism and actually predates the formation of Rabbinic Judaism.[30] Into the second century, the Nazarene sect of Judaism was widely accepted in the Jewish world as an authentic expression of Judaism.[31]

In addition, it can be argued that Messianic Judaism is more within the boundaries of Torah, the foundational document of Judaism, than other non-traditional forms of Judaism (see Appendix D).[32] Take Reconstructionist Judaism as an example. Reconstructionist Judaism formally removed God from Judaism,[33] claiming that the Torah is not the Word of God and Israel is not the Chosen People.[34] By contrast, Messianic Judaism proclaims the existence of the King of the Universe, upholds all Scripture as the Word of God, and affirms that Israel is God's instrument of blessing in the world. On these grounds, Messianic Judaism is arguably more in line with the central teachings of Judaism (biblically and historically) than Reconstructionist Judaism. If Reconstructionist Judaism and other non-faith expressions of Judaism are legitimate, then so is Messianic Judaism.[35]

Finally, there is a growing acceptance of Messianic Judaism in the American Jewish community (see Appendix D). The "pluralist" view, as represented by Rabbi Cohn-Sherbok and Rabbi Wine, anticipates a day to come when the mainstream Jewish community will more broadly recognize Messianic Judaism as an integral and vibrant expression of modern Judaism.

All of the above myths about Messianic Judaism ultimately stem from prejudice, insecurity, and *lashon ha-ra* (negative comments or rumors). As stated earlier, prejudice is irrational and rooted in the emotions. Over time, a person's views may change, especially if they are held them up to scrutiny or meet a Messianic Jew who shatters their stereotype. If you are an intermarried couple or a child of intermarriage, and would like to explore the Messianic Jewish option, don't let prejudice stand in your way. Visit a Messianic Jewish congregation and see for yourself what it's like. You may find it to be a good fit for your family.

# Endnotes

## Introduction

1. Phillips, "Children of Intermarriage: How 'Jewish'?," 81. See Chenkin, Kaplan, and Massarik 15.
2. Hevesy.
3. Commission on Reform Jewish Outreach, *Working With Interfaith Couples: A Jewish Perspective—A Guide for Facilitators*, 109–110.
4. Goodman-Malamuth and Margolis 72.
5. Samuelson 92; Wasserman 2; Brown, "Six Success Strategies for Intermarried Couples," 4.
6. From personal correspondence.
7. Yeshua is Jesus' original Hebrew name. See Barnstone 457–467.
8. Cohn-Sherbok xii.

## Chapter One

1. 1.5 million people are intermarried (Keysar, Kosmin, and Scheckner 48) and 1.5 million adults are the children of intermarriage (Mayer, Kosmin, and Keysar 5). Since two thirds of the offspring of intermarriage intermarry, a significant overlap exists between these two groups (Grossman 214). In addition, there are also 664,000 children under the age of 18 who are children of intermarriage (Keysar, Kosmin, and Scheckner 48).
2. Mayer, Kosmin, and Keysar 6.
3. Abrams 9. See Fishkoff 76.
4. Wertheimer 107.
5. Abrams 107.
6. Abrams 108. See Winer, Seltzer, and Schwager 131, 141.
7. Lazerwitz, et al. 101.
8. Lazerwitz, et al. 102.
9. Silverstein 45.
10. Jewish Outreach Institute 2.
11. Abrams 109–110.
12. Schneider 230.
13. Keysar, Kosmin, and Scheckner 49.
14. Abrams 111–112. See Mayer, *Children of Intermarriage*, 24, 29.
15. Mayer, "Will the Grandchildren of Intermarriage be Jews? The Chances are Greater than You Think," 78.
16. Sacks, *Will We Have Jewish Grandchildren?*, 2.

## Chapter Two

1. Petsonk and Remsen 111.
2. Seigel and Seigel 17.
3. Hawxhurst 8.
4. Petsonk and Remsen 17.
5. Petsonk and Remsen 321–322.
6. Commission on Reform Jewish Outreach of the Union of American Hebrew Congregations and the Central Conference of American Rabbis, *Outreach and the Changing Reform Jewish Community: Creating an Agenda for Our Future*, 86. Lazerwitz, et al., 100, notes that Jewish women today are as likely as Jewish men to intermarry.
7. McClain 135.
8. Lazerwitz, et al. 108.
9. Petsonk and Remsen 10.
10. Sacks, *Will We Have Jewish Grandchildren?*, 61.
11. Sacks, *Will We Have Jewish Grandchildren?*, 75.
12. McClain 17.
13. Commission on Reform Jewish Outreach of the Union of American Hebrew Congregations and the Central Conference of American Rabbis, *Outreach and the Changing Reform Jewish Community: Creating an Agenda for Our Future*, 7.

## Chapter Three

1. Seigel and Seigel 31.
2. In the ancient Near East, the wife was expected to embrace the religious identity of her husband's family. See Appendix A.
3. There is no evidence that a formal conversion ceremony existed for converts prior to the Second Temple period. The marriage ceremony itself implied the conversion of religious identity (Cohen, *The Beginnings of Jewishness*, 170). See Klayman, "Who is a Jew? The Concept of Conversion," 3–20.
4. According to the 1990 National Jewish Population Study, in the mainstream Jewish community there are approximately 65,000 people who "identify themselves as Jewish even though they were not born Jewish and did not undergo formal conversion. These people are Jewish by self-definition" (Hirt-Manheimer 253).
5. Schneider, 10, uses this definition.
6. Some rabbis encouraged a severing of all ties with the convert's family.
7. Baskin, "The Rabbinic Transformations of Rahab the Harlot," 141–157; Porton 258 n. 99; Bamberger 193–195, 214 n. 99.

8. Cohen, *The Beginnings of Jewishness*, 376–377.
9. See Appendix A for a discussion of formal versus informal conversion.

## Chapter Four

1. Cohen, *The Beginnings of Jewishness*, 242–243. See Klayman, "Who is a Jew? The Concept of Kin," 3–16.
2. Cohen, *The Beginnings of Jewishness*, 255.
3. This view is based on Ezra 9:1–2. See Cohen, *The Beginnings of Jewishness*, 243–244; Kaufmann 337–339; Fishbane 115–118.
4. Cohen, *The Beginnings of Jewishness*, 260–261.
5. Hayes 24–26, 228–230.
6. Seigel and Seigel 32. Bleich, 270–274, notes that while Maimonides sided with the majority view (*Mishneh Torah, Hilkhot Issurei Bi'ah* 12:1), the *Tur* sided with the minority position that only the Seven Nations are explicitly at issue in the Torah prohibition, albeit subsequent to conversion (*Tur Shulhan Arukh, Even ha-Ezer* 16).
7. Seigel and Seigel 33.
8. Patai and Patai 99–100.
9. Patai and Patai 104. See Yehiel 42.
10. Patai and Patai 103. See Hirschberg 169, 181, 199, 251, 318 n. 66.
11. Patai and Patai 102–103.

## Chapter Five

1. Poliakov 1483.
2. The *King James Version* of the Bible translates Acts 17:26 as "And hath made of one blood all nations of men." This translation, "one blood," is based on a variant reading that also stresses the concept of a human race.
3. UMJC Theology Committee, "Defining Messianic Judaism: Addendum 1. What do we mean by 'Jewish'?"
4. For a survey of modern views on race, see Harrison.
5. Parallel to the anthropological argument is the Kabbalistic view that Jews and Gentiles have different kinds of souls. See Wijnhoven 51. Many Orthodox Jews today believe that when a Gentile converts to Judaism he/she literally receives a Jewish soul. This has no basis in Scripture and is akin to racial theory on a metaphysical level.
6. Seltzer 11.
7. Patai and Patai 5.
8. Commission on Reform Jewish Outreach of the Union of American Hebrew Congregations and the Central Conference of American

Rabbis, *Outreach and the Changing Reform Jewish Community: Creating an Agenda for Our Future*, 96.

9. Siegel and Rheins 534.

10. See books by Bamberger, Braude, Feldman, Porton, Raisin, Epstein, Rosenbloom, Eichorn, Schwartz, Tobin, Jacob and Zemer, Homolka.

11. Rosenbloom 38.

12. Goodman and McKnight have challenged the majority view in arguing that Judaism did not become a missionary religion until the Rabbinic era. Feldman, 288–382, however, presents compelling evidence (following Moore, Bamberger, Braude, Raisin, Rosenbloom, and others) that Jewish missionary activity in the Second Temple period was widespread and successful.

13. Rosenbloom 93–117.

14. Rosenbloom 79; Wacholder 106.

15. Rosenbloom 79.

16. B. Sanh. 96b; Git. 57b; Sifre Num. 7 on 5:12; McKnight 32.

17. Prager, "Judaism Must Seek Converts," 91.

18. Nadich 10.

19. McClain 207. The 2001 AJIS Report estimated 170,000 converts (Mayer, Kosmin, and Keysar 20).

20. Hirt-Manheimer 4–5.

21. Hirt-Manheimer 5.

22. Hirt-Manheimer 253.

23. Primack 147–151.

24. Cowen v–vi.

25. See Blady, Parfitt, and Strizower.

26. Brook 305–306. See Wexler, *The Ashkenazic Jews*, 241–267.

27. Wexler, *The Non-Jewish Origins of the Sephardic Jews*, 229.

28. Patai and Patai 332.

29. McKeever presents this view in *Claim Your Birthright.*

30. See Appendix A for a discussion of formal versus informal conversion.

## Chapter Six

1. Phillips, "Children of Intermarriage: How 'Jewish'?," 93.

2. King, 3, concludes: "Most of the intermarried parents I met had told their children they were half-Christian and half-Jewish, or that they were both . . . Their Jewish/Christian children tended to know something about both religions but did not feel they belonged to either one." Goodman-Malamuth and Margolis, 33–34, confirm King's results in their case studies of Jewish/Christian children, concluding:

". . . most said that their interfaith parents had not presented more than a spotty, superficial view of Judaism and Christianity."

3. Petsonk and Remsen 194.

4. McClain 134, 137.

5. Shore 3.

6. Petsonk and Remsen 193–194.

7. Silverstein 45.

8. Mayer, *Love & Tradition*, 176.

9. Jewish spouses are generally unwilling to convert to Christianity for the sake of the children. According to the 1990 National Jewish Population Study, less than 1 percent converted (Lazerwitz, et al. 108–109).

10. These figures are from the 1993 Survey on Mixed Marriage conducted by Bruce Phillips. For the methodology of the study, see Phillips, "Children of Intermarriage: How 'Jewish'?," 82–85. The Phillips study is cited twice in the *2000 American Jewish Year Book* (DellaPergola, et al., "Prospecting the Jewish Future: Population Projections, 2000–2080," 128; Grossman 212–213).

11. Phillips, *Re-examining Intermarriage*, 49; Phillips, "Children of Intermarriage: How 'Jewish'?," 107–108. Phillips notes that the 1990 NJPS estimated 32 percent.

12. Phillips, "Children of Intermarriage: How 'Jewish'?," 108.

13. Phillips, "Children of Intermarriage: How 'Jewish'?," 108.

14. Phillips, "Children of Intermarriage: How 'Jewish'?," 107–108. "According to the NJPS of 1990, 20 percent of the children under 18 in intermarriages are currently Jewish" (Phillips, "Children of Intermarriage: How 'Jewish'?," 107). The Phillips study did not address marriages in which the non-Jewish spouse converted to Judaism (these were regarded as "in-marriages"), so the 18 percent figure would be slightly higher if the children of such parents were included (Phillips, *Re-examining Intermarriage*, 44).

15. "The largest category . . . of intermarried families, is the 'Christian' family, so named because it contains at least one identified Christian and no religiously identified Jew. It is made up of one of three possible combinations: (1) a 'Jewish Christian' married to a Gentile Christian; (2) a secular Jew married to a Gentile Christian; or (3) a Jewish Christian married to a secular Gentile. The 'Jewish Christians' identify as Christians by religion, and as Jews by ethnicity. In most cases they come from intermarried families of origin and were at least nominally raised as Christians" (Phillips, "Children of Intermarriage: 'How Jewish'?," 93).

16. Mayer, Kosmin, and Keysar 37.

17. Phillips, "Children of Intermarriage: How 'Jewish'?," 111.

## Chapter Seven

1. The Phillips study found that 12 percent of all intermarriages involve a Jewish Christian spouse married to a Gentile of no religion. An additional 28 percent of all mixed marriages are "made up of two Christians, one of whom is the adult child of a mixed marriage who was raised as a Christian" (Phillips, *Re-examining Intermarriage*, 47–48).

2. There are 808,500 adult children of intermarriage who were raised in a religion other than Judaism (Mayer, Kosmin, and Keysar 23). Of the total number of Jews raised from birth in other religions (JOR = 1,470,000), 396,900 (27%) have only a Jewish mother and 411,600 (28%) have only a Jewish father. In addition, there are 484,000 children of intermarried Jews who are being raised in a religion other than Judaism (Mayer, Kosmin, and Keysar 22–23); this figure is derived by taking the percentage of the intermarried population among Jews raised from birth in other religions (JOR = 55%) and multiplying it by the total number of Jewish children under 18 who are raised from birth in another religion (JCOR = 880,000). The total number of children of intermarriage is thus 808,500 + 484,000. On top of this are 102,900 adults who were raised by two Jewish parents in a religion other than Judaism (Mayer, Kosmin, and Keysar 23); the majority of these people are intermarried. In sum, the total number of adults and children of Jewish background who were raised in a religion other than Judaism is 1,395,400. According to the 1993 Survey on Mixed Marriage, the number of children raised in a religion other than Judaism or Christianity is statistically negligible; two percent were raised in *both* Judaism and a religion other than Christianity (Phillips, "Children of Intermarriage: 'How Jewish'?," 108). Thus, it is fair to say that at least 95 percent of all children of mixed marriage raised in a religion other than Judaism are being raised in Christianity. This extrapolates to more than one million Christians of Jewish background.

3. DellaPergola, "New Data on Demography and Identification Among Jews in the U.S.," 86.

4. Philip Cohen was editor of *The Messianic Jew*, a journal for the "Jewish Messianic Movement" in South Africa.

5. Cohen, *The Hebrew Christian and His National Continuity*, 37.

6. Kohn, "Ethnic Judaism and the Messianic Movement," 89.

7. Glaser 159.

8. Some intermarried couples, for example, are taught that the Church has replaced Israel or that there is no longer a Jew/Gentile distinction in the kingdom of God (Gal 3:11). For a Messianic Jewish response, see Juster 111–112 and Stern, *Jewish New Testament Commentary*.

9. In his study of adult children of intermarriage who were raised Christian, Phillips found that "one out of four reported that they lit Hanukkah candles, and almost one out of five attended a *seder*. This is not a fluke. The Jewish leanings of this group of Jews raised as Christians are evident throughout the analysis" (Phillips, *Re-examining Intermarriage*, 47–48). Additionally, Phillips (1997), 56, found that 15% were raising their children as "both Jewish and Christian." These parents "feel strongly that their children should know something about Jewish culture and history and they even feel strongly that their children should care about Israel. Their links to the Jewish people, though weak, are acknowledged" (Phillips [1997] 64).

## Chapter Eight

1. A revised and updated version of Gruzen's book was published in May 2001.
2. From the 1975 seminar "Jews and Christians Between Past and Future." The quote is thesis 56 on "The emergence of Christianity from Judaism."
3. Pritz 108, Paget 774. Meyers, 76, on the basis of archaeological evidence, conjectures that some "Jewish and (Jewish-) Christian communities apparently continued to live in harmony until the seventh century."
4. Oskar Skarsaune, Professor of Patristic Studies and Early Church History at the Free Faculty of Theology in Oslo, is conducting "a major ongoing research project called The History of Jewish Believers in Jesus from Antiquity to the Present" (Skarsaune 445). See www.casparicenter.org. The 2001 Colloquium "The Image of the Judaeo-Christians in Ancient Jewish and Christian Literature," sponsored by the Institutum Iudaicum, Brussels, November 18–19, is also indicative of the growing scholarly interest in early Jewish believers in Jesus. For published studies on the early Jewish Christians, see Paget, Taylor, Hagner (1997), Visotzky, Mimouni, Katz, Bagatti, Bauckham (1990, 1998 ["Jews and Jewish Christians..."]), Alexander, De Boer, Saldarini (1992), Boyarin, Segal, Horbury (*Jews and Christians...*), Schiffman (1981, 1985), Klijn (1973, 1974), Kraft, Murray (1974, 1982), Simon, Malina, Riegel, and Schonfield.
5. Ausubul 101. See Bockmuehl, Hagner (1984), Vermes (1973, 1983), Charlesworth (1991, 1997), Flusser (1969), Sanders, Young, and Lee.
6. Neusner (1987), Collins, Patai (1979), Charlesworth (1992, 1998), Oegema, Hurtado, Bauckham (*God Crucified*), Horbury (*Jewish Messianism...*), and Newman.
7. Ausubul 106.

8. Luke-Acts may be an exception to this statement. It is not clear if Luke was a Jew, a convert to Judaism, or a God-fearing Gentile.

9. Acts 11:20, 26; "Harnack makes the following observation: 'The name 'Christians' is the title of Gentile-Christians; at first and probably through a long period, Jewish-Christians were never called by this name.' In a footnote he explains that, to his knowledge, there is no old Christian document where Jews are called 'Christians.' This was entirely a Gentile designation" (Jocz 180).

10. Cook 6; Commission on Reform Jewish Outreach, *Working With Interfaith Couples: A Jewish Perspective—A Guide for Facilitators*, 180–184.

11. Cook 4–5.

12. Nerel, "Primitive Jewish Christians in the Modern Thought of Messianic Jews," 400–401.

13. Juster 1.

14. There is a difference in hermeneutical approach between Messianic Judaism and classic Gentile Christianity: "It has been said that Gentile Christian theology moves from the Pauline epistles backward and finds justification in the Old Testament, whereas Messianic Jewish theology should start with *Torah* and move forward to new *Torah* discoveries that would not have been found without the New Testament" (Stern, *Messianic Jewish Manifesto*, 90–91; see Gruber 5–13).

15. Cohn-Sherbok 178.

16. Phillips, *Re-examining Intermarriage*, 45; Phillips, "Children of Intermarriage: How 'Jewish'?," 101.

17. Klein and Vuijst 7–8.

18. Klein and Vuijst xxii. From an essay by David Biale in *Insider/Outsider: American Jews and Multiculturalism*.

19. Schiffman, "Intermarriage Can Have an Adverse Effect on Messianic Judaism," 112.

20. Samuelson 92; Wasserman 2.

21. Nerel, "Primitive Jewish Christians in the Modern Thought of Messianic Jews," 402.

## Chapter Nine

1. Kac, *The Messiahship of Jesus*, 36.
2. Kac, *The Messiahship of Jesus*, 27.
3. Hawxhurst 24.

## Chapter Ten

1. Commission on Reform Jewish Outreach of the Union of American Hebrew Congregations and the Central Conference of American Rabbis, *Outreach and the Changing Reform Jewish Community: Creating*

*an Agenda for Our Future*, 86. The gender gap has closed since 1989. Today, "Jewish men and women are now just about equally likely to marry non-Jews" (Lazewitz, et al. 100).

2. Lazerwitz, et al. 108.

## Chapter Fourteen

1. Mayer, Kosmin, and Keysar 5; Keysar, Kosmin, and Scheckner 48.
2. Goodman-Malamuth and Margolis 19.
3. Goodman-Malamuth and Margolis 189–190.
4. Mayer, "*Hold the Angst*: Sooner or Later the Children Grow Up," 3.
5. Klein and Nuijst 5, 7.
6. Goodman-Malamuth and Margolis 24.
7. Goodman-Malamuth and Margolis 43.
8. Eaton 60–61.
9. Harris-Shapiro 79.

## Chapter Fifteen

1. Kohn, "Ethnic Judaism and the Messianic Movement," 90.
2. DellaPergola, "New Data on Demography and Identification Among Jews in the U.S.," 86.
3. DellaPergola, "New Data on Demography and Identification Among Jews in the U.S.," 84.
4. Feher 140–142.
5. Harris-Shapiro 186.
6. Stern, *Messianic Jewish Manifesto*, 61.
7. Kinzer, *The Nature of Messianic Judaism*, 11.
8. UMJC Theology Committee, "Defining Messianic Judaism: Basic Statement," 1.
9. Pritz 108, Paget 774, Meyers 76.
10. Nerel, "Primitive Jewish Christians in the Modern Thought of Messianic Jews," 424.
11. Karaite Jews regard the Hebrew Bible as their sole authority for faith and life; Oral Torah (i.e. Rabbinic law as derived from Talmud) is not authoritative. See Schur 11. Pines, 48, suggests that "there exists some reason for thinking that at a certain period close relations existed between groups of Qaraites and groups of Jewish Christians."
12. According to Rabbinic tradition, even the Torah will undergo some change in the Messianic era. See Davies 50–83; Chayoun 96–98.
13. Ritterband 100–101.
14. See Mark 7:6–13. "It is crucial to understand that the highest authority and court of appeal for all teaching in Messianic Judaism is the Bible. . . . As Messianic Jews, we may gain wisdom and insight from

our Jewish tradition. The tradition, however, is to be tested by the Bible . . . that which is consistent with the Scriptures can be accepted; that which is inconsistent must be rejected. The Bible is the final rule of faith and practice." (Juster 158, 163).

15. Harris-Shapiro 42.

16. Cohn-Sherbok 211.

17. Feher 78.

18. Harris-Shapiro 108–109.

19. Feher 139.

20. Feher 103; Harris-Shapiro 142–143.

21. Harris-Shapiro 146.

22. Harris-Shapiro 96.

23. DellaPergola, "New Data on Demography and Identification Among Jews in the U.S.," 75.

24. For an example of Messianic Jewish *Rosh HaShanah* liturgy, see Cohn-Sherbok 113–117.

25. Cohn-Sherbok 118.

26. Feher 106.

27. For an example of Messianic Jewish *Sukkot* liturgy, see Cohn-Sherbok 110–111.

28. Cohn-Sherbok 110.

29. For an example of Messianic Jewish *Simchat Torah* liturgy, see Cohn-Sherbok 125–127.

30. Cohn-Sherbok 111.

31. For an example of Messianic Jewish Hanukkah liturgy, see Cohn-Sherbok 129.

32. Feher 107.

33. Harris-Shapiro 147. Messianic Jews recall the Messiah's birth in ways other than Christmas. Some recall it monthly on the *Rosh Chodesh* (New Moon) based on Col. 2:16–17. See Rudolph, *The Voice of the Lord: Messianic Jewish Daily Devotional*, Appendix A, iii. Others recall Yeshua's birth during the festival of *Sukkot*, a more likely time for the shepherds to be in the Bethlehem fields (Luke 2:8). It should not be forgotten that the celebration of Christmas was unknown to the Apostles; its origins can be traced to the time of Constantine in the fourth century and has little to do with the actual date of Yeshua's birth (Miles 20–23).

34. There are no statistics available as to what percentage of Messianic Jewish intermarried families have Christmas trees. However, the numbers are probably less than the mainstream Jewish community where 10–18 percent of Jewish-Jewish couples and 62–80 percent of Jewish-Gentile couples have Christmas trees. See McClain 140; Cohen, "Rais-

ing Children in an Interfaith Family: Mixed Marrieds Speak," 104–105.

35. Feher 109.

36. Cohn-Sherbok 130.

37. Easter is historically and theologically rooted in the celebration of Passover. It was originally observed on the same day as Passover and called *pascha* by the early Church Fathers. See Bradshaw and Hoffman, Bacchiocchi, Broadhurst, Saldarini (1984), Stallings, and Cantalamessa.

38. For an example of Messianic Jewish *Shavu'ot* liturgy, see Cohn-Sherbok 107–108.

39. Cohn-Sherbok 144.

40. For an example of Messianic Jewish *B'rit Milah* liturgy, see Cohn-Sherbok 144–145.

41. Harris-Shapiro 153–154. My father, Michael Rudolph, was the first Messianic Jewish *mohel* certified by the Union of Messianic Jewish Congregations.

42. For an example of Messianic Jewish *Bar/Bat Mitzvah* liturgy, see Cohn-Sherbok 149–150.

43. For an example of Messianic Jewish Wedding liturgy, see Cohn-Sherbok 151–153.

44. ". . . (as long as the cemetery is privately or corporately owned, rather than owned by a synagogue) cemetery officials generally won't inquire into the status of the dead person unless someone raises the issue" (Petsonk and Remsen 322).

45. Cohn-Sherbok 155.


## Appendix A

1. Some synagogues in the movement are under the authority of regional, national or international Messianic *beit din*s (courts of law). This may be the direction of the Messianic movement as standards of rabbinical ordination are increasingly defined by umbrella organizations like the Union of Messianic Jewish Congregations (UMJC) and the Messianic Jewish Alliance of America (MJAA).

2. Schiffman, "Intermarriage Can Have an Adverse Effect on Messianic Judaism," 113.

3. Riggans, "Messianic Jews and the Definition of Jewishness," 240, n. 6.

4. "Messianic Judaism has functionally decided to agree with the Reform Jewish ruling that descent from either parent who is Jewish makes one Jewish, if one maintains some connection with Jewish community and practice. This usage, although not officially sanctioned, seems to be almost universal among us . . ." Russ Resnik,

"Commentary on Defining Messianic Judaism: Addendum 1. What do we mean by 'Jewish'?"

5. Russ Resnik, "Commentary on Defining Messianic Judaism: Addendum 1. What do we mean by 'Jewish'?"

6. Hiat and Zlotowitz 43–48; Zlotowitz 129–135.

7. Cohen, *The Beginnings of Jewishness*, 156.

8. Hiat and Zlotowitz 43–48. For a critical response to the patrilineal argument and its implications, see Gordis; Bayme, "Patrilineal Descent Revisited," 137–145.

9. Cohen, *The Beginnings of Jewishness*, 266.

10. Qiddushin 3:12.

11. Bava Batra 109b. See Cohen, *The Beginnings of Jewishness*, 264.

12. Hyman 224.

13. Hirt-Manheimer 264.

14. Cohen, *The Beginnings of Jewishness*, 283.

15. McClain 197.

16. Alpert and Staub 57–58.

17. Hirt-Manheimer 264–265.

18. McClain 280.

19. Mayer, "American-Jewish Outreach in the 1990s and Beyond," 53.

20. Hawxhurst 150–151.

21. Mayer, "American-Jewish Outreach in the 1990s and Beyond," 53.

22. Hirt-Manheimer 266.

23. Cohen, *The Beginnings of Jewishness*, 267.

24. See Hayes, 27–34, for a discussion of views by Epstein, Milgrom, Klawans, Fishbane, and Olyan. I am not convinced by Hayes' argument that Ezra and Nehemiah instituted a "prohibition of intermarriage with all Gentiles" to preserve "genealogical purity." Even Hayes, 33, admits that "many postexilic biblical sources advance the integrationist approach characteristic of the First Temple period."

25. Klayman, "Who is a Jew? The Concept of Kin," 9–11.

26. Cohen, *The Beginnings of Jewishness*, 244.

27. Cohen, *The Beginnings of Jewishness*, 285–307.

28. Cohen, *The Beginnings of Jewishness*, 273. See Klayman, "The Offspring of Intermarriage: The Matrilineal Principle," 15–18.

29. Rudolph, "Intermarriage, Proselytes & The Next Generation." It is important to remember that formal conversion ceremonies did not exist until the Second Temple period (Cohen, *The Beginnings of Jewishness*, 109–110).

30. A precedent for covenant declaration is found in the complete edition of the *Shulchan Aruch* (Code of Jewish Law). See Yoreh Deah 268; trans. Eichhorn 108. According to the 1990 National Jewish

Population Study, in the mainstream Jewish community there are approximately 65,000 people who "identify themselves as Jewish even though they were not born Jewish and did not undergo formal conversion. These people are Jewish by self-definition" (Hirt-Manheimer 253).

31. McClain, 215, notes that some rabbis today use the term "common law Jew."

32. Cohen, *The Beginnings of Jewishness*, 265.

33. I am grateful to Carl Kinbar for pointing this out to me.

34. Stern, *Messianic Jewish Manifesto*, 175–180; Juster 192, 235; Rudolph, "Proselytes to Israel in a Messianic Jewish Congregation"; Fischer, "Messianic Jewish Conversion: Is it Viable?," 30–49; Fischer, "The Legitimacy of Conversion," 141–149; Schiffman, "Conversion of Gentiles Within Messianic Judaism."

## Appendix B

1. Luke may be the one exception (Col. 4:10–14). Some have suggested that he was a Gentile God-fearer who worshiped in the synagogue. Others question whether the Luke of Colossians 4 is the same person who wrote Luke-Acts.

2. Berger, *The Rebbe, the Messiah and the Scandal of Orthodox Indifference*, 53; Brown, *Answering Jewish Objections to Jesus: Theological Objections*, 228.

3. Reventlow 24; Kac, *The Messianic Hope*, 75.

4. Fishbane, "Midrashic Theologies of Messianic Suffering," 73–85; Patai, *The Messiah Texts*, 104–121, 165–170; Dubov 63–64;

5. Driver and Neubauer 258.

6. Driver and Neubauer 319–322,

7. Driver and Neubauer 153.

8. Driver and Neubauer 7.

9. Driver and Neubauer 9.

10. Driver and Neubauer 14–15.

11. Driver and Neubauer 399.

12. Driver and Neubauer 5.

13. Driver and Neubauer 11.

14. Driver and Neubauer 10–11.

15. Driver and Neubauer 374.

16. Driver and Neubauer 32.

17. Driver and Neubauer 386.

18. Driver and Neubauer 23–24.

19. Driver and Neubauer 99–100.

## Appendix D

1. For example, Rabbi Moshe Feinstein, the "single most influential halakhic decisor of the second half of the twentieth century," referred to Conservative and Reform rabbis as "deniers, sectarians, heretics, evil-doers, enticers [to sin] and corrupters" (Kellner 88). In 1945, the founder of Reconstructionist Judaism, Mordecai Kaplan, was denounced by Conservative rabbis and excommunicated by the Union of Orthodox Rabbis (of which he was not a member) for "expressing atheism, heresy and disbelief in the basic tenets of Judaism." They also burned the Reconstructionist prayer book (Raphael 184).
2. Berkman 2.
3. Rottenberg, "Those Troublesome Messianic Jews," 114–115. Though the opposition is strong, Messianic Jewish participation in the Jewish-Christian dialogue is growing, as evidenced by the recent exchange in Princeton Theological Review: Charry, "The Other Side of the Story," 24–29; Kinbar 30–37; Charry, "Response to Carl Kinbar," 38–39. See also Rottenberg, *Jewish Christians in an Age of Christian-Jewish Dialogue*; Glasser 105–117; Finto 189–193; Freedman 86; Kung 584–600.
4. Mayer, Kosmin, and Keysar 58.
5. Mayer, Kosmin, and Keysar 58; cf. 60, 67.
6. DellaPergola, "New Data on Demography and Identification Among Jews in the U.S.," 86.
7. Berkman 1.
8. Berkman 2.
9.  Cohn-Sherbok 209–210.
10. Cohn-Sherbok 212.
11. Cohn-Sherbok 212–213.
12. Werthheimer 79.
13. Mayer, Kosmin, and Keysar 6.
14. Harris-Shapiro 168.
15. Prager, "A New Approach to Jews-for-Jesus," 29.
16. Berger, *The Rebbe, the Messiah and the Scandal of Orthodox Indifference*, 2, 14–15.
17. Prager, "A New Approach to Jews-for-Jesus," 28.
18. According to Orthodox *halakhah*, Messianic Jews are Jews who have lost certain communal privileges due to apostasy. See Wyschogrod, "Letter to a Friend," 167–168; Harris-Shapiro 179–181; Cohn-Sherbok 200–201, 206.
19. October 24, 1999. Used with permission of the writer.
20. Berger, *The Rebbe, the Messiah and the Scandal of Orthodox Indifference*, 26.

21. Berger, *The Rebbe, the Messiah and the Scandal of Orthodox Indifference*, 89.
22. Berger, "The Rebbe, the Jews, and the Messiah," 24.
23. Grossman 226.
24. Berger, "The Rebbe, the Jews, and the Messiah," 25.
25. Berger, *The Rebbe, the Messiah and the Scandal of Orthodox Indifference*, 130–131.
26. Berger, "The Rebbe, the Jews, and the Messiah," 23–24, 149.
27. Wyschogrod, "Letter to a Friend," 166–168, 171.
28. See Novak 100.
29. Wyschogrod, "Response to the Respondents," 237.
30. Wyschogrod, "Response to the Respondents," 237.
31. Wyschogrod, "Response to the Respondents," 239.
32. See Rosenblum, "The ultimate Jewish pluralists."
33. Lockshin 137.
34. Samuelson 92; Wasserman 2.
35. Grossman 223.
36. Lockshin 144–146.
37. Kellner 88.
38. Kellner 89, n. 3; Keller 3–14; repr. in Bulka 253.

## Appendix E

1. Harris-Shapiro 17.
2. Webber 552. See Rupert 3–15.
3. For example, Reform Jewish *responsa* on Messianic Jews is stricter than Orthodox Jewish *halakhah*. See Jacob, *Contemporary American Reform Responsa*, 109–112; Cohn-Sherbok 206.
4. Harris-Shapiro 2.
5. Prager, *The Prager Perspective*.
6. Notably, *lashon ha-ra* about Messianic Judaism has made its way into literature on intermarriage, a testimony of the growing appeal of Messianic Judaism among intermarried couples. Silverstein addresses the Messianic Jewish option on page 2 of his book *Preserving the Jewish Family: After Intermarriage Has Occurred*; see Abrams 81.
7. For a thorough response to this argument, see Brown, *Answering Jewish Objections to Jesus: General and Historical Objections*, 9–15.
8. Cohn-Sherbok 182.
9. Silverstein 1–4; Cohn-Sherbok 182.
10. Cantor 164.
11. The recent New Testament translation by Barnstone uses "Yeshua" instead of "Jesus," as well as other Hebrew/Aramaic equivalents of

the Greek. No one, however, accuses Barnstone of being deceptive. Barnstone, like modern Messianic Jews, simply recognized the importance of restoring the authentic Jewishness of Jesus as depicted in the New Testament (Barnstone 9–27).

12. Feher 112.

13. By "emblem of the cross," I mean the *physical sign* of the cross that is worn or displayed by Christians. Messianic Jewish sensitivity regarding this emblem is akin to the feelings many blacks have regarding the Confederate flag. In both cases, the emblem is viewed by one party as inspirational and by the other as a symbol of persecution. Messianic Jews, of course, remember that Yeshua laid down his life for our sins by means of crucifixion, and that he taught his followers to crucify selfish desires.

14. Chayoun 96–98.

15. Harris-Shapiro 174–175.

16. Jacob, *Contemporary American Reform Responsa*, 109–110.

17. Cohn-Sherbok 167.

18. Kinzer, *The Nature of Messianic Judaism*, 5. See UMJC Theology Committee, "Defining Messianic Judaism: Addendum 2. A model for Gentile participation in Messianic Judaism," 2–4.

19. Harris-Shapiro 18. See Katz 43–76; Schiffman, "At the Crossroads: Tannaitic Perspectives on the Jewish-Christian Schism," 154; Boyarin 1–41.

20. "In a *responsum* about the status of a 'completed Jew' in the Jewish community, the Central Conference of American Rabbis adopted an even stricter stance than the Orthodox . . ." (Cohn-Sherbok 206). In full acknowledgement of the unorthodox position taken, the Reform *responsum* claims to "disagree with the *Talmud* and later tradition" (Jacob, *Contemporary American Reform Responsa*, 109–112).

21. Wyschogrod, "Letter to a Friend," 167–168.

22. Cohn-Sherbok 192. See *Encyclopedia Judaica* I, 212.

23. Novak 97.

24. Harris-Shapiro 180.

25. *Dabru 'Emet: A Jewish Statement on Christians and Christianity* was endorsed by over 150 rabbis and Jewish scholars. Its first declaration states: "Jews and Christians worship the same God. Before the rise of Christianity, Jews were the only worshipers of the God of Israel. But Christians also worship the God of Abraham, Isaac, and Jacob, creator of heaven and earth . . . as Jewish theologians we rejoice that, through Christianity, hundreds of millions of people have entered into relationship with the God of Israel" (Neuhaus 200).

26. Alexander 3.

27. Hyman 47.

28. Cohen, *Content or Continuity*, 31.

29. Cohn-Sherbok 205. *USA Today* reported in 1997: "A group of Ortho-dox rabbis declared on Monday that other branches of Judaism 'are not Judaism at all,' challenging the religious practices of millions of Ameri-can Jews. . . . The 600-member Union of Orthodox Rabbis of the United States and Canada, the oldest organization of rabbis in the USA, con-demned the more liberal Conservative and Reform branches for con-doning assimilation and intermarriage" (Sciaber 3A); Wertheimer xii–xiii.

30. Chilton and Neusner 1–18.

31. Harris-Shapiro 18.

32. Cohn-Sherbok 212.

33. One faculty member of the Reconstructionist Rabbinical College put it succinctly: "Although religion is paramount in the Reconstructionist definition of Jewish civilization, conspicuously absent from our defini-tion of Judaism is any mention of God. This is no accident" (Alpert and Staub 18).

34. McClain 182.

35. The consistency issue is not limited to Reconstructionist Judaism, "If Conservative Jews deny the belief in *Torah MiSinai*, Reform Jews reject the authority of the Law, Reconstructionist Jews adopt a non-theistic interpretation of the faith, and Humanistic Jews cease to use the Word 'God' in their liturgy, why should Messianic Jews alone be universally vilified?" (Cohn-Sherbok 209).

# Glossary

*Adonai*—Hebrew for "Lord." When in capital letters, it serves as a substitute for the ineffable Name of God, the Tetragrammaton.

*Aliyah*—Hebrew for "going up." All who recite the traditional blessings before and after the public reading of Scripture receive an *aliyah*, the honor of going up to the *bimah*. *Aliyah* also refers to the process of immigrating to Israel, i.e. going up to Jerusalem.

*Bar/bat mitzvah*—Hebrew for "son/daughter of the commandment." A rite of passage to adulthood (usually at age 12 or 13) when a Jew accepts upon himself/herself responsibility for the commandments of God.

B.C.E. and C.E.—respectively, these terms stand for "Before the Common Era" (a Jewish alternative to B.C.) and "Common Era" (a Jewish alternative to A.D.).

*Bimah*—Hebrew for "high place." A raised platform at the front of the synagogue.

*B'rit Milah*—Hebrew for "covenant of circumcision." A *bris* (Ashkenazic spelling) is the ritual act of circumcision in which a male child (usually eight days old) enters into covenant relationship with the God of Abraham, Isaac and Jacob (Gen. 17:11).

Chabad—A Hebrew acronym from the words *chochmah* (wisdom), *binah* (understanding), and *da'at* (knowledge). Chabad is the largest sect of ultra-Orthodox (Hasidic) Jews in the United States.

Christian—a follower of Jesus

*Dreydel*—Yiddish for "spinning top" (derived from the German *drehen* "to turn"). A Hanukkah top on which the Hebrew letters *nun, gimmel, hay,* and *shin* are inscribed, an acronym for the expression "a great miracle happened there." In Israel, *dreydel*s have the letter *pe*y instead of a *shin*, representing the Hebrew word *po* (here).

*Gefilte* fish—Yiddish for "stuffed fish." A mixture of fish (often whitefish, carp, and pike) ground up, seasoned, and cooked as little cakes.

Gentile—a member of a nation other than Israel; a non-Jew.

*Haggadah, haggadot* (pl.)—Hebrew for "telling." A handbook used at Passover *seder*s to recount Israel's exodus from Egypt, guiding participants through the order of the ritual meal.

*Halakhah*—Hebrew for "walk." The application of Jewish law so that Jews know how to walk before God.

*Hasid, Hasidim (pl.)*—Hebrew for "pious one." Hasidism was founded in 18th century Russia by Israel ben Eliezer, the Baal Shem Tov (Master of the Good Name). The Hasidic movement emphasizes Jewish mystical tradition, dynastic leadership (the *rebbe*), and joyful devotion to God through prayer, ecstatic worship, and study. Because Hasidic Jews typically stand out in appearance (e.g. males often grow sidelocks of hair called *peyot* and wear an old-world style of clothing), they are commonly regarded as "ultra-Orthodox" vis-à-vis "modern Orthodox" Jews.

High Holy Days—the fall festival season when *Rosh HaShanah, Yom Kippur,* and the intermediate *Yamim Noraim* (Days of Awe) are observed. These days are especially holy (set apart) because of the emphasis on prayer and fasting, leading up to the day when the High Priest was supposed to enter the Most Holy Place to make atonement for the sins of the nation (Lev. 16; 23:23–32).

*Huppah*—Hebrew for "cover or bridal chamber." A canopy under which a Jewish wedding takes place.

*In flagrante delicto*—Latin for "in the very act of committing the offense."

Interfaith option—see Jewish/Christian option.

JCC—Jewish Community Center.

Jew—according to some branches of Judaism, a person born to a Jewish father and/or mother and circumcised on the eighth day if male (see Appendix A); also a convert to Judaism.

Jewish Christian—commonly used as a designation for Jews who believe that Jesus is the Messiah. In the Messianic community, the word "Jewish Christian" takes on an additional nuance in light of modern Messianic Jewish history. The 20th century Messianic movement arose out of a milieu in which "Jewish Christians" (or "Hebrew Christians" as they often called themselves) viewed their Jewishness primarily as a matter of ethnicity. Pioneer Messianic Jews (such as Joseph Rabinowitz, Mark Levy, and Paul Levertoff) rejected this orientation and maintained that their Jewishness was primarily a matter of covenant faithfulness. They argued that Messianic synagogues needed to be established so that Jewish believers could live out their Torah obligations in a Jewish community context. Against this historical-theological backdrop, a "Jewish Christian" (in Messianic Jewish thought) is a person who is part of a church (rather than a Messianic synagogue).

Jewish/Christian option—also known as "Interfaith." Judaism and Christianity are observed in the household as separate and distinct religious traditions (hence, the use of the slash [/]); no attempt is made to reintegrate the two religions.

Jewish-Christian—by using a hyphen (-), "Jewish-Christian" emphasizes the coming together of people/things Jewish and Christian (e.g. intermarried couples, their children, Jews who follow Yeshua, theology, dialogue, etc.).

*Kashrut*—Hebrew for "fitness." The English word "kosher" derives from *kashrut* and refers to rules and regulations that pertain to dietary law in the Orthodox tradition.

*Ketubah*—Hebrew for "that which is written." A marriage contract signed at a Jewish wedding by the bride, groom, officiating rabbi and witnesses.

*Lashon ha-ra*—Hebrew for "evil tongue." Negative comments or rumors.

*Lubavitch*—Yiddish for "Lyubavichi." Lubavitch was a small town in Belorussia that became a center of the Chabad sect of Hasidism in 1813.

*Machzor*—Hebrew for "cycle." A prayer book for the High Holy Days.

*Matzah*—Hebrew for "unleavened bread." *Matzah* is eaten during Passover week to remember the haste with which our people had to leave Egypt (Exod. 12:14–20).

*Menorah*—Hebrew for "lampstand." A seven-branched candelabra reminiscent of the one that was lit in the Temple (Exod. 25:31–40).

Messianic Jew—a Jew who worships the Messiah Yeshua as *Ben-HaElohim* (the Son of God [John 20:31; cf. Luke 24:50–52; Heb. 1:1–6; Rev. 5:13–14]) and who embraces Jewish identity and Jewish communal life as a matter of covenant responsibility.

Messianic Judaism—a restoration of the Nazarene sect of Judaism in a twenty-first century context. Judaism, in all facets of its teaching, worship, and way of life, understood, scrutinized, and practiced in the light of Messiah Yeshua.

*Mezuzah*—Hebrew for "doorpost." A small box containing two hand-written biblical passages, Deut 6:4–9 and Deut. 11:13–21, affixed to the doorposts of homes.

*Mitzvot*—Hebrew for "commandments" given by God.

*Mohel*—Hebrew for "to cut." A person who cuts away the foreskin; one who performs the ritual act of circumcision according to Jewish tradition, through which male children enter into a covenant relationship with the God of Abraham, Isaac, and Jacob.

*Oneg Shabbat*—Hebrew for "Sabbath delight." Refreshments after the synagogue service; sometimes a light meal.

*Parashah, parashot* (pl.)—Hebrew for "exact amount." A specified portion of the Bible from the weekly synagogue Scripture reading cycle.

*Rebbe*—Yiddish, for "teacher." An exalted leader in the Hasidic community.

*Rosh HaShanah*—Hebrew for "Head of the Year." The traditional Jewish New Year, which is the beginning of a ten-day period of repentance leading up to Y*om Kippur* (Lev. 23:23–24).

*Seder*—Hebrew for "order." Refers to the order of the ritual meal eaten at Passover to remember the Exodus from Egypt.

*Shabbat*—Hebrew for "[day of] rest; Sabbath." *Shabbat* is the seventh day of the week (from Friday sunset to Saturday sunset). God commanded Israel to cease from work on this day and to assemble for worship (Exod. 20:8–11; Lev. 23:3).

*Shiva*—Hebrew for "seven." A seven-day period of mourning (Gen. 50:10).

*Shul*—Yiddish for "school." A local synagogue; a place where Jews pray and study the Torah.

*Sukkah, sukkot* (pl.)—Hebrew for "booth." A temporary shelter made of wood and foliage. Jews are commanded to dwell in a *sukkah* during the feast of *Sukkot* (Lev. 23:42).

*Sukkot*—The Feast of Booths, or Tabernacles, commemorating Israel's forty years in the desert before entering the Promised Land. During this period, Israel was vulnerable to the elements and fully dependent on God, a reality symbolized by their dwelling in *sukkot* (Lev. 23:33–43; Deut. 8).

*Tanakh*—Hebrew acronym from the words Torah (Teaching), *Nevi'im* (Prophets), and *K'tuvim* (Writings); i.e. the Hebrew Scriptures (see Luke 24:44).

*Tefillin*—Hebrew for "prayers." Small leather boxes containing Scripture on parchments that are bound to the forehead and arm of a Jew during morning prayers (except on *Shabbat* and festivals). The purpose of *tefillin* is devotional (Deut. 6:8).

*Torah*—Hebrew for "Teaching." Torah refers to the Five Books of Moses; the Law or Teaching of God.

*Yahrzeit*—Yiddish for "a year's time." The anniversary of someone's death, reckoned according to the Hebrew calendar.

*Yeshua*—Hebrew for "*Adonai* (the Lord) saves." Yeshua is Jesus' Hebrew name.

*Yom Kippur*—Hebrew for "Day of Atonement." The holiest day of the Jewish calendar; a fast day, the culmination of a ten-day period of repentance and prayer for the forgiveness of sin (Lev. 16; 23:26–32).

# Bibliography

Abrams, Elliot. *Faith or Fear: How Jews Can Survive in a Christian America*. New York: The Free Press, 1997.

Alexander, Philip S. "'The Parting of the Ways' from the Perspective of Rabbinic Judaism." *Jews and Christians: The Parting of the Ways A.D. 70 to 135*. Ed. James D. G. Dunn. Grand Rapids: Eerdmans, 1992. 1–26.

Alpert, Rebecca T. and Jacob J. Staub. *Exploring Judaism: A Reconstructionist Approach*. Wyncote: The Reconstructionist Press, 1997.

Ausubul, Nathan. *The Jewish Book of Knowledge*. New York: Crown, 1964.

Bacchiocchi, Samuele. *God's Festivals in Scripture and History: The Spring Festivals*. Berrien Sprngs: Biblical Perspectives, 1995.

Bagatti, Bellarmino. *The Church from the Circumcision: History and Archaeology of the Judaeo-Christians*. Jerusalem: Franciscan Printing Press, 1984.

Bamberger, Bernard J. *Proselytism in the Talmudic Period*. Cincinnati: Hebrew Union College Press, 1939.

Barnstone, Willis. *The New Covenant: Commonly Called the New Testament* I. New York: Riverhead, 2002.

Baskin, Judith. "The Rabbinic Transformations of Rahab the Harlot." *Notre Dame English Journal* 2 (1978–79): 141–57.

Bauckham, Richard. "Jews and Jewish Christians in the Land of Israel at the Time of the Bar Kochba War, With Special Reference to the Apocalypse of Peter." *Tolerance and Intolerance in Early Judaism and Christianity*. Eds. Graham N. Stanton and Guy G. Stroumsa. Cambridge: Cambridge University Press, 1998. 228–238.

————. *God Crucified: Monotheism & Christology in the New Testament*. Grand Rapids: Eerdmans, 1998.

————. *Jude and the Relatives of Jesus in the Early Church*. Edinburgh: T&T Clark, 1990.

Bayme, Steven. "Patrilineal Descent Revisited." *Contemporary Debates in American Reform Judaism: Conflicting Visions*. Ed. Dana Evan Kaplan. New York: Routledge, 2001. 137–145.

Berger, David. *The Rebbe, the Messiah and the Scandal of Orthodox Indifference*. Portland: The Littman Library of Jewish Civilization, 2001.

————. "The Rebbe, the Jews, and the Messiah." *Commentary*. September 2001. 23–30.

Berger, Leigh Paula. "Messianic Judaism: Searching the Spirit." Ph.D. diss. University of South Florida, 2000

Berkman, Jacob. "Speech by Reform Rabbi Encourages Messianic Jews, Outrages Others." http://baltimorejewishtimes.com. August 15, 2000.

Bernstein, Howard. "Evangelizing Jews: Messianic Jews Versus Jews for Jesus." Toronto: Annual meeting of the Association for the Sociology of Religion, August 1997.

Blady, Ken. *Jewish Communities in Exotic Places*. Northvale: Aronson, 2000.

Bleich, J. David. *Contemporary Halakhic Problems Volume II*. New York: KTAV, 1983.

Bockmuehl, Markus. "Halakhah and Ethics in the Jesus Tradition." *Early Christian Thought in its Jewish Context*. Eds. John Barclay and John Sweet. Cambridge: Cambridge University Press, 1997. 264–278.

Boyarin, Daniel. *Dying for God: Martyrdom and the Making of Christianity and Judaism*. Stanford: Stanford University Press, 1999.

Bradshaw, Paul and Lawrence Hoffman. *Passover and Easter: Origin and History to Modern Times*. Notre Dame: University of Notre Dame, 1999.

Braude, William G. *Jewish Proselytizing: In the First Five Centuries of the Common Era*. Providence: Brown University, 1940.

Broadhurst, Donna and Mal Broadhurst. *Passover: Before Messiah and After*. Carol Stream: Shofar Publications, 1987.

Brook, Kevin Alan. *The Jews of Khazaria*. Northvale: Jason Aronson, 1999.

Brown, Michael L. *Answering Jewish Objections to Jesus: General and Historical Objections*. Grand Rapids: Baker Books, 2000.

————. *Answering Jewish Objections to Jesus: Theological Objections*. Grand Rapids: Baker, 2000.

Brown, Rupert. *Prejudice: Its Social Psychology*. Oxford: Blackwell, 1995.

Brown, Scott. "Six Success Strategies for Intermarried Couples." *The Chosen People*. Special Seeker's Edition. 1999.

Bulka, Reuven. *Dimensions in Orthodox Judaism*. New York: KTAV, 1983.

Cantor, Ron. *I Am Not Ashamed*. Gaithersburg: Messiah's Mandate of Tikkun International, 1999.

Charlesworth, James H., Herman Lichtenberger, and Gerbern S. Oegema, eds. *Qumran-Messianism*. Tübingen: Mohr Siebeck, 1998.

————— and Loren L. Johns, eds. *Hillel and Jesus: Comparative Studies of Two Major Religious Leaders.* Minneapolis: Fortress Press, 1997.

—————. *The Messiah: Developments in Earliest Judaism and Christianity.* Minneapolis: Fortress, 1992.

—————, ed. *Jesus' Jewishness: Exploring the Place of Jesus in Early Judaism.* New York: The Crossroad Publishing Company, 1991.

Charry, Ellen T. "The Other Side of the Story." *Princeton Theological Review* 3 (2001): 24–29.

—————. "Response to Carl Kinbar." *Princeton Theological Review* 3 (2001): 38–39.

Chayoun, Yehudah. *When Moshiach Comes: Halachic and Aggadic Perspectives.* Spring Valley: Feldheim, 1994.

Chenkin, Alvin A., Saul Kaplan, and Fred Massarik. *Initial Findings of the National Jewish Population Survey.* New York, 1972.

Chilton, Bruce and Jacob Neusner. *Judaism in the New Testament.* New York: Routledge, 1995.

Cohen, Henry. "Raising Children in an Interfaith Family: Mixed Marrieds Speak." *Making Jewish Outreach Work: Promoting Jewish Continuity Among the Intermarried.* Ed. Egon Mayer. New York: The Jewish Outreach Institute & The Center for Jewish Studies. The Graduate School of the City University of New York, 1996.

Cohen, Philip. *The Hebrew Christian and His National Continuity.* London: Marshall Brothers, n.d.

Cohen, Shaye J. D. *The Beginnings of Jewishness: Boundaries, Varieties, Uncertainties.* Berkeley: University of California Press, 1999.

Cohen, Steven M. *Content or Continuity? Alternative Bases for Commitment.* New York: American Jewish Committee, 1991.

Cohn-Sherbok, Dan. *Messianic Judaism.* New York: Cassell, 2000.

Collins, John L. *The Scepter and the Star: The Messiahs of the Dead Sea and Other Ancient Literature.* New York: Doubleday, 1995.

Commission on Reform Jewish Outreach. *Working With Interfaith Couples: A Jewish Perspective—A Guide for Facilitators.* New York: Union of American Hebrew Congregations and the Central Conference of American Rabbis, 1992.

Commission on Reform Jewish Outreach of the Union of American Hebrew Congregations and the Central Conference of American Rabbis. *Outreach and the Changing Reform Jewish Community: Creating an Agenda for Our Future.* New York: Union of American Hebrew Congregations, 1989.

Cook, Michael. "Judaism and Christianity: The Parting of the Ways." *Keeping Posted* 3 (December 1973): 3–7.

Cowen, Ida. *Jews in Remote Corners of the World.* Englewood Cliffs: Prentice-Hall, 1971.

Davies, W.D. *Torah in the Messianic Age and/or the Age to Come.* Journal of Biblical Literature Monograph Series. Philadelphia: Society of Biblical Literature, 1952.

De Boer, Martinus C. "The Nazoreans: Living at the Boundary of Judaism and Christianity." *Tolerance and Intolerance in Early Judaism and Christianity.* Eds. Graham N. Stanton and Guy G. Stroumsa. Cambridge: Cambridge University Press, 1998. 239–262.

DellaPergola, Sergio, Uzi Rebhun, and Mark Tolts. "Prospecting the Jewish Future: Population Projections, 2000–2080." *American Jewish Year Book.* Eds. David Singer and Lawrence Grossman. New York: American Jewish Committee, 1993. 103–146.

———. "New Data on Demography and Identification Among Jews in the U.S." *Jewish Intermarriage In Its Social Context.* Ed. Paul Ritterband. New York: The Jewish Outreach Institute & The Center for Jewish Studies. The Graduate School of the City University of New York, 1991.

Driver, Samuel R. and Adolf Neubauer, trans. *The "Suffering Servant" of Isaiah According to the Jewish Interpreters.* New York: Hermon, 1968.

Dubov, Nissan Dovid. *To Live and Live Again: An Overview of Techiyas HaMeisim Based on the Classical Sources and on the Teachings of Chabad Chassidism.* Ed. Uri Kaploun. Brooklyn: Sichos in English, 1995.

Eaton, Tony. "Forum: Should Messianic Jews Intermarry?" *Kesher: A Journal of Messianic Judaism* 9 (Summer 1999): 32–64.

Eichorn, David Max. *Conversion to Judaism: A History and Analysis.* New York: KTAV, 1965.

Epstein, Lawrence J. *Readings on Conversion to Judaism.* Northvale: Jason Aronson, 1995.

Feher, Shoshanah. *Passing Over Easter: Constructing the Boundaries of Messianic Judaism.* Walnut Creek: Alta Mira, 1998.

Feldman, Louis H. *Jew and Gentile in the Ancient World: Attitudes and Interactions From Alexander to Justinian.* Princeton: Princeton University Press, 1993.

Finto, Don. *Your People Shall Be My People: How Israel, the Jews and the Christian Church Will Come Together in the Last Days.* Ventura: Regal, 2001.

Fischer, John. "The Legitimacy of Conversion." *Voices of Messianic Judaism: Confronting Critical Issues Facing a Maturing Movement.* Ed. Dan Cohn-Sherbok. Baltimore: Messianic Jewish Publishers, 2001. 141–149.

——————. "Messianic Jewish Conversion: Is it Viable?" *Kesher: A Journal of Messianic Judaism* 6 (Winter 1998): 30–49.

Fishbane, Michael. "Midrashic Theologies of Messianic Suffering." *The Exegetical Imagination: On Jewish Thought and Theology.* Cambridge: Harvard University Press, 1998. 73–85.

——————. *Biblical Interpretations in Ancient Israel.* Oxford: Clarendon, 1985.

Fishkoff, Sue. "Reaching Out to the Intermarried" *Moment* 5 (2000): 56–61, 76–77, 84–86.

Fleischer, Ruth I. "The Emergence of Distinctively Jewish Faith in Jesus, 1925–1994." Ph.D. diss. King's College, University of London, 1995.

Flusser, David. "The Emergence of Christianity from Judaism." *Jews and Christians Between Past and Present.* Baarn, Holland: Instituut voor Internationale Excursies, 1975.

——————. *Jesus.* Trans. Ronald Walls. New York: Herder and Herder, 1969.

Freedman, David Noel. "An Essay on Jewish Christianity." *Journal of Ecumenical Studies* 1 (1969): 81–86.

Glaser, Mitchell L., "A Survey of Missions to the Jews in Continental Europe 1900-1950." Ph.D. diss. Fuller Theological Seminary, Faculty of the School of World Mission, 1998.

Glasser, Arthur F. "Messianic Jews, Dialogue, and the Future." *Christians and Jews Together: Voices from the Conversation.* Eds. Donald G. Dawe and Aurelia T. Fule. Louisville: Theology and Ministry Worship Unit, (PCUSA), 1991. 105–117.

Goodman, Martin. *Mission and Conversion: Proselytizing in the Religious History of the Roman Empire.* Oxford: Clarendon, 1984.

Goodman-Malamuth, Leslie and Robin Margolis. *Between Two Worlds: Choices for Grown Children of Jewish-Christian Parents.* New York: Pocket, 1992.

Gordis, Robert, ed. "Children of Mixed Marriages: Are They Jewish? A Symposium on Patrilineal Descent." *Judaism* 1 (Winter 1985): 32–40.

Grossman, Lawrence. "Jewish Communal Affairs." *American Jewish Year Book.* Eds. David Singer and Lawrence Grossman. New York: American Jewish Committee, 1993. 208–241.

Gruber, Dan. *Torah and the New Covenant.* Hanover: Elijah Publishing, 1998.

Gruzen, Lee F. *Raising Your Jewish/Christian Child: How Interfaith Parents Can Give Children the Best of Both Their Heritages.* New York: Newmarket, 1990.

Hagner, Donald A. "Jewish Christianity." *Dictionary of the Later New Testament & Its Development.* Eds. Ralph P. Martin and Peter H. Davids. Downers Grove: InterVarsity, 1997. 579–587.

──────. *The Jewish Reclamation of Jesus: An Analysis & Critique of the Modern Jewish Study of Jesus*. Grand Rapids: Academic, 1984.

Harrison, Faye V., ed. "Contemporary Issues Forum: Race and Racism." *American Anthropologist* 3 (1998): 609–631.

Harris-Shapiro, Carol. *Messianic Judaism: A Rabbi's Journey Through Religious Change in America*. Boston: Beacon, 1999.

──────. "Syncretism or Struggle: The Case of Messianic Judaism." Ph.D. diss. Temple University, Department of Religion, 1992.

Hawxhurst, Joan C. *The Interfaith Family Guidebook: Practical Advice for Jewish and Christian Partners*. Kalamazoo: Dovetail, 1998.

Hayes, Christine. *Gentile Impurities and Jewish Identities: Intermarriage and Conversion from the Bible to the Talmud*. Oxford: Oxford University Press, 2002.

Hevesy, Nikki, prod. *Joined Together?: Discovering a spiritual basis for unity in your interfaith marriage* (video). New York: Chosen People Productions, 2002.

Hiat, Phillip and Bernard M. Zlotowitz. "Biblical and Rabbinic Sources on Patrilineal Descent." *Journal of Reform Judaism* 1 (Winter 1983): 43–48.

Hirschberg, H. Z. *Yisrael ba'Arav*. Tel Aviv: Mossad Bialik, 1946.

Hirt-Manheimer, Aron, ed. *The Jewish Condition: Essays on Contemporary Judaism Honoring Rabbi Alexander M. Schindler*. New York. Union of American Hebrew Congregations, 1995.

Homolka, Walter, Walter Jacob, and Esther Seidel, eds. *Not By Birth Alone: Conversion to Judaism*. London: Cassell, 1997.

Horbury, William. *Jews and Christians in Contact and Controversy*. Edinburgh: T&T Clark, 1998.

──────. *Jewish Messianism and the Cult of Christ*. London: SCM, 1998.

Hurtado, Larry. *Early Christian Devotion and Ancient Jewish Monotheism*. Philadelphia: Fortress, 1988.

Hyman, Meryl. *Who is a Jew?:Conversations, Not Conclusions*. Woodstock: Jewish Lights, 1998.

International Bible Society. *The Holy Bible: New International Version*. Grand Rapids: Zondervan, 1984.

Jacob, Walter and Moshe Zemer, eds. *Conversion to Judaism in Jewish Law: Essays and Responses*. Pittsburgh: Rodef Shalom, 1994.

──────. *Contemporary American Reform Responsa*. New York: Central Conference of American Rabbis, 1987.

Jewish Outreach Institute. "Jewish Population Projections: The Impact of Jewish Outreach on the Intermarried and 2001." Cited

30 December 2002. http://www.joi.org/library/research/ impact7.shtml.

Jocz, Jakob. *The Jewish People and Jesus Christ*. London: SPCK, 1949.

Juster, Daniel. *Jewish Roots: A Foundation of Biblical Theology for Messianic Judaism*. Shippensburg: Destiny Image, 1995.

Kac, Arthur. *The Messianic Hope*. Grand Rapids: Baker Book House, 1981.

—————, ed. *The Messiahship of Jesus: Are Jews Changing Their Attitudes Toward Jesus?* Grand Rapids: Baker Book House, 1980.

Kasdan, Barney. *God's Appointed Customs: A Messianic Jewish Guide to the Biblical Lifecycle and Lifestyle*. Baltimore: Messianic Jewish Publishers, 1996.

—————. *God's Appointed Times: A Practical Guide for Understanding and Celebrating the Biblical Holidays*. Baltimore: Messianic Jewish Publishers, 1993.

Katz, Steven T. "Issues in the Separation of Judaism and Christianity After 70 C.E.: A Reconsideration." *Journal of Biblical Literature* 1 (March 1984): 43–76.

Kaufmann, Yehezkel. *Religion of the Religion of Israel* 4. Trans. C.W. Efroymson. New York: KTAV, 1977.

Keller, Chaim Dov. "Modern Orthodoxy: An Analysis and a Response." *Jewish Observer* (June 1979): 3–14.

Kellner, Menachem. *Must a Jew Believe Anything?*. Portland: The Littman Library of Jewish Civilization, 1999.

Keysar, Ariela, Barry A. Kosmin, and Jeffrey Scheckner. *The Next Generation: Jewish Children and Adolescents*. Albany: State University of New York Press, 2000.

Kinbar, Carl. "Missing Factors in Jewish-Christian Dialogue." *Princeton Theological Review* 3 (2001): 30–37.

King, Andrea. *If I'm Jewish and You're Christian, What Are the Kids?: A Parenting Guide for Interfaith Families*. New York. Union of American Hebrew Congregations, 1993.

Kinzer, Mark. *The Nature of Messianic Judaism: Judaism as Genus, Messianic as Species*. West Hartford: Hashivenu Archives, 2001.

Klayman, Seth. "Who is a Jew? The Concept of Conversion." *The Messianic Outreach* 1 (Fall 1999): 3–20.

—————. "Who is a Jew? The Concept of Kin." *The Messianic Outreach* 3 (Summer 1999): 9–11.

—————. "The Offspring of Intermarriage: The Matrilineal Principle." *The Messianic Outreach* 4 (Summer 1998): 15–18.

Klein, Daniel and Freke Vuijst. *The Half-Jewish Book*. New York: Villard, 2000.

Klijn, A. F. J. "The Study of Jewish Christianity." *New Testament Studies* 20 (1974): 419–431.

————— and G. J. Reinink. *Patristic Evidence for Jewish-Christian Sects.* Leiden. Brill, 1973.

Kohn, Rachel L. E. "Ethnic Judaism and the Messianic Movement." *Jewish Journal of Sociology* 29 (1987): 85–96.

—————. "Hebrew Christianity and Messianic Judaism on the Church-Sect Continuum." Ph.D. diss. McMaster University, Department of Religious Studies, 1985.

Kraft, R. A. "In Search of 'Jewish Christianity' and its Theology, Problems of Definition and Methodology." *Recherches de science religieuse* 61 (1972): 81–96.

Kung, Hans. "Jewish Christianity and Its Significance for Ecumenicism Today." *Fortunate the Eyes that See: Essays in Honor of David Noel Freedman in Celebration of His Seventieth Birthday.* Eds. Astrid B. Beck, et al. Grand Rapids: Eerdmans, 1995. 584–600.

Lazerwitz, Bernard, J. Alan Winter, Arnold Dashefsky, et al. *Jewish Choices: American Jewish Denominationalism.* SUNY Series in American Jewish Society in the 1990s. Eds. Barry A. Kosmin and Sidney Goldstein. New York: State University of New York Press, 1998.

Lee, Bernard J. *The Galilean Jewishness of Jesus: Retrieving the Jewish Origins of Christianity.* New York: Paulist, 1988.

Lockshin, Marty. "Judaism, Christianity and Jewish-Christianity: What the Future May Hold." *Cult and Culture: Studies in Cultural Meaning: Studies in Cultural Meaning.* Actes du colloque du 29 au 31 octobre 1997. Les Cahiers du C.I.C.C. 8, Juillet 1999. 137–148.

Malina, Bruce J. "Jewish Christianity or Christian Judaism: Toward a Hypothetical Definition." *Journal for the Study of Judaism in the Persian, Hellenistic, and Roman Periods* 7 (1976): 46–57.

Mayer, Egon, Barry A. Kosmin and Ariela Keysar. *American Jewish Identity Survey, 2001.* AJIS Report: An Exploration in the Demography and Outlook of a People. New York: The Graduate Center of the City University of New York, February 2002.

—————. "*Hold the Angst*: Sooner or Later the Children Grow Up." *The Inclusive* 2 (2000): 1–3.

—————. "Will the Grandchildren of Intermarriage be Jews? The Chances are Greater than You Think." *Moment* 2 (1994): 78.

—————. "American-Jewish Outreach in the 1990s and Beyond: The Coming Revolution in Demography and Communal Policy." *The Imperatives of Jewish Outreach: Responding to Intermar-*

*riage in the 1990's and Beyond.* A Publication of the Jewish Outreach Institute & The Center for Jewish Studies. New York: The Graduate School of the City University of New York, 1991. 37–62.

————. *Children of Intermarriage.* New York: American Jewish Committee, 1989.

————. *Love & Tradition: Marriage Between Jews and Christians.* New York: Plenum, 1985.

McClain, Ellen Jaffe. *Embracing the Stranger: Intermarriage and the Future of the American Jewish Community.* New York: Basic Books, 1995.

McKeever, James. *Claim Your Birthright.* Medford: Omega, 1989.

McKnight, Scot. *A Light Among the Gentiles: Jewish Missionary Activity in the Second Temple Period.* Minneapolis: Fortress, 1991.

Meyers, Eric M. "Early Judaism and Christianity in the Light of Archaeology." *Biblical Archaeologist* 2 (June 1988): 68–79.

Miles, Clement A. *Christmas Customs and Traditions: Their History and Significance.* New York: Dover, 1976.

Mimouni, Simon C. and F. Stanley Jones, eds. *Le Judéo-Christianisme Dans Tous Ses États.* Lectio Divina Hors Serie. Actes Du Colloque de Jérusalem 6–10 Juillet 1998. Paris: Les Éditions du Cerf, 2001.

Moore, G. F. *Judaism in the First Centuries of the Christian Era: The Age of the Tannaim.* 3 vols. Cambridge: Harvard University Press, 1927–1930.

Murray, Robert. "Jews, Hebrews and Christians: Some Neglected Distinctions." *Novum Testamentum* 24 (1982): 194–208.

————. "Defining Judaeo-Christianity." *Heythrop Journal* 15 (1974): 303–310.

Nadich, Judah. *Rabbi Akiba and His Contemporaries.* Northvale: Aronson, 1998.

Nemoy, Leon, trans. *Karaite Anthology: Excerpts from the Early Literature.* New Haven: Yale University Press, 1952.

Nerel, Gershon. "Primitive Jewish Christians in the Modern Thought of Messianic Jews." *Le Judéo-Christianisme Dans Tous Ses États.* Lectio Divina Hors Serie. Actes Du Colloque de Jérusalem 6–10 Juillet 1998. Eds. Simon C. Mimouni and F. Stanley Jones. Paris: Les Éditions du Cerf, 2001. 399–425.

————. "Messianic Jews in Eretz Israel, 1917–1967: Trends and Changes in Shaping Self Identity" (in Hebrew). Ph.D. diss. Hebrew University, 1995.

Neuhaus, Richard John. "Dabru 'Emet: A Jewish Statement on Christians and Christianity." *The Chosen People in an Almost*

*Chosen Nation: Jews and Judaism in America*. Ed. Richard J. Neuhaus. Grand Rapids: Eerdmans, 2002. 199–206.

Neusner, Jacob. *Death and Birth of Judaism*. New York: Basic Books, 1987.

Newman, Carey, James Davila, and Gladys Lewis, eds. *The Jewish Roots of Christological Monotheism*. Leiden: Brill, 1999.

Novak, David. "When Jews are Christians." *The Chosen People in an Almost Chosen Nation: Jews and Judaism in America*. Ed. Richard J. Neuhaus. Grand Rapids: Eerdmans, 2002. 92–102.

Oegema, Gerbern S. *The Anointed and His People: Messianic Expectations from the Maccabees to Bar Kochba*. Journal for the Study of the Pseudepigrapha. Supplement Series 27. Sheffield: Sheffield Academic, 1998.

Paget, James Carleton. "Jewish Christianity." *The Cambridge History of Judaism* III. Eds. William Horbury, W. D. Davies and John Sturdy. Cambridge: Cambridge University Press, 1999. 731–775.

Parfitt, Tudor. *The Thirteenth Gate*. Bethesda: Adler & Adler, 1987.

Patai, Raphael and Jennifer Patai. *The Myth of the Jewish Race*. Revised Edition. Detroit: Wayne State University Press, 1989.

—————. *The Messiah Texts*. Detroit: Wayne State University Press, 1979.

Petsonk, Judy and Jim Remsen. *The Intermarriage Handbook: A Guide for Jews & Christians*. New York: Arbor House, 1988.

Phillips, Bruce A. "Children of Intermarriage: How 'Jewish'?" *Studies in Contemporary Jewry An Annual* XIV. Ed. Peter Y. Medding. New York: Oxford University Press, 1998. 81–127.

—————. *Re-examining Intermarriage: Trends, Textures & Strategies*. New York: The American Jewish Committee and The Susan and David Wilstean Institute of Jewish Policy Studies, 1997.

Pines, Shlomo. *The Jewish Christians of the Early Centuries of Christianity According to a New Source*. The Israel Academy of Sciences and Humanities Proceedings II. Jerusalem: Central, 1966.

Poliakov, Leon. "Theory of Race." *Encyclopaedia Judaica* 13. Jerusalem: Keter, 1974. 1483–1486.

Porton, Gary G. *The Stranger Within Your Gates: Converts and Conversion in Rabbinic Literature*. Chicago: The University of Chicago Press, 1994.

Prager, Dennis. "A New Approach to Jews-for-Jesus." *Moment Magazine* (June 2000): 28–29.

—————. *The Prager Perspective*. January 15, 1999.

—————. "Judaism Must Seek Converts." *Readings on Conversion to Judaism*. Ed. Lawrence J. Epstein; Northvale: Jason Aronson, 1995. 79–97.

Primack, Karen, ed. *Jews in Places You Never Thought Of.* Hoboken: KTAV, 1998.

Pritz, Ray. *Nazarene Jewish Christianity: From the End of the New Testament Period Until Its Disappearance in the Fourth Century.* Leiden: Brill, 1988.

Raisin, Jacob S. *Gentile Reactions to Jewish Ideals.* New York: Philosophical Library, 1953.

Raphael, Marc Lee. *Profiles in American Judaism: The Reform, Conservative, Orthodox, and Reconstructionist Traditions in Historical Perspective.* San Francisco: Harper & Row, 1985.

Reventlow, Henning Graf. "Basic Issues in the Interpretation of Isaiah 53." *Jesus and the Suffering Servant: Isaiah 53 and Christian Origins.* Eds. William Bellinger and William Farmer. Harrisburg: Trinity Press International, 1998.

Riegel, S. K. "Jewish Christianity: Definitions and Terminology." *New Testament Studies* 24 (1978): 410–415.

Riggans, Walter. "Messianic Jews and the Definition of Jewishness." *Roots and Branches: Explorations Into the Jewish Context of the Christian Faith.* Bedford: PWM Trust, 1998.

——————. "Messianic Judaism and Jewish-Christian Relations: A Case Study in the Field of Religious Identity." Ph.D. diss. University of Birmingham, 1991.

Ritterband, Paul. "…Only by Virtue of Its Torah." *Jewish Intermarriage In Its Social Context.* Ed. Paul Ritterband. New York: The Jewish Outreach Institute & The Center for Jewish Studies. The Graduate School of the City University of New York, 1991. 100–101.

Rosenbloom, Joseph R. *Conversion to Judaism: From the Biblical Period to the Present.* Cincinnati: Hebrew Union College Press, 1978.

Rosenblum, Jonathan. "The ultimate Jewish pluralists." *Jerusalem Post.* January 9, 1998. Cited 30 December 2002. Repr. http://www.jewishmediaresources.org/article.

Rottenberg, Isaac C. "Those Troublesome Messianic Jews." *The Chosen People in an Almost Chosen Nation: Jews and Judaism in America.* Ed. Richard J. Neuhaus. Grand Rapids: Eerdmans, 2002. 103–116.

——————. *Jewish Christians in an Age of Christian-Jewish Dialogue.* Self published by the family and friends of Isaac Rottenberg in honor of his 70th birthday, 1975.

Rudolph, David J., ed. *The Voice of the Lord: Messianic Jewish Daily Devotional.* Baltimore: Messianic Jewish Publishers, 1998.

Rudolph, Michael. "Intermarriage, Proselytes & the Next Generation II." A paper presented at the Union of Messianic Jewish Congregations Conference, 1998.

_____. "Proselytes to Israel in a Messianic Jewish Congregation."
       1988.

Sacks, Jonathan. *Will We Have Jewish Grandchildren?: Jewish Conti-
       nuity and How to Achieve it*. London: Vallentine Mitchell &
       Co., 1994.

Saldarini, Anthony. "Jews and Christians in the First Two Centuries:
       The Changing Paradigm." *Shofar* 2 (Winter 1992): 16–34.

_____. *Jesus and Passover*. New York: Paulist, 1984.

Samuelson, Fran. "Jewish-Christian Congregations: A History and
       Comparative Study." M.A. thesis. Wesley Theological Semi-
       nary. March 15, 2000.

Sanders, E. P. *Jesus and Judaism*. Philadelphia: Fortress, 1985.

Schiffman, Lawrence H. *Who Was a Jew?: Rabbinic and Halakhic Per-
       spectives on the Jewish-Christian Schism*. Hoboken: KTAV,
       1985.

_____. "At the Crossroads: Tannaitic Perspectives on the Jewish-
       Christian Schism." *Jewish and Christian Self-Definition: Vol-
       ume Two, Aspects of Judaism in the Graeco-Roman Period*. Eds.
       E.P. Sanders, et al. London: SCM, 1981. 115–156.

Schiffman, Michael. "Intermarriage Can Have an Adverse Effect on
       Messianic Judaism." *Voices of Messianic Judaism: Confront-
       ing Critical Issues Facing a Maturing Movement*. Ed. Dan
       Cohn-Sherbok. Baltimore: Messianic Jewish Publishers, 2001.
       111–116.

_____. "Conversion of Gentiles Within Messianic Judaism."
       *Hashivenu Forum 2*. Chicago. October 17–19, 1999.

Schneider, Susan Weidman. *Intermarriage: The Challenge of Living
       with Differences Between Christians and Jews*. New York: The
       Free Press, 1989.

Schonfield, Hugh. *The History of Jewish Christianity*. London:
       Duckworth, 1936.

Schur, Nathan. *History of the Karaites*. New York: Peter Lang, 1992.

Schwartz, Yoel. *Jewish Conversion: Its Meaning and Laws*. New York:
       Feldheim, 1995.

Sclater, Anne. "Rabbi group: Only Orthodoxy is Judaism. Group con-
       demns more liberal practices of other branches." *USA Today*.
       April 1, 1997. 3A.

Segal, Alan. "Jewish Christianity." *Eusebius, Christianity, and Judaism*.
       Eds. Harold Attridge and Gohei Hata. Leiden: Brill, 1992. 326–
       351.

Seigel, Robert A. and Debbie Herman Seigel. *Intermarriage: A Guide
       for Parents*. Miami: The Rashi Press, 1979.

Seltzer, Carl C. "The Jew—His Racial Status." *Harvard Medical Alumni Bulletin* (April 1939): 11.

Shore, Alan. "Putting the 'Faith' in Interfaith Marriage." *The Chosen People*. Special Seekers Edition. 1999.

Siegel, Richard and Carl Rheins, eds. *The Jewish Almanac*. New York: Bantam, 1980.

Silverstein, Alan. *Preserving Jewishness in Your Family: After Intermarriage Has Occurred*. Northvale: Aronson, 1995.

Simon, Marcel. *Versus Israel: A Study of the Relations Between Christians and Jews in the Roman Empire AD 135–425*. London: The Littman Library of Jewish Civilization, 1996.

Skarsaune, Oskar. *In the Shadow of the Temple: Jewish Influences on Early Christianity*. Downers Grove: InterVarsity, 2002.

Soloff, Asher. "The Fifty Third Chapter of Isaiah According to the Jewish Commentators, to the Sixteenth Century." Ph.D. diss. Drew University. Department of Religion, 1967.

Stallings, Joseph. *Rediscovering Passover: A Complete Guide for Christians*. San Jose: Resource Publications, 1995.

Stern, David H. *Complete Jewish Bible*. Clarksville, Maryland: Jewish New Testament Publications, 1998.

—————. *Messianic Jewish Manifesto*. Clarksville, Maryland: Jewish New Testament Publications, 1997.

—————. *Jewish New Testament Commentary*. Clarksville, Maryland: Jewish New Testament Publications, 1996.

Strizower, Schifra. *Exotic Jewish Communities*. New York: Thomas Yoseloff, 1962.

Taylor, Joan E. "The Phenomenon of Early Jewish-Christianity: Reality or Scholarly Invention?" *Vigiliae Christianae* 44 (1990): 313–334.

Tobin, Gary A. *Opening the Gates: How Proactive Conversion Can Revitalize the Jewish Community*. San Francisco: Jossey-Bass, 1999.

UMJC Theology Committee. "Defining Messianic Judaism." Affirmed by the Delegates to the 23rd Annual UMJC Conference on July 31, 2002. Cited 30 December 2002. http://www.umjc.org/aboutmj/mjdefined.htm.

Vermes, Geza. *Jesus and the World of Judaism*. Philadelphia: Fortress, 1983.

—————. *Jesus the Jew: A Historian's Reading of the Gospels*. Glasgow: William Collins Sons & Co., 1973.

Visotzky, Burton L. "Prolegomenon to the Study of Jewish-Christianities in Rabbinic Literature." *AJSR* 14 (1989): 47–70.

Wacholder, Ben Zion. "The Halakah and the Proselytizing of Slaves During the Gaonic Era." *Historia Judaica* 18 (1956): 89–106.

Wasserman, Jeffrey S. "Messianic Jewish Congregations: A Comparison and Critique of Contemporary North American and Israeli Expressions." Ph.D. diss. The Southern Baptist Theological Seminary, December 1997.

Webber, Howard, pub. *Webster's II New Riverside Dictionary.* Beacon Street: Houghton Mifflin, 1984.

Wertheimer, Jack. *A People Divided: Judaism in Contemporary America.* Hanover: Brandeis University Press, 1993.

Wexler, Paul. *The Non-Jewish Origins of the Sephardic Jews.* Albany: State University of New York Press, 1996.

————. *The Ashkenazic Jews: A Slavo-Turkic People in Search of a Jewish Identity.* Columbus: Slavica, 1993.

Wijnhoven, Jochanan H. A. "The Zohar and the Proselyte." *Readings on Conversion to Judaism.* Ed. Lawrence Epstein. Northvale: Aronson, 1995. 47–68.

Winer, Mark L., Sanford Seltzer and Steven J. Schwager. *Leaders of Reform Judaism.* New York, 1987.

Wyschogrod, Michael. "Letter to a Friend." *Modern Theology* 2 (April 1995): 165–171.

————. "Response to the Respondents." *Modern Theology* 2 (April 1995): 229–241.

Yehiel, Asher ben. *Responsa* (in Hebrew). Jerusalem: n.p., 1965.

Young, Brad H. *Jesus the Jewish Theologian.* Peabody: Hendrickson, 1995.

Zlotowitz, Bernard M. "A Perspective on Patrilineal Descent." *Judaism* 1 (Winter 1985): 129–135.